Touched by His Hand

The Reflections of

Phillip Keller

Touched by His Hand

The Reflections of Phillip Keller

As a Tree Grows

Still Waters

Sea Edge

Sky Edge

INSPIRATIONAL PRESS

NEW YORK

Previously published in four separate volumes:

First Inspirational Press edition published in 1996.

Inspirational Press, A division of BBS Publishing Corporation
450 Raritan Center Parkway, Edison, NJ 08837

Inspirational Press is a registered trademark of BBS Publishing Corporation.

Published by arrangement with W. Phillip Keller and Kregel Books..

Distributed by World Publishing
Nashville, TN 37214
www.worldpublishing.com

Library of Congress Control Number: 96-77426
ISBN: 0-88486-373-5

Printed in the United States of America.

Contents

Book I

As a Tree Grows

Reflections on Growing in the Image of Christ

Contents

Foreword

DEEP WITHIN THE innermost heart of every earnest child of God there lies a compelling urge, an aroused desire, to become more like Christ in character.

The pages that follow show in simple layman's language how one can grow in godliness. By comparing parallel principles of natural growth in the life of a tree with supernatural truth in the life of a believer the manner in which a Christian character develops is made clear.

This method of demonstrating divine truth through natural phenomena was frequently used by Christ himself when he walked among men. Being the author of both the natural and supernatural realms it was the most effective means of conveying His truth to human hearts.

May these woodsman's insights into how the child of God can "grow like a cedar in Lebanon" assist the reader to become more like the Master.

W. PHILLIP KELLER

1
The Cedars of Lebanon

The righteous shall flourish like the palm tree: he shall grow like a cedar in Lebanon.

—Psalm 92:12

WHAT A CLEAR, concise statement! "The righteous [the man or woman right with God; a person in whom has been implanted a new, spiritual life by God's Spirit] *shall grow* like a cedar in Lebanon."

The cedars of Lebanon are referred to frequently in Scripture. They are unique trees of breathtaking beauty, massive size, rich fragrance, and high-quality timber. Their natural habitat is the high mountainous country of Lebanon where they grow luxuriantly.

The cedars of Lebanon are used as a symbol of all that is to be desired in Christian character. They stand for that which is fine and noble and strong. They represent beauty of life, vigor of character, fragrance of personality, and impeccability of conduct.

If I am utterly honest with my own heart I shall discover that my character as a Christian is not of this caliber. I lack the qualities which would ordinarily make me stand out above my fellows as the cedars stand tall above the lesser trees and vegetation growing about their base.

This need not be so. We have the authority of God's declaration that it is normal for anyone who has *new* life from above, implanted within the soul by the Spirit of God, to grow into a mature Christlike individual. "The righteous shall grow . . . like a cedar in Lebanon."

A tiny cedar seedling, by growing steadily and surely, matures into a mighty monarch of the mountain forest. But the tragedy is that some never get much beyond being tiny, stunted seedlings. They are alive; they are true trees; but they are virtually standing still. There is no growth.

For the cedars to become impressive trees, inspiring in their stature, strong in their timber, they must grow far beyond seedling or even sapling stage. They simply have to put on annual growth rings to produce towering trunks from which fine lumber can be cut. And this they do naturally and quietly without fanfare or frustration. It is a normal process. Similarly there should be a natural growth in the Christian's character.

In the Old Testament the details of the construction of Solomon's temple in Jerusalem are carefully recorded. We are told that the outer walls were of stone, a product of the earth, earthy. All of the stonework on the inside of the temple was to be covered with cedar boards and beams. This timber was obtained from the magnificent cedars of Lebanon. King Solomon went to great expense and labor to have these trees cut and transported from the mountains of Lebanon down to Jerusalem because there was no substitute for this wood.

Then, finally, the cedar lining of the walls was in turn overlaid with pure gold. Thus the temple became a suitable sanctuary for the Most High God.

This is a precise picture of the normal Christian. My physical body is of the earth, earthy. "For dust thou art, and unto dust shalt thou return" (Genesis 3:19). This is the counterpart of the temple's outer walls of stone.

As an infant I entered the world with an earthborn frame of flesh within which resides an undeveloped character bearing a most remarkable capacity for God and for growth.

The cedar boards and beams were produced from living trees that had grown in the high mountains. So, likewise, through the growth of godly character it is intended that I should become a fit habitation for God himself. To be suited for this noble service my life must possess qualities comparable to those of the cedars of Lebanon.

What are these special characteristics, and why was it imperative that cedar be used in the temple?

First of all, this timber is rich-grained, lustrous, and beautiful to behold. Is this true of my character? Is there a glow, an attractiveness, to my life?

Second, cedar has a delicate aroma, a delightful fragrance. This perfume permeated the whole building. Are those around me conscious of the fragrance of Christ in my character?

Third, the cedar is famous for its repulsion of insects of all sorts.

Moths and beetles and termites avoid it. Its presence has a purifying influence. Does mine, in a sordid, corrupt world?

Fourth, the cedar of Lebanon is a very durable wood, being quite impervious to decay. If my character is Christlike it will have this enduring quality. It will not be weak or soft or rotten.

Inside Solomon's splendid temple the cedar boards were in turn overlaid with pure gold. In God's language gold represents purity, holiness, righteousness—the righteousness of God himself. There is applied to my character the righteousness of Christ Jesus—the overlaying of my life with the holiness of himself. Thus I become a fit habitation for God. "Ye are the temple of the living God; as God hath said, I will dwell in them, and walk in them" (2 Corinthians 6:16).

This, then, being the parallel, how do the cedars of Lebanon grow into maturity for such a noble purpose? If they, through patient growth, produced fine material for the temple, then I, too, through growth must be capable of developing a character for holy service.

A tree grows, as does a soul, not by internal striving, but by continuous response to certain external stimuli outside itself. In the natural as in the supernatural (spiritual) realm there are specific conditions which must be present to insure optimum growth. These will now be examined individually as they apply to the character of a Christian.

2
Life

God gave us eternal life, and this life is in His Son. He who possesses the Son has that life; he who does not possess the Son of God does not have that life.

—1 John 5:11–12, Amplified Bible

AN OBVIOUS TRUTH, though one that is sometimes forgotten, is the fact that growth is impossible without *LIFE* being present. Only a live organism is able to grow. Therefore, it follows that the first requirement for growth is *life*.

The life of a cedar commences in the cone of a parent tree. Within the tiny seed, packed tightly inside the cone of the mature tree, lies the minute life-germ implanted there through the complex and mysterious reproductive process of heredity.

When the cone has ripened and fully matured it opens under the impulse of sunshine, moisture, and moving air. The small seed is released to the wind and floats down to earth where it will find its seedbed upon the forest floor. Lying there so very small and insignificant it holds within itself *life*; it possesses a potential cedar tree within its very germ. Yet to the untrained eye of the casual passerby it may appear inert and unpromising.

All that is required, however, is for the appropriate natural environment to exert its influence on the life within the seed and it will begin to be a tree. As the germ responds to the stimuli of moisture, warmth, air, and light which surround it, germination takes place and growth commences.

This is how a tree begins.

This is how the life of a tree develops.

But, what is life?

We really do not know! Immense sums of money and millions of man-hours of research have been spent attempting to discover what *life* really is. We know what it does and how it responds to various stimuli, and on this basis we have produced a fairly simple scientific definition for it:

Life is the capacity of an organism to correspond with its environment.

So when the tiny, viable seed finds itself surrounded by an array of stimuli such as moisture, air, warmth, light, and others which comprise its total environment, it responds. It germinates. It begins to grow. One day a slender rootlet emerges and starts to grow down into the soil. Soon after, a frail shoot pushes out and upward reaching toward the sun. A seedling is under way! If all goes well its root will penetrate the forest floor while at the same time its first frail leaves will spread themselves in the air. Slowly, surely, and with quiet persistence it grows first into a seedling, then a sapling, then a sturdy tree, and at last a forest monarch.

All this growth, all this maturity, is the outcome of correspondence between the tree and its environment.

In truth it may be said that not only does the tree penetrate directly into its environment but also that, as we shall see in later chapters, the components of the environment actually enter intimately into the tree thus producing normal growth. This is correspondence between the two.

Now, just as the parent cedar produces certain cones carrying viable seeds that have implanted in them the life germ of a new cedar, so God the Father, by his Holy Spirit, implants in the hearts of some men—those who believe—the very life of Christ, the *LIFE* of God himself from above. How?

"It is the spirit which gives Life; the flesh confers no benefit whatever. The words I have spoken to you are spirit and Life. But there are some of you who do not believe." (John 6:63–64, Weymouth N.T.)

This "inheritance" of eternal life is a mystery and marvel that even surpasses the hereditary process within the seed of a cedar. No more does the frail, minute, inert-looking seed lying on the ground resemble the magnificent tree towering above it than does a newborn Christian (believer in Christ) resemble the mighty God, the Heavenly Father, whose will it is that he, likewise, should develop into his likeness. It is not the outer appearance which matters. It is, rather, the imparting of God's own life to mortal man, enabling him to have correspondence with God, that counts.

The vital question is, Do I have this *LIFE*?

The verse at the head of this study puts it very plainly.

"He who does not possess the Son of God does not have that life."

Beneath the giant, outstretched limbs of the parent cedar there may be thousands of seeds scattered upon the earth. Yet out of these only a few dozen may be viable (possessing life). All were produced by the tree, but not all will become new trees. Some lack *life*.

The same is true of people. God makes it very clear that, though he is the Father of all men by creation, only those to whom *the life of Christ* has been vitally imparted are spiritually alive. All others are dead. This sobering truth confronts every individual.

We stand in amazement before the realization that God the Father purposes, desires, and wills that we should develop our inherent capacity to become like himself. Yet this is only possible if first we have his life in us. He yearns to give us the *GIFT OF LIFE*. Nothing thrills him more than to see us accept Christ who becomes our *NEW LIFE*. This remains one of the moving mysteries of human history (*see* Ephesians 1). The realization that the all-wise, all-loving, all-righteous, all-powerful One should choose to impart to man not only his own divine life but also the capacity to mature into his own likeness overwhelms the human heart.

This new, inner life is in reality the very Spirit of Christ himself imparted to mortal man. This is what is meant by "receiving Christ" into the heart. It is achieved through the invasion of man's spirit by the Spirit of the living God. Only the Spirit of God occupying and controlling the spirit of a man makes that man capable of responding to the stimuli which, surrounding him on every side, emanate from God. This correspondence with God is the normal Christian life. It is what Scripture calls walking with God or "fellowship . . . with the Father" or being "alive unto God."

A genuine Christian moves and lives and has his being in God (Acts 17:28). God becomes his very environment. And it is only in this atmosphere that he grows in Christ.

3
Water

Blessed is the man that trusteth in the Lord, and whose hope the Lord is. For he shall be as a tree planted by the waters, and that spreadeth out her roots by the river, and shall not see when heat cometh, but her leaf shall be green; and shall not be careful in the year of drought, neither shall cease from yielding fruit.

—Jeremiah 17:7–8

THE VITAL LIFE processes of an organism are dependent on moisture in its cells. Water is essential to survival. A flourishing tree may be 80 percent moisture, which means that there must be a continuous supply available from its environment if growth is to proceed normally.

Water spells the difference between a desert and a forest. It spells the difference between a dry, shriveled, stunted tree and the splendid form of a towering cedar of Lebanon. Water is actually the essence of life within a growing tree.

Not only is moisture essential as that which combines with the air to produce carbohydrates for growth, but it is also the means of food and energy exchange within the tree. In addition, it guarantees mineral and vitamin absorption through both the leaves and roots. It determines the health and vigor of the tree.

A healthy tree has its cells turgid and charged with moisture. The sap which circulates throughout the tree is a complex combination of minerals, carbohydrates, vitamins, and proteins in suspension. The constant movement of this moisture through the tree from cell to cell conditions and controls its health.

All trees, like the cedars of Lebanon, may derive water from their environment in a variety of ways. The water may be in the form of the still, silvery dew that descends during the night to settle softly on the outstretched boughs. It may be in the clouds and mists and fog that sweep in off the sea to swathe the forest in misty veils. It may be the summer showers or the winter snows. It may come through underground springs or rushing streams that cascade down the mountainside, where roots reach out to draw refreshment from the flow.

But a point to remember is that the tree does not hoard this moisture for itself. The vast network of running roots beneath the soil often exceeds the outspread canopy of trunk, branches, and leaves spread to the sky. And vast quantities of water are lifted through the framework of the tree to be transpired out into the surrounding air. This moisture, along with the discharge of oxygen, is what gives the forest atmosphere such a fresh fragrance.

Again we discover striking parallels in the life of the eager, earnest Christian who is thirsting after righteousness, eager to grow into the likeness of Christ.

God's Word tells us explicitly that such shall be satisfied. "Blessed are they which do hunger and thirst after righteousness: for they shall be filled" (Matthew 5:6).

Again, in Isaiah 44:3, "For I will pour water upon him that is thirsty, and floods upon the dry ground."

In the spiritual realm, what is the counterpart of water to a tree?

It is life eternal. It is everlasting life. It is the very resurrection life of Christ himself imparted to mortal man. It is new life in Christ made available to me by his death and through his blood shed on Calvary.

Throughout Scripture we have the picture given to us of Christ himself being the true fountain of living water (Jer 2:13). He is shown as the source and spring of everlasting life which is poured out continuously to thirsty men and women (Rev 22:1). Without this invigorating flow of life I am spiritually desiccated (dried up). I live amid a world in which the mark of death and decay lies upon everything that surrounds me. I am like a tree in a desert spot languishing for water.

But Christ deigned to come down into this earthly domain of death. He chose to deliberately pour out his life in his blood in order to deliver me from death. Now, through his resurrection power, his life eternal flows forever to those who will draw on it.

As a tree by the waters grows, in spite of drought all around it, so I, by drawing upon the life of Christ, grow into his strength and beauty despite the dominion of death all around me.

How do I do this in a practical way?

In Scripture, *to drink is to believe.*

First, I believe that by Christ's shed blood the *penalty* of death which would otherwise be mine for past sins has been canceled at Calvary.

Second, I claim a daily energizing through the resurrection life of

Christ made real in me by his Spirit. This keeps me from the *power* of sin and evil, which would otherwise stunt my Christian life.

The moisture which a tree took in last week will not suffice for today. Likewise, I, too, must draw daily on the water of divine life—even on Christ's refreshing stream.

This process of receiving continuously the very life of Christ is to be made keenly aware of his presence and power within. I have the work of Calvary cleansing me from the *guilt* of sins, and I have the resurrection life of Christ (made real in me by the Spirit) ever keeping me from the *grip* of sin. Thus I live a triumphant life of true health and holiness in God. This is how I rise above the world.

Just as water is lifted high in the tallest cedar against all the downward pull of gravity, so the triumphant life of Christ is uplifted in me through the upwelling life of his Spirit within. He it is who counteracts all the downward drag of sin and death in the decadent world around me (*see* Romans 8:2).

To live thus, cleansed and enlivened by the water of life which flows continually from Christ for thirsty men, is to live and grow up in him. What is more, it is to have springing up from within my innermost being a surge of life that flows out (is transpired) to those around me in refreshment and benediction.

"The man who believes in me, as the scripture said, will have rivers of living water flowing from his inmost heart" (John 7:38, Phillips translation).

4
Light

All things were made by him;
and without him was not any
thing made that was made.
In him was life; and the life
was the light of men.
And the light shineth in
darkness; and the darkness
comprehended it not.

—John 1:3–5

IN THE PHYSICAL realm of plants, shrubs, and trees, light is the key to life. Without light there can be only degeneration and death.

If we study the association of trees and shrubs in a forest we will soon discover that each one is competing with its fellows for light. *Each* is stretching out its limbs and leaves to capture the maximum amount of available sunlight.

The lower limbs and smaller trees growing in the understory of the forest where there is only feeble light filtering through the overhanging foliage will be stunted and sickly and susceptible to disease.

On the upper surface of each leaf or needle are an innumerable array of stomata with light-absorbing cells. By means of the complex process of photosynthesis sunlight is used by the leaf to produce carbohydrates for its growth.

This explains why, in order to flourish and grow, a leaf automatically responds to light falling upon it and turns toward it.

Almost all of us have seen plants in a window turn all their leaves toward the sun. A leaf that does not respond to this outer stimulus is sick.

Likewise most of us have seen plants that were kept in a basement or darkened room where there was insufficient light. They were yellow and sickly and made no strong growth.

It is worthy of mention here that the basis of all plant and animal life upon our planet is inexorably locked up with light. Light is the catalyst which accounts ultimately for the production of organic growth in all its diverse forms. It is this response to light that stimulates and accelerates growth. It enables a seedling to grow from a tiny green spike, pushing its way up through the damp mold of the forest floor, to a majestic monarch of a tree that combs the clouds with its upstretched limbs.

The majestic cedars of Lebanon, their great, widespread limbs reaching into the sunny skies of northern Palestine, are in reality stretching toward the sun. Every live twig and needle they possess turns to the precise position where it will benefit most from the sunlight streaming down upon it.

Response to sunlight year after year is part of the secret of their stature.

In the realm of the supernatural (spiritual) life the same identical principle of growth holds true. We are told emphatically in the verses at the head of this chapter that God is life and this life was the light of men.

Elsewhere the Word of God states plainly:

"The Lord God is a sun . . ." (Psalm 84:11).

He is the source of all life, both physical and spiritual. He surrounds us on every side with the radiance of himself.

Spiritual light, divine light, God-given light, can reach our hearts in a number of ways.

First and foremost there is the earthly life, ministry, death, resurrection, and message of Jesus Christ. He was the literal expression of divine life and light in human form.

Second, there is the written Word of God in Scripture, which again is referred to as light.

Then there is the spoken message and live reality of godly preachers, teachers, and Christian friends conveying light to our hearts.

Finally there is the realm of nature, which reveals the unity, beauty, and wisdom of the character of God himself.

Through all these media light is continually being shed about me. Now the important and crucial question is: Do I respond to the light that falls upon my heart and mind? Do I turn toward it? Do I reach out for it and hold myself in readiness to react to its stimulus?

How does one respond to spiritual light so that its entrance will produce growth of character?

Here is a simple illustration. Suppose my character is continually marred by my caustic tongue. Not only can it carve up my acquaintances but it continually brings reproach on my Master.

Then one day the light of God's Word on this matter suddenly streams into my aroused consciousness from James 3.

I am faced with two choices. Either I can turn away from this light, spurn it, ignore it, excuse myself by saying, "Oh, well, that's just a weakness of mine." Or I can turn toward God on this point in repentance. I can allow the light to penetrate to the bottom of my being about this matter. I reach out in genuine repentance (an absolute, sincere decision to quit) and embrace the light. At the same time I ask that the gracious Holy Spirit empower me to control my conduct.

This is faith in action.

Faith in action is the Christian's response to light. And the moment I respond thus, God gives power (for light is energy) to grow on this point.

To merely feel sorry for having offended someone with my tongue and then to return and do the same again is neither to repent, nor to respond to light, nor to grow in this area of my life.

It is in fact to fold up and wilt just as a leaf does which refuses sunlight. This denotes that I am sick and weak.

The remarkable truth about exposure to light, whether in the natural or supernatural, is that the growth produced by it is the actual transmutation of light. The tree itself is transformed into a light-storing, light-giving body. This is shown when we burn a slab of wood and see its flames give off light energy accumulated through many summers of patient growth.

Likewise, my character is charged and transformed into the very character of God when continually exposed to him. Paul stated this clearly when he said, "And all of us, with unveiled faces, reflecting like bright mirrors the glory [character] of the Lord, are being transformed into the same likeness, from one degree of holiness to another, even as derived from the Lord the Spirit" (2 Corinthians 3:18, Weymouth N.T.).

5
Heat

And they said one to another, Did not our heart burn within us, while he talked with us by the way, and while he opened to us the scriptures?

—Luke 24:32

THE NEXT REQUIREMENT for growth is heat. A tree may be flooded with light but unless the temperature is above 40 degrees F. there will be little or no growth.

When trees grow at very high altitudes on mountains or on the fringe of the true Arctic zones they are dwarfed and stunted by cold. A transect taken from one of these little scrawny trees may show it to be several hundred years old, yet it may be no more than six or eight feet high.

But the cedars of Lebanon have the benefit of being native to a warm and sunny climate. They enjoy a long growing season during which the weather is balmy and conducive to growth most of the year.

As in the case of light, the tree or its leaves are incapable of growth, even in the summer, unless there is a proper internal response to the warmth around them. Only a healthy tree is sensitive to the stimulus of heat.

Each stoma of a leaf has two guard cells at its entrance which open or close in response to temperature change. When they open it is possible for air to enter the leaf, allowing the process of photosynthesis to proceed. This process is said to be the most important on the planet, since all plant as well as animal life depends upon it for growth and sustenance.

A healthy, vigorous tree is sensitive to the temperature around it. It responds eagerly to warmth, allowing the full flow of air to enter its stomata, thus producing maximum growth.

Turning to the Christian life, it is a sad but true observation that there are innumerable Christians with stunted, dwarfed characters like a tree at timberline. They may have been exposed to a tremendous amount of light all their lives but there has been virtually no growth. In fact, some have literally stood still, unmoving and unchanged, from the time of their beginning a new life in Christ. They are really not more than seedlings or spindly saplings from which little timber can come to fashion a temple of the Most High.

This lack of maturity in Christian character brings contempt upon the church. Many who claim to have known the Lord for twenty, thirty, or forty years have characters which are a mockery because there has been no growth, no change, no transformation into the likeness of Christ.

In looking back to my youth, I am reminded again and again of the tremendous impact made on my own life by watching the growth in my father's Christian character. As a small lad I knew him to be a hard-driving, hotheaded, impulsive, impatient man. But as I grew up and passed through my teens I watched, awe-struck, at the steady transformation taking place in my father. It was obvious that the love of God was being shed abroad more and more in his life and in responding to that love, his character was changed. He became one of the most gentle, endearing, considerate, and warmhearted people I ever knew.

In the Christian life, the counterpart of physical warmth is love or affection. It is the other side of the character of God himself—"for God is love" (1 John 4:8).

Just as God is light, which reveals to us his character of holiness, purity, justice, and righteousness, so God is love, which discloses his character of compassion, mercy, tenderness, and kindness.

There are Christians who know all about God in a clinical way. They can dispute over doctrines and discuss all the details related to the divine life. There is no end to the light they have, but it has never produced growth because it was not combined with a warm, personal love for Christ.

Just as a tree surrounded with summer sunlight grows rapidly in response to light and warmth, so can I grow as a Christian the moment I respond to the love of God which surrounds me on every side.

The love of God to men is a continuous outpouring just as are the warm rays of sunlight from the sun. This outpouring finds expression in a myriad of forms. It is the food I eat, the heat for my home, the air I breathe, the water I drink, my friends and my family, my faculties of sight, sound, and sense. In fact, "every good and every perfect gift is from above, and cometh down from the Father of lights" (James 1:17).

God's love to us, however, found its most poignant and sublime expression in his own Son who came to live among men, then die and rise again, to make it possible for us to share his eternal life.

How then do I respond to this love? How do I react so that it will produce growth in my character?

As with light so with love, I must hold myself open to allow it to enter—for love begets love.

This is done by deliberately maintaining what I call "an attitude of gratitude."

If I determine, by God's help, to discover something good from him for which to be genuinely grateful in every event and circumstance of life, it will surprise me to feel my heart warmed toward him. This will result in an inner glow of gratitude.

Instead of complaining I will find myself thanking him for his kindness and mercy and love each day.

To do this is to grow in love and affection and warmth, not only to Christ but also to those around me.

True appreciation is one certain way to give great pleasure and love back to my Heavenly Father.

What is more, in this sort of inner climate, compounded of love and appreciation, the gracious Holy Spirit comes into my being eager to produce his own fruits of a sunnier clime.

This is to know what it is to have our hearts burn within us, moved by a warm, compelling affection for Christ—growing in gratitude and graciousness.

6
Air

And the Lord formed man of the dust of the ground, and breathed into his nostrils the breath of life; and man became a living soul.

—Genesis 2:7

IN THE DISCUSSION of growth in response to light it was pointed out that the critical process of photosynthesis involves the combination of carbon dioxide and water into carbohydrates under the stimulus of sunlight.

The carbon dioxide for this purpose is drawn by the plant directly from the atmosphere which surrounds it, and is absorbed by the stomata of the leaf when the guard cells open.

As the plant extracts the carbon dioxide from the air, it discharges back into the atmosphere pure oxygen. In part, this is how the oxygen content of the atmosphere is maintained. The balance of the oxygen content of the air which is so essential to all life on earth is controlled to a very large extent by the growth processes of plants and trees.

It is also this discharge of oxygen into the atmosphere which gives that special quality of purity and freshness to forest and mountain air. There is an exciting invigoration and keen stimulation to the atmosphere of forested country.

Most of us are acquainted with the perfumelike pungence of a pine or fir forest that is breathing deeply of summer air. The trees are growing at a maximum rate, drawing heavily from the warm, sunlit air that surrounds them. No matter what species the tree may be, this is the season of setting and forming and ripening its fruit.

Again, as with light or warmth, the degree of growth and its effect on the tree are related to the response of the tree to the air around it.

Scientific experiments have demonstrated that a tree absorbs much more than merely carbon dioxide from the air that moves about its limbs. Borne upon the winds, especially those from off the sea, or ocean, are minute particles of minerals in suspension of mist and fog. These are picked up from the wind-plowed surfaces of the sea to be carried aloft in clouds. Nutrients are thus combed from the atmosphere by the eager, grasping, waving branches that bow and bend beneath the whispering winds.

This is also part of the secret of the majestic growth of the giant cedars of the high country.

Throughout the Word of God the gracious Holy Spirit is likened to air, to atmosphere, to the wind. "The wind breathes where it will, and thou canst hear the sound of it, but knowest nothing of the way it came or the way it goes; so it is, when a man is born by the breath of the Spirit" (John 3:8, Knox translation).

To every true child of God come continually the soft solicitations of the Holy Spirit. He comes with gentleness yet with an insistent desire to be allowed admittance into the innermost recesses of the life and heart and intellect.

In the providential plan of God the choice of whether or not an individual will allow the gracious Spirit to enter is a matter of personal cooperation. As pointed out in the preceding chapter, if we are warm in our affection and love and gratitude to God we provide a welcome climate within. Here the Spirit finds it not only easy to enter, but also conducive to the production of his own exotic fruits.

"The Spirit, however, produces in human life fruits such as these: love, joy, peace, patience, kindness, generosity, fidelity, tolerance and self-control" (Galatians 5:22, Phillips translation).

If we would grow and produce these fruits, the one thing we must do is draw deeply of the Spirit of Life himself who is willing to enter the waiting heart that is open to him with a warm welcome.

How is this done in practical experience?

The areas of my spiritual life which can be made open and available to him are my mind, my intellect, my emotions, and my will.

These all have their seat in my conscious and subconscious mind. It is perfectly possible for me to deliberately respond to the wooing of the gracious Spirit as he speaks to my innermost mind. Or, conversely, I can spurn and reject his overtures. If I do the latter he is easily grieved and quickly withdraws. He will not force an entrance or impose himself upon me.

If I wish to have a Christian mind marked by the qualities of the mind of Christ, it is proper for the production of such a mind to come about by the inner working of the gracious Spirit in my mind. My appetites, my desires, my ambitions, my motives, will be molded and made up of impulses which had their origin with him. The degree to which this is done daily in my life is proportional to the degree to which I deliberately allow him to enter and control my mind, emotions, and will.

Not only will this result in my thinking upon those things which are pure and lovely and of good report but it will mean my entire life exudes a wholesome aura of decency and uplift and integrity. To be with me will be akin to walking amid the cedars of Lebanon—which are both noble and fragrant—trees of the high places. This is to know something of the secret growth in godliness.

The question is, have I ever sincerely and earnestly invited the Holy Spirit to occupy and take control of my mind in this manner? He awaits my invitation to enter and begin his own winsome work of growth. It is he who will give me a godly disposition.

"For it is God which worketh in you both to will and to do of his good pleasure" (Philippians 2:13).

7
Weather

Praise the Lord from the earth,
ye dragons, and all deeps: fire,
and hail; snow, and vapours;
stormy wind fulfilling his word:
mountains, and all hills; fruitful
trees, and all cedars.

—Psalm 148:7–9

WEATHER IS A most important and ever present part of any environment in which a tree grows. Up to this stage in our studies we have discussed the specific components which comprise weather as a whole: heat, light, moisture, air.

There is, however, an overall sense in which weather is a direct physical force influencing the growth of a tree. Storms, hail, blizzards, sleet, snow, frost, or lashing winds make an inescapable impact upon all plant life, but especially on trees that are long-lived. They must stand exposed to the whims of weather year after year, unable to escape or evade its onslaught, facing its fury with quiet fortitude.

Often as a boy I would lie in the shade of some sturdy tree that stood alone, green and strong beneath the blazing sun, wondering what it would be like to be a tree. I knew that for the tree there could be no release from the spot in the soil to which it was rooted. It simply had to stand there silently, enduring the burning heat and searing drought of summer. When autumn winds lashed its limbs, stripping off its tattered leaves, there was still no escape. Under the blast of winter blizzards, with their weight of snow and frost and sleet, it could only bow its branches, sometimes bent to its tired trunk, and wait patiently for release. And then again, March gales and April storms would whip it mercilessly, glazing it in ice before its buds at last began to burst anew in spring. Always, patiently, heroically, it endured all sorts of weather.

Not until later in life, when I began serious mountain climbing, did I fully understand what weather could do to wood. High up on the hills, well above the forest stands, where individual trees stood exposed on some rugged ridge, I found trees of exquisite beauty and matchless character. There they stood, their forms twisted and battered into striking shapes. Here was the stuff to delight an artist, the beauty to challenge a photographer.

But beside this, all the fury of sleet and wind and snow and sun had fashioned an inner beauty beyond belief.

Here was wood with grain of luster and lovely lines. Wood with whirls and curves that would delight the heart of a wood-carver—even those old craftsmen who carved the flowers and fruits that were to adorn the inner sanctuary of Solomon's temple.

Turning to the normal life of the Christian we are confronted with the simple fact that in this life we are going to have troubles. Jesus himself said, "In the world ye shall have tribulation: but be of good cheer; I have overcome the world" (John 16:33).

The life of our Lord himself was, outwardly, a continuous series of testings and turmoil. He was a virtual storm center about which there raged relentlessly all the fury of his enemies and detractors. Yet within there was the quiet acceptance of every adversity as a part of the Father's will.

In another place he told his followers in very straightforward language, "If the world hates you, ye know that it hated me before it hated you" (John 15:18).

One of the fallacious concepts that has crept into the church is that if a man becomes a Christian, then everything in life's garden will suddenly become agreeable and delightful; that there will be nothing but blessing and prosperity and peacefulness.

This is simply not so, and more especially for the man or woman courageous enough to take an open stand, set apart from the crowd, where the blasts of criticism, scorn, and ridicule of a cynical world will be felt at their fiercest.

But exactly as in the case of the cedar that clings alone to its rocky cliff, there will be incorporated into that character a strength, a hardiness, a toughness, and a rugged vitality matched only by its beauty and attractiveness that sets it apart from its fellows. Outwardly a Christian's life may appear the worse for wear and tear. Even our Master was a man of sorrows and acquainted with grief. But oh, what a figure set apart he was—sinners were drawn to him and children loved him.

The growth of such character is possible only under adversity. It is something that can be produced only under the inexorable stress and strain of stormy weather. The tree which responds vigorously to the wrenching winds and bending snow grows tough and strong and durable. Inwardly there is the continuous, quiet, unspectacular growth in godliness. The inner life becomes rich, lustrous, and mellow. Built into the very fiber and grain of the soul are a charm and beauty that only blustery weather could possibly produce.

Most of us want to avoid the hard things, the adverse winds, the testing times. Let us not. They are God's method of making special timber for adorning his sanctuary.

The individual whose life has been exposed to stormy weather and survived the strain is most often the one with a quiet inner calm, a sweet serenity of spirit.

Beyond and above this, the picturesque trees above timberline—the battered, beaten, bent, and beautiful trees of the high country—possess the finest aroma. Their wood is impregnated with pitch and resins that act as lubricants between the flexing fibers of their wind-tossed timber. When this wood is sawn and planed and shaped under the master craftsman's cutting tools, its fragrance fills the air and all the building.

Such perfume is produced only by adversity.

God give me grace to thank you for hardship.

When I do, my life and spirit will grow beautifully winsome—not bitter or cynical.

8
Fire

Open your doors, O Lebanon, that the fire may devour your cedars! Wail, O fir tree and cypress, for the cedar has fallen; because the glorious and lofty trees are laid waste! Wail, O you oaks of Bashan, for the thick and inaccessible forest [on the steep mountainside] has in flames been felled.

—Zechariah 11:1–2, Amplified Bible

THE ONCE MAGNIFICENT forests of Lebanon are today but a tiny fragment, a sad remnant of their former splendor. It is true man's wasteful and indiscriminate cutting accounts for much of the loss. Solomon alone sent 183,300 hewers, fellers, and workers into those fine forests. But the other cause of their decline has been from burning. Some of the forest fires were started through carelessness of shepherds, settlers, or woodcutters. Others were ignited by natural causes like lightning.

The growth of forest trees all over the world is closely linked with fire. Fire is a determining factor in the survival of certain species. For instance, some trees are fire-resistant. Their thick, tough, corklike bark will scarcely burn at all, so that they can withstand hot fires that would destroy other species. The oaks of dry regions are typical of this fire-resistant type, so are the Douglas firs of our Pacific region. This does not mean that they will not burn at all; it simply implies that they can endure and survive where their fellows sometimes succumb.

One of the species most sensitive to fire are the cedars. Not only do they burn readily and intensely but, once fire has swept through their stand, they are often supplanted by other trees. Or if other species are not growing adjacent to them, their stand may be replaced by inferior forms of brush and undergrowth. Though cedars grow in moist, well-watered regions, they are, nevertheless, extremely susceptible to fire damage and are readily fire-killed.

In many forests, fires burn more fiercely and with greater devastation because brush and brambles and undergrowth become established around the trees. A very clear picture of this is given in Judges 9:15: "And the bramble said unto the trees, if in truth ye anoint me king over you, then come and put your trust in my shadow: and if not, let fire come out of the bramble, and devour the cedars of Lebanon."

Lightning also frequently strikes trees that stand out in exposed sites on ridges or open country. If a tree has dead or dry wood it may be set ablaze. Green, vigorous, luxuriant trees are not so apt to burn, though they may be scarred or split or shattered by the electrical discharge that goes to ground.

The likelihood of such a calamity befalling a strong, green, vigorously growing tree is much less than for one which is dried up, diseased, or cumbered with dead wood. The rich, dense foliage of a healthy cedar, moreover, so shades the soil beneath it that it precludes brush and brambles from encircling it. So the chances of its being burned are more remote.

In the Word of God, fire, especially as it is used in the Old Testament, represents the great judgments of God in administering justice to mortal man. Fire especially applies to his own children, those who are his chosen ones, those who have known him but who have gone astray.

As Christians we are inclined to forget that our Heavenly Father who is all love and mercy and compassion to us is at the same time altogether righteous, holy, just, and severe in disciplining those who disobey.

In a very real sense one of the most serious difficulties an earnest Christian faces in his conduct on earth is found in the area of his intimate contact with non-Christians.

In this realm lies the ever present temptation to become too closely involved with the life, enterprise, and interests of the world. Many of these associations may appear perfectly legitimate and even worthwhile, but they may not necessarily be of merit in God's mind. Like the brambles and underbrush entwining themselves around the trunks of the cedars, they slowly but inexorably enmesh us in an apparently harmless though potentially flammable association.

The Christian who is keen for God and growing in Christ should not allow the entanglements of the world to wrap themselves around him. This is precisely what happened to "righteous Lot," who, when fire fell on Sodom and Gomorrah, was stripped of everything and came within a hairsbreadth of losing his own life. It was only the angels' direct intervention and Abraham's prayers for his survival that saved him from disaster.

When we become too closely identified with the world in which we live, disaster may stalk us and even engulf us in its rushing fury, just the way fire sweeps through the underbrush to set the cedars alight.

God makes it very clear that judgment must first begin with his own people (1 Peter 4:17–18). And we must consistently remind ourselves that though he is longsuffering, and patient in his dealing with us, there are times when a Christian who compromises with the world will be punished promptly and with awesome severity. On occasion, like a bolt of lightning flashing from a thundercloud, death may even descend to consume the living tree. This is what happened to Ananias and Sapphira, who dropped dead when they tried to deceive God over a real estate transaction (Acts 5:1–11).

Jesus entreated his Father that though we are in the world, we would not be of it (John 17:14–17). We can do no better than pray the same prayer ourselves. Moreover, God expects us to use the discretion he has given us to detect dangerous situations when they present themselves. He expects us to have the simple courage to refuse unnecessary entanglements.

This is best assured when we are growing steadily in him.

Because the cedars are relatively thin-barked trees, readily susceptible to fire, they are a valid example of the Christian life. In my growth in God there needs to be a keen sensitivity to the reproof and correction of the Spirit. Otherwise, judgment, when it comes, will prove to be a burning experience. It will leave an indelible scar, like those on a charred tree, on my careless character.

"For our God is [indeed] a consuming fire" (Hebrews 12:29).

9
Space

I will bring healing to their crushed spirits; in free mercy I will give them back my love; my vengeance has passed them by. I will be morning dew, to make Israel grow as the lilies grow, strike roots deep as the forest of Lebanon. Whose branches shall spread, it shall become fair as the olive, fragrant as Lebanon cedar.

—Hosea 14:4–6, Knox translation

IN SCIENTIFIC TERMINOLOGY there is a law which states that nature will not tolerate a vacuum. This applies equally whether the vacuum be created by artificial, mechanical means within a laboratory retort, or whether it be in a biological sense in the natural realm.

For example, when a forest fire has swept through a stand of timber, leaving in its wake a bare burn that is bereft of life, a biological blank or vacuum has been created. Or if during a gusting gale trees are uprooted and crash to the earth leaving great gaps in the forest canopy, a biological vacuum has been established.

Nature will not tolerate such a situation. At once biological processes are set in motion to restore some sort of life and growth to the barren spot. It may commence with only lowly mosses, lichens, and annuals. Subsequently grass and pioneer plants such as poplar, willow, and other short-lived trees will invade the space. These are but forerunners of the climax vegetation of tall, long-lived trees that will eventually supplant the pioneers to produce a permanent forest.

This is but a bird's-eye view of the continuous contest which proceeds in the plant kingdom for space, for room to grow, for a place to spread in splendor.

Trees that grow together too tightly in dense groves will actually smother and stunt each other. If in the fierce competition to find space for their spreading limbs and roots some succumb, the vacancy left by their death is promptly occupied by the surviving trees around. This immediate response to space is one of the most powerful impulses that control and determine the degree of growth in a virile tree.

A vigorous cedar of Lebanon, its head towering well over one hundred feet into the sun, its massive, widespread horizontal limbs far outstretched for air and dew and mist, its roots reaching far in search of water and nutrients from the soil, requires a tremendous amount of space in order to thrive. This is especially true of individual trees which often produce a number of trunks from the same base, spreading themselves splendidly in a display of green glory.

There were no other trees in all of Palestine to compare with the magnificent cedars of Lebanon. To those who saw them they were a thrilling sight as they grew to such grandeur on their rock-ribbed mountains. And one of the most important reasons why they attained such stature was that they had space—ample, open room—in which to flourish.

Coming now to the Christian life, it is interesting to observe the same law of response to space at work in human hearts.

Jesus himself made reference to it in his parable about the sower and the seed. He emphasized how, in the growth of some plants, they were actually choked out by the competition from others (*see* Matthew 13:7, 22). There was simply a lack of sufficient space in which to survive.

In the Christian life, as in the life of a tree, we must face the fact that we are continually crowded and surrounded by earthly attractions, by human philosophies, by people with worldly concepts.

Now God has very definite, though at times drastic, measures for eliminating some of this competition from our lives. He literally clears away the encroaching trees and undergrowth by his fires of discipline or storms of suffering and sorrow.

If a loved one or a friend or a business associate begins to gradually dominate my life and cramp my Christian growth, God may see fit to remove him or her. The sudden gap left in my life may seem an appalling loss, but he did it in love to make more room for me to grow in himself. He wants me to respond with new affection and fresh devotion to Christ.

Perhaps my profession, my career, my business, has become the overshadowing thing in my life. It is stifling my growth in God. It dominates my desires. I find myself becoming indifferent to Christ's claims. A falling off in correspondence with God becomes apparent in my conduct.

God in mighty mercy and jealous love for his child may bring my career tumbling down around me. My business may be blown away in the winds of adversity. Then suddenly there is space and time and opportunity for me to spread myself before him in repentance. Only there will I sense the depth of his concern for me. Our beautiful head passage from Hosea puts it so clearly: crushed spirits will be healed, love will be restored, and the still dews of his quietness will be upon my outstretched limbs. Again, the very roots of my being will lay hold afresh on Christ, they will draw their strength from God. Out of it all, my life will exude the fragrance of a revitalized and vigorous growth.

It should be emphasized that everything depends upon how I respond to this outer stimulus of space that God clears around me.

I can recoil from the apparent disaster of his discipline, growing bitter, scarred, and cynical. Or I can reach out to grasp God, spreading myself penitently in his presence to grow stronger than ever: this because I realize it is he who has done it in love.

Some of the finest and most noble cedars stand all alone, set apart among their crowded fellows. The man or woman who grows mighty in God discovers, too, that he must be set apart from the clamorous commotion of the common crowd.

10
Minerals

As therefore you have received the Christ, even Jesus our Lord, live and act in vital union with Him; having the roots of your being firmly planted in Him, and continually building yourselves up in Him, and always being increasingly confirmed in the faith as you were taught it, abounding in it with thanksgiving.

—Colossians 2:6–7, Weymouth translation

AT THE BEGINNING of this series of studies it was stated that a tree *does not grow itself*. Rather it grows in response to certain stimuli or specific conditions which surround it.

Now that portion of a tree which we refer to as the root system that is below the surface of the ground is surrounded by soil. Reduced to very simple terms we may say that soil consists of inorganic matter and organic matter. Or in layman's language we call them minerals and humus.

Minerals in the soil are derived from the weathering of rock. They have their origin either in the bedrock upon which the soil rests, or they have been transported from afar and distributed across the land by glaciation, flooding, wind erosion, or other physical forces of weathering.

It is perfectly proper to say, therefore, that rock in the form of minerals comprises a most important part of a tree's total environment. It is, moreover, common knowledge that the vigor and quality and strength of any vegetation are determined in large measure by the mineral content of the soil upon which it is growing. A tree rooted in rich soil produces rich foliage and strong growth. One struggling on sickly, thin, leached-out land will be correspondingly weak and stunted.

It is no accident or mere chance that the cedars of Lebanon are trees of tremendous size and strength. Their natural habitat is the mineral-rich mountains of Syria. Those high rock ridges are ideal for timber.

The tireless roots of the forest giants penetrated and honeycombed the soil that lay upon those mountains, drawing from it minerals which would be built up into the very tissues and fibers of the timber. It was not just happenstance that these cedars have towering trunks that stand like tall spires upon the mountainside. Their roots are bound up with the very soil upon which they grow.

What a sublime picture this is of the Christian whose life is now rooted and grounded in Christ Jesus!

Again and again throughout Scripture the inspired writers have used the metaphor of our God as a rock. For example: "I will publish the name of the Lord: ascribe ye greatness unto our God. He is the Rock, his work is perfect" (Deuteronomy 32:2–4).

In the spiritual realm the strength and stamina of my character will depend upon the sort of material from which it is built. It will be conditioned by the source from which I draw spiritual sustenance. The decision as to where I choose to sink my spiritual roots and on what I prefer to feed my mind and heart and soul rests with me.

Christ Jesus offers himself as a sure rock upon which a man can establish his character. In the verse at the head of this study I am told clearly and concisely that the very roots of my being have been *planted in him* just as God chose to plant the cedars in the high hills of Lebanon.

Having been established in such a setting with all the resources of Christ made available to me, there is no reason why I shouldn't grow except for my own indolence, my reluctance to put out an effort to search for the riches in him just as the tree roots search the soil.

One of the interesting things about the root system of a tree is that very often it actually exceeds in size and scale the total mass of the trunk, limbs, and leaves which can be seen above the ground. It is not unusual for a tree to have miles of roots and rootlets.

The great tasks of this underground network are not only to anchor the tree to the ground but—much more important—to search out and absorb the available nutrients in the soil. By a very complex process the minerals are absorbed through the root hairs at the tips of the rootlets which are always growing rapidly. This material is then taken up into the tree and built into the very fibers and tissues of the trunk and branches. This is what gives strength and sturdiness to the entire tree. Yet it must be remembered that all this goes on below ground in silence and without fanfare.

Similarly, if we would grow up into Christ, if we would be built up in him, there must be a quiet searching of his Word; there must be an assimilation of the riches available to us in secret, diligent study.

From cover to cover the Bible is a bold declaration of the precious provisions made for man by his Heavenly Father. It is a revelation of all our resources in Christ. It is rich with promises and truths and eternal principles upon which I can draw for strength of character and stamina of conduct. These are my legitimate heritage. It is up to me to take them, to claim them for myself just as a tree absorbs the minerals from the soil in which it grows.

As I assimilate God's Word it becomes incorporated into the very fiber of my makeup. It becomes life and strength to me. The decision for me is a very simple one. Will I or will I not study the Scriptures? They contain the riches which are mine in Christ Jesus.

If I commit whole chapters to memory, making them mine, I will soon discover God's gracious Spirit doing the building up of my character with the material that I have taken into my mind and heart. Thus I grow from strength to strength.

Rather than learning random verses it is well to master whole *blocks* of the Bible. This gives continuity and coherence to the material in mind. Here are twenty-four passages which if mastered—one each month for only two years—will provide material that can completely transform the fabric of a Christian's life. One cannot absorb these and not grow!

Exodus 20:1–21	Malachi 3	Romans 8
1 Samuel 2:1–10	Matthew 5	1 Corinthians 13
Psalm 1	Matthew 6	Galatians 5
Psalm 23	Matthew 7	Ephesians 6
Psalm 51	John 3	Philippians 3
Proverbs 20	John 14	Colossians 1
Isaiah 40	John 15	Hebrews 12
Isaiah 53	John 16	Revelation 21

Another suggestion for uncovering treasures from the Bible is to read a passage daily in at least two different translations (the more the better). Each reading comes then as a new rendering that reveals the truth and riches not previously discovered.

Finally there is the thrill of what I sometimes call "taking an energetic hike in Scripture"—reading an entire book rapidly at a single sitting to sense its surging story and message for my heart. This will disclose delights and previous new truths of great worth.

11
Humus

For if we have been planted together in the likeness of his death, we shall be also in the likeness of his resurrection.

—Romans 6:5

THE PRECEDING STUDY stated that soil is composed of organic and inorganic compounds, that is to say, of humus and minerals. Humus, to put it very simply, is dead or decaying vegetable matter. It is derived from the broken-down cellular structure of plants and trees. Humus is composed of the leaves, twigs, buds, bark, wood, roots, and fruit that have fallen back to the earth to be incorporated into the soil through the processes of decay.

Humus is as important for healthy soils and vegetation as are the minerals. Soils high in humus grow trees and plants with a "bloom." Their foliage shines and glistens with a rich sheen that sets them apart from those grown on poor land.

Humus represents the critical link in the so-called energy conversion cycle which is made up of birth, growth, death, decay, and rebirth. All of life is dependent upon this complex process. It explains why we say there can be no life or growth without there first being death. In fact, the entire biota (living world) is conditioned by death. Life can only come from preexisting life which is made available through death. For example, in a forest a tree takes root, runs its life course, comes to the end of its growth, then one day under a fierce storm crashes back to the earth. Immediately the agents of decay go to work on the mass of splintered wood, reducing it to humus. Soon other tree seedlings take root in the decomposing material and a new array of life emerges from the dead form. Through the death of one, new life has been imparted to many others.

It is startling to discover this same principle running throughout the Bible. From beginning to end we find the theme that spiritual life is dependent upon sacrificial death. The supreme and universal application of this principle came at Calvary. God himself saw that it was imperative he himself should die in the form of his own Son in order that there might be made available to all men of all time the opportunity for them to be born anew into his life, or as the head verse puts it, "planted together in the likeness of his death." This then enables us to grow up into the life of his resurrection. For it is on the very life of Christ that we draw our sustenance, exactly as the young cedar derives new life from the prostrate form of its predecessor.

This is all a great mystery, but nevertheless a fact. It is one of the thrilling realities we accept and act on by simple faith. For just as new seedlings strike root and grow luxuriantly upon the fallen trunk of a former forest monarch, so there is life and growth available to me through the sacrificial death of the Lord of Glory. Young Christians are sometimes bewildered by this principle, yet we are told plainly, "Since by man came death, by man came also the resurrection of the dead. For as in Adam all die, even so in Christ shall all be made alive" (1 Corinthians 15:21–22).

Now there is a second aspect to the part being played by death in the growth of any living organism. Actually from the time of birth or even germination every living thing is dying. If we stand long enough under one of the giant cedars we will notice a continual dropping of cast-off limbs, twigs, bark, needles, and ripened cones. This material falls in a steady rain beneath the tree adding to the humus of the soil in which it is growing. Not only does it contribute to its own good but also that of all the lesser trees and shrubs growing about its base. Still another benefit is that this removes what would otherwise become diseased.

This daily dying, though it might appear a painful process to the tree, is one of its most wholesome growth activities. Likewise in my daily spiritual life I have to discover that there are areas of my character which can be improved only by severe pruning, either through outright death or by God's cutting hand.

As Jesus put it to his disciples, "Let . . . [a man] deny himself [die to his own desires], and take up his cross [that will cut him from his claim to himself], and follow me" (Mark 8:34).

How do I do this in actual practice?

First, I simply recognize the fact that as a Christian there are some desires of the old life to which I must die. Most of these are selfish and self-centered attractions. Paul tells us to reckon ourselves dead to them.

For instance, my natural inclination may be to love exaggerating and telling tall stories. All that this achieves is the inflation of my ego. As a Christian I have to take the position that this tendency simply does not have a place in my conduct. I positively reject it. I count (reckon) myself estranged from it, as having no place for it in me. Immediately at that point it drops off like a falling leaf or dead branch and I become more Christlike on that characteristic.

But many of us are not resolute enough nor earnest enough in our dealings with God to live this way. Then for our own good he steps in and prunes us in what sometimes can be a painful process.

Often after a terrible storm one can walk under the trees and see a veritable carpet of limbs, leaves, twigs, and other debris lying beneath the trees.

How does this work in my spiritual life?

Assume that I continue to indulge my appetite for telling tall stories. One day I may discover that someone has caught me in an outright lie and the upshot is that I am terribly humiliated and mortified. I am in a very real sense broken up over the matter. Now I can do one of two things. Either I can deny it, resent it, protest my innocence, and pretend it was not intended; or I can humble myself, apologize, confess my wrong, and reach out to take this mortification willingly. If I do this the cross has been applied and in dying to myself on this point I have grown into Christ's likeness.

This very simply is the meaning of dying daily. It may not always be that I am in the wrong. Sometimes it happens that I am accused without a cause. Still it is right for me to accept this cross with gladness. My Lord did when there was no fault found in him. To do this is to be made one with him, to be identified with him, to grow in *Him*. Thus from death come resurrection life and newness of character.

As a Christian progresses along this path, over his life steals that ineffable glow resembling the rich foliage of a tree growing in soil charged with humus. The world has less and less claim on his character; he discovers that the old desires are losing their attraction. He is set free from the world. *He is alive unto God.*

12
Perils

Therefore as a fire devoureth the stubble, and the flame consumeth the chaff, so their root shall be rottenness, and their blossom shall go up as dust: because they have cast away the law of the Lord of hosts, and despised the word of the Holy One of Israel.

—Isaiah 5:24

EVERY LIVING ORGANISM is surrounded by perils of some sort. This is the very pattern and essence of biological behavior on this planet. The whole life and existence, whether of individuals or entire species, is conditioned by danger of death. The instant a man or a tree is born it is set on course to die. It is surrounded on every side by the agencies of death which, for lack of a better, all-inclusive term, I have called "perils." Only so long as the life forces of growth and renewal within the organism exceed the destructive forces of disintegration and death from without will it survive.

It is the principle of preying on and being preyed upon which underlies all existence. As pointed out in the chapter on humus, all life is governed by the energy conversion cycle whereby the continuous cycle of birth, growth, life, death, decay—birth, growth, life, death, decay, and so on, proceeds uninterrupted. The Buddhists, without hope in God, refer to this as "being chained to the wheel of life." A more apt expression would be "chained to the wheel of death."

In the design of natural life it can be clearly seen how any living organism is continually surrounded by perils that potentially spell death. In the case of a tree there are innumerable diseases that may attack the foliage, the trunk, the blossoms, the seed, or the roots. To survive in their own struggle for existence the bacteria or virus that produces the disease must perpetuate itself at the expense of the life of the tree.

The same thing is true of the insect pests which often attack trees. Bark beetles may be riddling the trunk, or nematodes invading the root system, or moths, aphids, and leafhoppers feeding on the foliage.

Sometimes the peril is more conspicuous than the subtle danger from insects or disease. Storm-broken wood may be invaded by the spores of fungi, mosses, or lichens that begin their deadly work of decay.

Beyond this the peril may be outright physical damage and destruction from animals: seedlings gnawed by rodents; a sapling shredded by a buck polishing the velvet from his antlers for the fall rut; a mature tree damaged by a porcupine feeding on his favorite bark.

All of these, whether moss or mouse, buck or bacteria, are really predators preying upon the tree. Whether or not it survives or succumbs to these outer stimuli depends directly upon one thing and one thing only—the health and vitality of its inner life. A strong, sturdy, rapidly growing tree will react swiftly and surely to the attacks made upon it. Disease organisms will not find a footing; spores of decay will be discouraged; damage from animal depredations will be rapidly repaired.

But let it be repeated. All this is possible only if and when the tree itself is in optimum health, when there is surging through it the full force of a vigorous, energetic inner life.

The cedars in Lebanon are unique in possessing properties that make their wood resistant to insects, virtually impervious to decay, and extremely durable. This is why they are capable of growing into fine fragrant timber suitable for the temple.

In the economy of God, he saw clearly that because death dominated the earth, the only way its power and domination could be broken was for himself, in Christ, to enter directly into the cycle of birth, growth, life, and death upon our planet. Christ Jesus was born of a virgin, grew up among men, lived and moved among us, then died for us. But, marvel of marvels, his body did not decay (Psalm 16:10). Instead of being chained to the cycle, he shattered its power and rose directly from the dead. No wonder Christians shout, "Death is swallowed up in victory. O death, where is thy sting? O grave, where is thy victory?" (1 Corinthians 15:54–55).

What a triumph!

The shackles that had chained men to the wheel of death on this planet have been snapped.

This is the magnificent overcoming life made available to man through the resurrection of Christ.

This inner life must surge through me in full flowing strength if I am to triumph over the attacks of evil all around me.

The Christian life is a perilous life; it is threatened with danger and destruction on every hand.

> We are troubled on every side, yet not distressed; we are perplexed, but not in despair; persecuted, but not forsaken; cast down, but not destroyed; always bearing about in the body the dying of the Lord Jesus, that the life [resurrection] also of Jesus might be made manifest in our body (2 Corinthians 4:8–10).

This is the exact picture of how a virile Christian responds to the stimuli of perils which encircle him.

How do I realize this resurrection life within?

How do I acquire this vitality to counteract all the forces of evil and sin and despair that surround me in a dying and despairing world?

By calmly claiming and acting on God's own declaration: "Ye are of God, little children, and have overcome them: because greater is he [Christ] that is in you, than he [Satan] that is in the world" (1 John 4:4).

This takes trust, simple faith, implicit confidence in God. Faith is more than mere belief; it is an absolute conviction, an implicit confidence that gives me the grit *to act on* and *respond to* the declarations of divine truth.

Now if I want my faith in God to grow, the way to stimulate it vigorously is to remind myself always of his absolute faithfulness and utter reliability to me, his child.

God cannot betray either himself or his children.

As I act on this realization, he unfailingly imparts to me, by the Spirit, his own abounding resurrection life of growth in godliness that counteracts every peril and perplexity. I know of a surety that *he is alive* and because he is alive I, too, shall live.

It is when I lose confidence in God's Word to me that I leave myself wide open to an invasion of doubt and sin and despair that can only result in rottenness and weakness within (see head verse).

"This is the victory that hath overcome the world, even our faith" (1 John 5:4, A.S.V.).

13
Darkness

And if thou draw out thy soul to the hungry, and satisfy the afflicted soul; then shall thy light rise in obscurity, and thy darkness be as the noon day: and the Lord shall guide thee continually, and satisfy thy soul in drought, and make fat thy bones: and thou shalt be like a watered garden, and like a spring of water, whose waters fail not.

—Isaiah 58:10–11

BECAUSE OF THE physical laws which control the rotation of the earth upon its own axis, it is a natural phenomenon that there should be both light and darkness upon the planet.

Depending upon the season of the year and the geographical location of any given tree, it will be exposed to light for a portion of each twenty-four-hour period and plunged into darkness for the balance of the time. This is one of the straightforward facts that make night, or darkness, one of the stimuli that condition its growth.

During darkness, photosynthesis, which can only proceed under the impulse of light, ceases. Respiration, however, goes on. Respiration is the process whereby carbohydrates, especially dextrose, formed by photosynthesis, are oxidized (burned slowly) within the tree to energize all its vital life functions. This process takes oxygen out of the air and combines it with dextrose to produce energy, giving off ordinary water and carbon dioxide as by-products.

In other words, the tree's response to darkness is active life. During darkness ample energy is generated to fulfill the essential functions of life processes within the tree.

Darkness also normally provides respite from excessive heat. It evens out and moderates temperatures within a tree so that photosynthesis can proceed at an optimum rate when sunlight is available, assuring maximum growth. High internal temperatures (exceeding 120 degrees) can be very damaging to even the sturdiest tree.

Darkness brings dew and refreshment to the foliage of the tree. In mountainous country like Lebanon, where the forests lie close to the sea, nighttime brings its banks of cloud and mist and fog that enshroud the trees in refreshing coolness, saturating the cedars with mineral-laden moisture from the ocean deeps.

In short, darkness is the time during which a tree restores its strength, replenishes its energy, refreshes its fevered life, and finds respite from the heat and activity of the day.

Among Christians there is a decided aversion to darkness. Probably this is because in the Bible darkness is so often associated with evil. Because of this we draw back from the very thought of darkness as if it could contain nothing but ill.

In a spiritual sense we must discover the meaning of darkness in two dimensions, especially as it relates to the formation of Christian character. First there is the darkness of unbelief all around us: the darkness of a world separated from God who is the source of all light; the darkness of men and women who grope for that light, but who have not met the Man of Galilee in the light of his own glorious life and compassion for them.

How am I to respond to such darkness around me? Will I recoil from it? Will I withdraw from those unfortunate ones who walk in such darkness? Or will I go out into it eagerly seeking to lead some of them to my Master? If I do, the outcome will startle me. Even that darkness will be transformed into light and life and energy when men meet my Master. (Read the head verse carefully.)

One of the tremendous personal thrills, known only to a true child of God, is the delight of introducing a soul in darkness to his own Heavenly Father and Christ Jesus his Saviour, the light of the world. Such an experience energizes and vitalizes a Christian's entire life beyond the power of words to describe. It makes his inner life a bright adventure despite the darkness around him.

The second aspect in which a Christian must understand darkness pertains to his own personal life. We are given no guarantee by God that all our days on earth will be nothing but brightness. It is an inexorable law of life, as sure as the rotation of the earth, that for all of us there are going to be some tears and sighs, some sorrow and sadness, some dark periods of disappointment and despair.

Often these are times and events over which we have no control whatever. They come as swiftly and surely as darkness in the desert. How am I going to respond to their apparent oppression? How will I react to these seeming reverses that come to me as stimuli in disguise?

Am I going to rebel against them because they bring a sudden lull into my feverish activity, because they bog down my busy life, because they curtail my ambitious aspirations?

Or, contrariwise, will I accept them calmly as coming from the hand of my Heavenly Father for my own well-being? After all, it is perfectly possible to walk in the dark unafraid, undisturbed, and undismayed—"for thou are with me."

Christians at times are so caught up in being busy about many things that God deliberately lets darkness descend around them just so he can have a chance to take a quiet walk with them alone for a change. There in the coolness and stillness, frustrated souls are refreshed, the fever of life is forgotten, and men become "like a watered garden."

In the darkness lies part of the secret to a character that is wholesome, fruitful, radiant, yet balanced in its godly behavior. For some of us it is only in the darkness we dare draw so close to Christ that we later come away with the myrrh and frankincense of his own presence upon us.

It is only in the darkness that I discover something of the sweet fellowship of his suffering—taste a little of the awesome agony he endured for me in the darkness of Gethsemane.

In the darkness I understand at last something of those wondrous words, "not my will, but thine."

14
Rest

And he shall be like a tree planted by the rivers of water, that bringeth forth his fruit in his season; his leaf also shall not wither; and whatsoever he doeth shall prosper.

—Psalm 1:3

ONE OF THE conditions most frequently forgotten in thinking about the growth of a tree is rest. Or, to put it in technical terminology, dormancy. In northern climes winter is the period or season of rest. In tropical regions it is generally the hot, dry season of the year when trees and plants find respite from rapid growth.

It is important to understand that dormancy is not death. A tree may appear to be dead, it is true. The leaves of deciduous trees will be all stripped off in the fall leaving a stark skeleton. The tree is nevertheless very much alive—but at rest.

In the case of conifers and evergreens like the cedars of Lebanon the needles are not all shed at once, so that the tree appears to be green and growing at all seasons. Actually this is not so, for during winter these trees, too, are dormant and at rest.

In the design of living things, whether plants or animals, it has been ordained that their bodily structure and strength should be rested and restored periodically. This is conducive to optimum growth. In this connection it is of interest to note that even God himself saw fit to rest after completing his creative enterprise throughout the universe.

Dormancy in a tree occupies a specific season. This season of rest is the one which just precedes the springtime of active and accelerated growth. It is really the time of peaceful preparation for the drastic demands of growth. It is the time of rebuilding wornout cells and reconditioning tired tissues. All of this is in preparation for the upsurge of the vigorous spring.

In a certain sense the period of rest is one of the most important throughout the entire year. It is the season when a tree becomes fully refitted for the exhausting demands that will be made upon it during the long, rigorous growing season when new wood is added to its structure and fresh fruit is borne upon its boughs.

So we may say in all accuracy that in order to grow and flourish in season a tree must also rest and relax out of season.

Precisely the same principle applies in the total spiritual, mental, and emotional life of the Christian. There is an erroneous concept common to many children of God that to be effective they must be always active. There is the idea abroad that one must be always "on the go for God."

Yet even our Lord and Master, Jesus Christ, when he moved among us as the God-Man, found it imperative to withdraw from the activity of his busy life and take time to rest. Again and again we find him slipping away to some quiet spot on a mountainside or across the lake where he could be alone and still for refreshment of body, mind, and spirit. These were interludes of quiet communion with his Father.

In each of the preceding chapters it has been emphasized that man has his part to play in the decisions which determine his growth in character. *When I deliberately set myself* TO DO *what God requires of me, responding positively to the stimuli from himself, then he performs his part in seeing to it that* MY LIFE DOES TAKE ON THE CHARACTER OF CHRIST.

This is equally true of rest. It is in the very makeup of life that we are bound to encounter times when we have gotten beyond our strength and stamina. Then we will hear the Spirit's gentle voice saying, "Come ye yourselves apart . . . , and rest a while" (Mark 6:31).

Again the vital question is, "Will I or won't I respond to this warm invitation?" I can claim to be too busy; that there simply isn't time; that there are too many others depending on me; that I'm tough and can take it; or that I'd rather wear out than rust out.

Each of these may be legitimate and logical replies but they are not necessarily either wise or godly.

Proof of this lies in the number of Christians who collapse under the strain and pressure and tension of twentieth-century society.

Sometimes God, in a mercy which we cannot comprehend, has to deliberately compel us to take an enforced rest for a season. Illness, sudden reverses, or chilling consequences come like the dark, cold grip of winter upon a Christian, compelling him to cease from his busyness.

Then we hear the plaintive cry, "Why did this have to happen to me?" or "Why am I out in the cold?" "What is the sense of all this suffering?" "Why can't I keep going for God?"

The answer is a simple one.

I do not honestly believe God is capable of doing his work in the world without my feverish human efforts.

When I reach the place where I have implicit confidence in God's ability to manage not only the affairs of the world but also mine, as I entrust them to him, I will have found the place of rest.

This is borne out very clearly in Hebrews 4:9–10: "There remaineth therefore a rest to the people of God. For he that is entered into his rest, he also hath ceased from his own works [busyness], as God did from his."

It is not always easy to simply step aside into solitude and rest and quietness. But unless I learn how, my entire growth in God will be endangered.

As a simple first step in this direction may I suggest the reader take twenty minutes each day to go out and walk alone—a brisk walk—only smiling to strangers—deliberately looking for the beauty and handiwork of God in the natural world about him, and inwardly adoring the Lord for who he is. Leave the worries and work at home or in the office. It will prove to be a tonic, a rest that results in growth in God.

Most of us have never learned the humble though powerful practice of concentrating on Christ. Outside, walking alone, away from the usual surroundings which remind us of our feverish workaday world, we can give our hearts a chance to center their interest and affection on him.

It is a simple, humble habit. Perhaps it is too ordinary for most men.

But to walk with God means just that—daily.

This in essence is the secret of rest. It is the time of waiting, of communicating with God the Father, of coming to Christ, of being inwardly conscious of the Holy Spirit's gentle voice entreating me to lift up my soul to him who, when he was among us, said, "Come unto me, all ye that labour and are heavy laden, and I will give you rest" (Matthew 11:28).

And having come, I will be refreshed and fitted for new growth in God during future days.

Book II

Still Waters

To
our little mountain lake

Contents

Preface

ALMOST EXACTLY TEN years have elapsed since I picked up a pen and started to write again after the great loss of my first wife, Phyllis. That was an unsure and trembling start. In fact, then I often wondered if, in truth, I could complete another book.

But the intervening ten years have seen not just one book, but ten, come into full flowering. Some of these have gone on to become national and international bestsellers under our Father's good hand.

Ursula, my second wife and courageous little companion, has shared wholeheartedly in these endeavors. To her I express my hearty gratitude. It has not all been an easy road. Writing is a tremendously demanding discipline. It carries with it discouraging disappointments, as well as deep delights.

From time to time it is imperative that an author should pause to rest, to sharpen his skills, to hone the tools of his trade. To do this requires something that may differ slightly or radically from the form of work he may employ most of the time.

It is akin to the veteran woodsman who is wise enough to stop and rest from his chopping and sawing. He will perch up on a stump, take a file from his pocket to touch up the teeth of his saw, draw out a whetstone to hone the edge of his axe razor sharp. Then, refreshed and restored, he will return to work doubly equipped.

Still Waters has been just such an interlude; it has been a labor of love. Time was set aside to record this interlude for the sheer joy of writing. The theme is one that has enriched my own spirit.

My most earnest hope is that it might in some significant way inspire and enrich the reader.

W. PHILLIP KELLER

1
The Search for "Still Waters"

THOSE WHO HAVE read some of my previous books, such as *Canada's Wild Glory, Splendour From the Land, Under Desert Skies* and *A Shepherd Looks at Psalm 23,* will know that I am a man with an intense, unrelenting love for the land. But beyond this basic, fundamental fondness for earth and trees, plants, shrubs, grass and livestock, the whole out-of-doors is essentially my home territory. It is there I feel a unique oneness with all things wild and free.

A number of my books have dealt with this dimension of life. *Africa's Wild Glory, Under Wilderness Skies, Travels of the Tortoise* and *Mountain Splendor* have all endeavored to share with the reader some of the powerful impulses and deep delights that have made my life in the outdoors such an incredible adventure. They have recounted some of the exciting experiences of living close to the land. They have revealed those values and ideals that are essential for the preservation of wild places and wildlife, which are an integral part of our wholeness as a society.

For several years my work and responsibilities made it imperative for me to live in the city. True, it was not a large metropolis, but it was still an urban environment. My wife and I rented a spacious suite in a modern high-rise building. We were fortunate to find one with pleasant views across the valley and within easy walking distance of the lake. Had it not been for the opportunities to slip away quietly for long tramps along the beach, my stay in the city would have been much more painful than it was.

In the apartment, I tasted the sort of life that is the lot of millions upon millions of city residents. We enjoyed all the conveniences and comforts associated with a man-made environment. There were thermostats and double-glass windows and electric doors and wall-to-wall carpeting and air conditioning to control the indoor climate.

There were double bathrooms, gleaming with tile and chrome

fixtures. Built-in appliances such as oven, dishwasher, stove, refrigerator, washer and drier all made for the most modern mode of existence. Two telephones, one beside the bed, kept us in immediate contact with the entire city and all of its busy life. Underground security parking, electric doors, elevators and paved drives insured that we were sheltered from the elements of wind, snow, sleet or rain.

Yet, amid all this apparent affluence and seeming security, a strange sensation of insecurity hovered in the background. There was a profound, pervading promise of vulnerability to our pretty place. Fortunately we were reluctant to purchase property of this sort; rather we rented. This at least reduced the risks of becoming enmeshed and terribly trapped in an unwholesome environment.

The word *unwholesome* was chosen with great care, for I never felt completely at ease in this artificial, urban environment. In a sense I felt caged in. I was cramped and constricted by my surroundings of steel, stucco, concrete and asphalt. They tended to cut me off from contact—intimate contact—with the earth. My feet were always insulated from the touch of soil and grass and leaves and twigs and sand and rock. My face craved the kiss of the sun, the caress of the wind or the stimulation of snow and rain. The air I breathed was stale, often charged with fumes of carbon monoxide or industrial wastes. The water I drank came through the pipes so contaminated with chlorine it was scarcely potable, much less palatable to one who has drunk deeply from mountain streams. Most of the food I ate was procured from the supermarket, its origin often thousands of miles away in some foreign land.

Somehow I sensed that my dependence upon others to supply me with power, light, heat, water, food and shelter from afar made me very vulnerable. One lightning strike or one labor strike, and my artificial man-made world could imprison me helplessly in the midst of modern devices.

Because of all this, a deep subconscious unease often lay upon my spirit. My wife, Cheri (her pet name), and I would sometimes speak of this deep disquiet in our more somber moments. She, as a young girl, had gone through the agony and anguish of a great war in Europe. She knew firsthand what it was to be cut off by catastrophe from the elemental resources of the land. She had stood in line for hours, shivering in the cold, waiting for a meager handout of bread or milk or meat. She had felt the awesome, gnawing hunger pangs of unsatisfied appetite. She had been sent on errands to the countryside, to exchange the finest of laces and linens for a sack of potatoes or a pound of butter.

Beyond all of these vague, yet sinister, aspects of our vulnerability lay the very tangible and tough realities of day-to-day living. Because of inflation; because of increased labor costs; because of the accelerating energy crisis; because of international monetary exchanges, the bills we had to pay from month to month kept going up and up. Charges for power, heat, light, food, water, telephone and transportation escalated steadily.

I am too free a spirit to be trapped by the tensions of my times. And, as we contemplated a change, I decided that we would search for some still waters, where the tyranny of twentieth-century urban life would not intrude. We would look for a spot somewhat removed from the noise and confusion of city living. It would not be easy to find. Privacy, seclusion and peace are rapidly becoming the rarest commodities in a crowded world. The place where a person could still, at least to a degree, derive his life and sustenance from his immediate surroundings for his own strength was not easy to stumble across.

But we would try.

I wanted to get back to basics.

There was a longing to re-establish contact with the land. Again I would draw my sustenance and comfort directly from the resources of the earth around me. With the strength of my body and keen awareness of my mind, I wanted to sense and know what it was to be a free and independent man, moving in gentle harmony with the outdoor seasons and natural environment that supported me.

This quest for a quiet life was more than just a move from the city to the country. It involved more than merely relocating ourselves geographically in a rural setting.

There was also a deep inner hunger, a fierce longing, for stillness and silence and serenity. I needed space for my soul to rest from the rush and clamor of city tensions.

One of civilization's most formidable forces, which had exacted an enormous toll of tension from me, was traffic noise. The unrelenting roar of trucks, screech of cars and staccato gunfire of motorbikes gunning up the hill past our place made many nights a nightmare. The drone of city traffic, power mowers, powerboats, power street sweepers and air traffic overhead beat upon our eardrums all day long.

Even though subconsciously I endeavored to shut out this intrusion, the noise pollution preyed upon me. It generated a revulsion in my inner being, which resented the racket that beat about me with such remorseless intensity. Sigurd Olson expressed this exasperation very pointedly in his book *Singing Wilderness*:

> More and more do we realize that quiet is important in our happiness. In our cities the constant beat of strange and foreign wavelengths on our primal senses beats us into neuroticism, changes us from creatures who once knew the silences to fretful, uncertain beings immersed in a cacophony of noise which destroys sanity and equilibrium.

But beyond all these considerations, the search for still waters was in a sense a search for spiritual refreshment: to be still and know God; to sense His presence; to commune with Him quietly, without undue haste or rush.

Just to sit softly in the twilight beside a lake or on a bluff or rock in some quiet glade and be glad He, too, was there sharing the setting with me; this I sought.

There are those who claim that to try and go back to our beginnings is to live life in reverse. They assert vehemently that we cannot turn back the clock and reduce the tempo of our times.

Perhaps for the vast multitudes born and cradled in the complexity of great cities, this is true. Perhaps from the hour of their conception they have been subtly conditioned, even in their mothers' warm wombs, to the world of stress and strain around them. But for me, this was not so. I was born and reared in the great, open, sweeping expanses of Africa's plains and bush. I am a product of the wilds, a son of the wilderness. Wide vistas, open spaces, long views, the warm sun, vagrant winds and star-filled nights in untamed country are the fabric fashioned into my rough character. It was upon these that my boyhood soul was built into manhood. And if long removed from them, even as a man in his twilight years, I ached for them with profound pain.

No, indeed, finding still waters in our busy, boisterous twentieth century would not be easy.

For it was also a search for simplicity. It was a quest for basic human self-reliance.

I was deliberately turning my back upon the easy life of reliance on others to meet my needs. With the output of my own strength, the use of my own wits, the exertion of my own muscles, I would seek independence amid a pathetically dependent society.

In so far as it was possible and practical, I wanted to dig my own garden, grow much of my own food, gather my own fuel and nourish my own soul with the natural beauties about me. I wanted to live in serenity and in dignity. For me, peace of mind, stillness of spirit and soundness of health were more important than any prestige or prominence that hectic city life might proffer.

The mute question was, could such a way of life be rediscovered? Could it be grasped again by a man well advanced in years? Could it be tasted and relished, even if only briefly, before that last call came to go home where change and decay no longer dismay?

2
The Find

TO FIND THE sort of spot we dreamed about would not be easy. Twenty-five years ago it would have been much, much easier. But with the passing of time, most of the desirable properties had been taken up and developed to a high degree.

There had been many years of prosperity, affluence and rapid urban growth. Investors had large sums to spend on real estate. Land values soared to unheard-of heights, and many wealthy families were looking for some quiet corner in the country where they could have a second home. These rural retreats were often little more than status symbols. To own a summer house in the hills or beside a lake was to parade one's prosperity, just as owning a second car was at one time a mark of financial success.

In spite of the enormous competition, we set out in earnest to see what was available. In the usual manner, we followed the newspaper advertisements, watched For Sale signs along the roads, allowed agents to drag us from place to place, trying to persuade us to buy something not really suited to our needs. But we were not to be diverted or dissuaded from our dream. I refused to buy something not suited to us.

It was a discouraging search. So many times we seemed to be hot on the trail of a tempting spot, only to discover that it had enormous disadvantages or drawbacks. Sometimes properties were blatantly misrepresented. The advertisement would sound so appealing, but the place itself would turn out to be appalling.

Then, one gentle spring day, I returned to a little lakeside cottage that had been given only a cursory glance several months before. It looked rather dilapidated, and the original asking price had been outrageous. But suddenly, because of illness, the owner had been compelled to sell, and now the value asked had been substantially reduced, to a more reasonable level.

The morning I went to take a second look, I discovered that the adjoining land was also for sale. Together, the two properties would provide the sort of privacy and seclusion that we sought. But I was still not sure the cottage was capable of accommodating us comfortably. It looked to be not much more than a thin shell of a structure, suited to a few fleeting summer weeks. The question was, could it be converted into a reasonably suitable permanent residence? We would have to look inside.

The location left something to be desired. It was down a short dead-end road, rather too close to a main arterial road to suit my taste. Fortunately, a thick screen of assorted trees and native shrubs surrounded the place. The cottage, when the leaves were out, could not be seen from the main highway. It sat tucked away on a little shelf of sward beside the lake, unknown and unnoticed by most of those who drove past.

To a degree, this was not altogether undesirable. At least we were convenient to an all-weather road. There would be no need to fight sleet and ice and deep drifts of winter snow to get in and out during adverse weather. I had endured more than my share of such roads in previous places I had owned across the years.

Second, even though I sought a place of peace and quiet for writing, I did not wish to become totally detached from the tempo of my times. Too many authors and thinkers and scholars ensconce themselves in ivory-tower isolation. They lose touch with the tough realities of their generation. For me, the muffled rumble and roar of traffic that filtered down through the trees would be a constant, solemn reminder of the stern, competitive, noisy, high-speed world in which I live.

To a degree, depending upon the atmospheric conditions and direction of the wind, the sounds of speeding vehicles would rise or diminish. Sometimes they were so muted they could scarcely be heard. On other occasions their noise seemed to be unduly amplified by the lake surface or the towering cliffs behind. Yet seldom were the lap of water or rustle of leaves inaudible.

On the whole, despite the proximity of the paved highway, peace and tranquility prevailed in this gentle spot. Sufficiently so that as I strolled around its untidy and rather neglected grounds, I could clearly hear the spring songs of the western meadowlarks nesting in the sagebrush hills above us. I could also hear the clear, piercing, plaintive notes of a loon on the lake. They were sounds that surmounted all those other sounds and spoke peace to my spirit.

Down at the water's edge, there was the soft lap of water on stones—the lazy lullaby of the lake washing back and forth on the rocks in front of the cottage. It was an intimate, satisfying sensation to sit there watching the wind-stirred riffles run up to my feet, yet seldom break the satin-smooth surface of the water.

Between breezes, the lake would lie perfectly still. It was cupped in a warm valley between gaunt, gnarled ridges of rock and shale. Their bold battlements of brown and gray formations were mirrored in the still waters with immaculate, flawless perfection.

I had never been on a property that seemed to have such an intimate interaction with a body of water. Most homes and houses built on beaches or shorelines stand back a bit from the water's edge. It is as if they stand there as onlookers at a respectable distance. They enjoy the view, but prefer not to come too close.

Here it was totally different. The lake almost embraced the cottage on two sides. It sang on the tiny sand beach only a few feet from the door. It rippled in the reeds that ran along the edge of the grass glades. Sunlight glancing off its surface flooded the great windows facing it. The presence of the lake itself was astonishingly pervasive. It was everywhere around, moving and breathing. It was an environment that was relatively new and exciting to one, like myself, who had never lived in such close association with a mountain lake.

I felt inexorably drawn under its spell. Quickly I began to discover that this could be a stimulating spot to live. I had read that lakes were too placid, too serene, too quiet to stimulate a writer, but a few hours beside this body of water convinced me otherwise. Here one was in immediate contact with a whole web of life that was in constant motion. Its many moods, its changing seasons, its abundant bird life, its varied habitats suited to all sorts of animals, made it a miniature world of endless delight and wonder.

I stumbled across several stubs of poplar that still bore the chiseled tooth marks of beavers. As I scrambled along the shore, a beautiful dark mink darted along a log. On the path behind the cottage, a coyote had left his droppings in the gravel. At night his wilderness cry would echo across the lake from the brown bluffs above us.

I found an open glade, cleared from the woods that flourished along the shore. Its soil was dark, rich, mellow with the accumulated leaf mold of uncounted centuries. It had been carved from the wilderness by some sturdy pioneer long since forgotten. With sweat and skill and the labor of love, it could be made into a bountiful garden for fruit and vegetables.

The longer I looked around, the more convinced I was that at last we had found our spot. It was wild enough, untamed enough, to appeal to my wilderness spirit. A black bear had been seen swimming across the lake a few days before. The wild bighorn sheep were lambing on the rock bluffs overlooking the cottage. And across the lake, bands of mule deer came down at dawn to drink, their shining coats reflected in the still waters.

But the cottage itself remained a question. A few days later we were shown inside. To our unbounded surprise and delight, it was far, far better than its weathered exterior had indicated.

It was of sturdy open-beam construction. It was not a shack at all, but an all-cedar cottage, with great expanses of glass opening onto the lake. An atmosphere of spaciousness, warmth and charm came from the softwood interior. The native cedar shone satin smooth and gave off the rich aroma of forest fragrance.

Cheri and I looked at each other. A knowing look of mutual approval and agreement passed between us. *This was it. We had found it. The search was over!* No words were spoken, but these were the sentiments of our spirits, sure and certain.

The previous occupants had been temporary tenants, and, as is always the case, the cottage showed signs of neglect and carelessness. It would take time and work to restore its luster. Minor interior alterations would have to be made to suit our lifestyle. There were no proper clothes cupboards. Heating arrangements were inadequate for winter weather. Floor coverings would have to be replaced. Insulation of the roof and walls would have to be undertaken.

None of these were unduly difficult. By fall, when the great black birches turned their greenery into flaming gold, the little cottage would be a snug home, sheathed and sealed against winter storms.

Sitting on the open sun deck in the gentle spring sunshine, we wrote out an offer to purchase the property. In a few days it would be ours. It was the opening of a brand-new chapter in our lives. We had no idea just how rich and full and exciting its pages would be. It was another step of adventure on the trail of a life already replete with great satisfactions and enormous thrills.

In a very genuine and sincere sense, we knew it was the place of our heavenly Father's arrangement for us. Often we had turned to Him, seeking definite direction in our decisions. It is far too easy to stumble into traps when purchasing property. He had been our senior counselor and consultant. The clear guidance He gave brought us to something better than we had ever imagined.

One of our deep desires was that this spot should be not just an inspiration to us, but to all others who visited us, who had a chance to taste its tranquillity.

Standing beneath the birches, looking across the shining loveliness of the lake, its name came to me clearly: "We will call it 'Still Waters,' for it is our Lord who led us here."

3
The Fireplace

BECAUSE "STILL WATERS" in its original state was basically only a summer cabin, it lacked any proper heating arrangement for winter weather. There was a small fireplace that would take the chill off a cool June evening, but it was far from adequate to face the fury of a fierce northerly in November.

It was obvious something much more substantial would have to be provided to pour heat into the place at a steady pace, no matter how ruthless the storms were that raged around our rough walls.

Since the energy crisis has crept up on our contemporary world, hundreds of thousands of home owners have turned back to wood and coal in search of fuel savings. A whole new generation of efficient wood- and coal-burning stoves, heaters and fireplaces has found a ready market among embattled people aroused by ever-increasing fuel costs.

So I went in search of some sort of fireplace unit, heater or stove that would serve several purposes at once with a maximum of efficiency. It was nearly as difficult as deciding on a new car. There are a multitude of models, designs and makes to choose from. They are promoted and advertised with beautiful literature and beguiling brochures. But to find the type best suited to our needs meant more than just looking at lovely pictures put out by the manufacturers.

After reading all we could and tramping through all the stores, I came across the unit that impressed me the most. It was simple in design, yet elegant in appearance. Made of heavy, quarter-inch steel, fully lined with heavy firebrick, it could serve as a cook stove, heater or open fireplace.

But the price seemed prohibitive.

Though only one unit remained for sale, I procrastinated about purchasing it. Finally the decision could not be deferred any longer. That day I quietly bowed my head and requested supernatural guidance from God, my Father, in proceeding to purchase it.

When I asked to be shown the unit, I was taken out to the warehouse by a young man from the company whom I had not met before. He quickly assured me this particular model was the finest and only trouble-free unit they had ever stocked. This helped to harden my resolve.

Then, almost in the same breath, he went on to inform me that he was the son of the owner of the company. It was his special privilege to extend a discount to any customer. He would be glad to knock off 10 percent then and there, if I would take it off his hands. Would I! My heart leaped with gratitude, the sale was consummated and I walked out of the store breathing deeply, "Thank You, Father!"

The little heater, not even three feet high or wide, weighed nearly a quarter of a ton. It was not the sort of thing one just picks up or pushes around at will. It was a piece of equipment you quickly learned to respect.

A kind friend came over to help move it inside, but the two of us could hardly budge it, so we called upon our wives to help us. Heaving, straining, shoving and pushing, we finally got it into place. It was terribly tricky, fitting the smoke pipes just right. I had measured their length to the exact fraction of an inch. But by tipping the stove gently on one side, we were able to insert them at an angle, and then slide the unit into place. All of us were puffing and heaving with the exertion, but the heater stood square and straight and sure in its place when we were through.

It turned out to be one of those pieces of equipment that work to perfection. In fact, it so far surpassed our expectations that we still marvel at its efficiency and rave to our friends about its performance.

Adorning its black bulk are beautiful, gleaming, stainless-steel knobs. Its name, too, is emblazoned in bold shining silver across the front. The fire screen used when an open fire is desired is also fabricated from glowing stainless steel, so that the entire unit stands as a handsome piece to enhance our home.

I had a friend, who is a skilled tinsmith, construct a metal tray in which the stove would stand. This I filled with glacial stones and rocks from the hills above us. Each stone was selected with loving care for its sparkle, color and shape. These were each washed carefully in the lake, then arranged around the base in a beautiful, natural mosaic of mountain rocks.

Behind the fireplace, to protect the wooden walls from its heat, I decided to place a single rugged slab of granite. A friend and I went to the edge of a gaunt canyon back of our cottage. There an outcrop of beautiful rock had split into sheets of stone that could be pried off the basement formations. With enormous care, I picked out a piece that I felt would exactly suit the cottage.

It was no easy thing to carry this giant slab of stone out of the hills. We made a crude cradle of poles and ropes to carry it. Then, stumbling along a few steps at a time, we slowly struggled up the canyon trail.

Now the rock stands serenely back of the heater, adorned with patches of lovely lichens and bits of moss that remind us of the rugged hills from whence it came.

Because of the basic design of the heater, which uses a steel baffle, it burns a minimum of fuel with a maximum of heat. In ten minutes time, even a moderate fire begins to warm the entire cottage. Once the heavy steel unit, along with the giant slab of granite behind it, are hot, they remain so for hours, permeating the whole place with that gentle, living, vibrant heat that is so uniquely characteristic of wood fuel. Its aroma fills our home, and the fragrance of the fire lends an ancient aura of goodwill and good cheer to the atmosphere.

When I come back to the cottage—whether from working in the garden, hiking in the hills or canoeing across the lake—I am welcomed by the pungent perfume of wood smoke. There is something warm and wonderful in its enchantment, akin to being greeted at the door by the open arms and warm embrace of a loving woman.

We spend hours and hours of quiet contentment beside this fireplace. Its flames dance up the chimney in bright hues of gold, yellow, red, blue and sometimes even green, when a piece of wood streaked with fungus or lichens is licked by the fire.

The flames flicker and play in reflection on the windowpanes.

They play and dance, too, in the eyes and faces of those who sit quietly before them, borne away in daydreams of delight.

Even cutting and gathering wood for this fireplace is no chore. It uses so little and burns so efficiently that my woodpile for the winter was ten times bigger than I needed. Few are the things in life which have so far surpassed our happiest hopes.

4
Inside "Still Waters"

WHEN WE FIRST came to "Still Waters," the cabin itself posed somewhat of a problem. It had been used only for casual summer interludes. Though built of the best native cedar planks, it was still not much more than a mere shell, meant to shelter its occupants from the elements.

Being of open-beam construction, with great expanses of glass overlooking the lake, it was a handsome summer retreat. But the very attributes that worked to its special advantage in warm weather made it equally unsuitable for winter residence. With its single-layer board walls, high open-loft ceilings and giant windows, there was ample air movement and space to moderate summer's scorching heat.

All of this, however, would have to be altered to make it habitable when winter winds hauled down across the lake from the north. Amid snow and ice and driving sub-zero sleet, it would need to be much more snug and tight against the weather.

To accomplish this, we sought the services of a veteran carpenter. With his long experience and great drive, he quickly converted it from a mere cabin to a snug, comfortable cottage. Assisted by his two young and sturdy nephews, he performed a modern miracle in less than a week of work.

First he put on a double roof, fully insulated. This would retain all the heat that formerly escaped upwards and outwards through the single tongue-and-groove cedar roof. Then he double glazed all the giant windows. The glass was put in with meticulous precision, fully sealed and charged with desiccant between the air spaces, to prevent fogging or condensation.

Finally, he insulated all the outside walls and sheathed them again in satin-lustered native cedar. It made for a beautiful weather-tight structure. With painstaking care, he personally selected each piece of cedar that went on the walls.

When the whole transformation was complete, the cottage stood glowing in its natural wood tones. No one would ever suspect that it had been so dramatically altered, since its entire beautiful interior remained untouched, in its native woodsy splendor. Smooth cedar planking, rich with its warm hues of brown, red and bronze, gave the little home an aura of coziness and contentment.

We removed one large set of sliding glass doors that opened onto the deck. In its place we installed a huge picture window that gives an unobstructed view over the lawns and lake to the rugged hills beyond.

The alterations were done in midsummer, at the hottest time of the desert year. Immediately, we noticed that the modifications improved the liveability of the cottage. Its double roof and walls kept out the blazing heat, and the double glass tempered the burning summer sun. So we had gained dramatically in every direction, much to our delight.

The elderly carpenter and his youthful helpers were excellent craftsmen. They worked with vigor and zest, despite the appalling heat. An occasional plunge in the lake would cool them off. And when the day's work was done, one knew that their time had been spent to the optimum.

The refurbishing of the cottage was a tremendous treat. So often it is common to hear people complain about shoddy workmanship and slipshod labor. But we were given a delectable taste of old-fashioned craftsmanship at its best. A certain pride of accomplishment and inherent skill in workmanship had been apparent in the whole project. When the men were done, we were left with the distinct impression that this had been a labor of love.

Inside the cottage, a pronounced atmosphere of peace and serenity prevails. There is something distinctly warm and woodsy about it. It blends beautifully with the birches and boulders and beaches around it. It is almost as if part of the outdoors has been brought indoors. One blends with the other. The inside is not separated from the outside by superficial barriers. Looking in is as much an extension of one's view as looking out is a widening of one's vision.

On the wooden walls there hang gorgeous genuine oil paintings of mountain scenes and native wildlife. These have come into our care through the unique artistry of my friend Karl Wood. Acclaimed and recognized as one of Canada's foremost mountain painters, his exquisite work lends an atmosphere of authentic mountain grandeur to our cottage.

There are other unique furnishings, too, which are essentially a part of our native upland world of forests, lake and hills. A beautiful wood-burl table, fashioned from a giant Douglas fir and mounted on elk antlers, graces the living room. The antlers were a pair of crown-royals that I picked up on a remote ridge in the northern Rockies on my first expedition into that rugged wilderness.

On my desk stands a handsome lamp. Its base is a rich, dark-red slab of native juniper, its pedestal a twisted greasewood stem. And adorning it are a pair of California quail: a cock and hen beautifully posed.

From the open-beamed ceiling hangs a cheerful chandelier created from two sets of dainty whitetail-deer antlers. Often we look across the lake and watch these deer feeding at the water's edge. Now several sets of their cast-off crowns grace our home, flooding it with charm and good cheer.

Here and there on the walls there are other mounted birds. A gorgeous golden-breasted meadowlark, singing his heart out, reminds us of our songsters on the sagebrush benches above us. The waxwing is one of hundreds that come winging through the valley to gorge themselves on wild-rose hips and mountain-ash berries.

All these mounts have been prepared and fashioned by my friend Abe Braun. Though now semiretired, he is among the finest taxidermists on the continent. His superb workmanship is found from the Yukon to Panama. For our part, we feel honored to have a few pieces of his superb craftsmanship in our care. It lends enormous atmosphere to our home.

We are people who find deep pleasure in common things: a twisted piece of driftwood, a gnarled, wave-washed root; a slab of stone, shattered and shining with minerals; a spray of maple leaves, scarlet and gold; sprigs of pine and fir, redolent with resin and the fragrance of the forest; bouquets of wild desert flowers gathered from the hills; a gnarled piece of beaver wood, cut by chisel-sharp teeth; giant ponderosa pinecones and dainty spruce cones.

These are all a part of the wild world in which we live and work and play. They are the warp and woof of our mountain realm. We relish them, revel in them, then happily pass them on to friends or visitors.

Inherently there is something very sure and very satisfying in these common bonds between the earth and us. We sense and know instinctively that we are not separated from the source of our sustenance and inspiration by man-made barriers. Here there is an intimacy with the earth that sustains us, the environment that supports us, the surroundings that inspire us and set our spirits singing.

Inside "Still Waters," there is a profound awareness of belonging—in a primitive, pristine way—to the world around us. Even the manner in which the cottage snuggles into its lakeside setting among the trees and shrubs and rocks and grass lends the feeling of being native to the landscape. It does not impose or intrude upon its surroundings. It is so much at peace in its place that many have passed it by for years, not even knowing it was there, resting quietly among its friendly trees.

This little cottage by the lake is a place of quiet contentment. To those friends and visitors who come within its walls, it speaks serenity. Here is stilled the rush and noise of urban life, and in its place there descends the stillness of nature's gentle ways.

Always, our hope and prayer and desire remain that anyone setting foot within our wooden walls will go away richer than when they came: richer in memories of a few moments of repose, in which they sensed the gentle touch of God's gracious Spirit on their souls.

To help achieve this end, we make sure that music plays a prominent part in our lives. But this *music* of which I speak is not all of the man-made sort.

Many of the melodies played around "Still Waters" are as ancient as our hills, as ageless as our desert stars. This music caressed and cheered this valley centuries before the first Indians set foot upon its hot, sandy beaches. It is music that comes drifting in on the breezes through our open windows; it is a medley of songs that soothes our spirits as we step to the open door.

There are the tremulous notes of meadowlarks and orioles, chickadees and song sparrows. There are the haunting, long-drawn cries of the loons on the lake, the coyotes on the cliffs. There is the strident, stirring sound of Canada geese on wing, as well as sandhill cranes and flights of ducks crossing the sky in spectacular flocks.

Added to these are the lap of waves on rock and sand: the rhythmic splash of water shattering on stone. The rush and gush of white-crested waves, pushed and plowed by the wind at work on the lake, stirs our souls.

That same wind whistles and sings and whoops its way through the trees. The branches bend and bow and billow in the blustery breezes. They brush and rub their leaves together in a symphony of sound that makes sleep come sweetly and the rest refreshing.

We are rich with melodies of a hundred sorts. To these we add the joy of music of our own making. Despite our limited space, a modest organ graces our home. Cheri, in her own winsome way, was able to purchase the instrument at a fraction of its original price. From it we draw hours of pleasure, playing our favorite songs and hymns.

Added to all this, we can tune into a high-fidelity good-music station. The strains of majestic symphonies and the great classics are received within our warm walls, bringing to them inspiration and uplift for all who are within earshot. And because of all this, we know ourselves to be blessed.

5
Tree Planting

CLOSE BEHIND "Still Waters" runs a busy highway. It is one of the main north-south travel routes through our mountain country. Because of the tourist influx drawn by the sunny skies, beautiful beaches, lovely lakes, mighty mountains and the bountiful fruit of the valley, this is a busy, noisy thoroughfare in summer. The rest of the year, it is less congested and thunderous.

To help screen ourselves from the traffic sounds, it was decided to plant trees along the road. There were trees there already, but it seems one can never have too many, if it is privacy and seclusion that are desired. To a degree, the native poplars, birches and junipers already supplied a leafy screen. But we wanted even more privacy.

I decided on planting Lombardy poplars for an avenue of stately, rapidly growing trees. A nearby nursery supplied me with a fine set of sturdy specimens. A friend came to help dig the deep holes. One morning's hard work saw all the slim-shaped trees, still bare of leaves, standing in place, erect and graceful. Digging the holes helped us to discover that our soil was deeper, darker and of better content than I had ever supposed.

There is something sacred about planting trees. There is permanency, hope and a long look down the years ahead in this rite. It is sacramental, in the sense that one is aware the trees may very well be there long after the planter has passed on. Standing in their place beneath the blazing summer sun, bent beneath winter snows, they will grace the landscape long years after I am gone.

There is love and affection and compassion bound up with growing trees. They must be watered and staked and pruned and sprayed, to forestall the adversity of their environment and predators. Beautiful trees take more than just being plunked in place to thrive. So between trees and men there begins to emerge a bond of affection and endearment.

I watched the row of Lombardies with commingled awe and delight. In the first summer's growth, they shot up nearly six feet. Great, green, gorgeous leaves unfurled from their swelling buds to flutter like emerald flags, blowing in the breeze. I cut back the most advanced shoots to thicken up the growth, making their dense branches an even better sound barrier.

By late fall, they were a galaxy of gold, each leaf gilded yellow, flashing back the sunlight that struck its surface. In a few years the avenue would be a landmark in the valley, a sight to gladden the spirit of any passersby.

I also planted some trees of heaven. These are a vigorous, large-leaved tree, with a distinctly tropical appearance. Yet they are tough enough to endure a cold winter. They thrive on marginal land and can endure dire drought. In late summer, their foliage changes to a rich bronze that is arresting in its diversity.

An amusing aspect of this little venture was that the trees came from a friend who had kindly dug them up from a roadside site. He placed them carefully in boxes and then brought them to me. At the time, all the young saplings were stripped and bare of leaves, so I planted each in its special spot with the utmost care.

To my chagrin, in a few weeks, when the little trees leafed out, I discovered that several of my supposed trees of heaven were in fact the dreaded poison oak, a local shrub that thrives in our area of the country. I am very susceptible to poison oak, so these interlopers were soon torn from the soil, though not without a hearty laugh. In their dormant winter condition, they had looked very much like the little tree saplings.

Speaking of poison oak, it is worthy of mention that the finest antidote to its painful blisters is the application of ordinary Crest toothpaste. This is worth remembering, because many of the more expensive remedies provide little or no relief at all.

I also planted a variety of native and exotic junipers, some of which were dug from the hills around us. They are tough, hardy trees with beautiful foliage of various hues and forms. I have always admired these durable, graceful trees, which thrive under semidesert conditions in the toughest terrain. I sometimes layer the lower limbs of special trees in the mountains, in the hope that one day I shall return to retrieve a new sapling started in this simple way.

Maples are also among my favorites. The only native maple that does well in our high country is the hardy little vine maple. In many places, it really is not much more than a multistemmed bush. The largest specimen I ever saw was no more than thirty feet high, with the largest stem about ten inches across. It had been bulldozed out of the ground to make a logging road. I cut it up for the fireplace. Its hard, dense wood gave off heat equal to the best of coal.

I dug up and replanted one of these little maples in our rockery. In fall its foliage will flame from yellow to orange and finally crimson. It will be a thing of glorious beauty against the blue backdrop of the lake.

I also planted a delicate, split-leaved, scarlet Japanese maple. Whether it can withstand the cutting winter winds that whip across the lake to lash its limbs with snow and sleet remains to be seen. Time alone will tell. For one summer, at least, its feathery foliage gave us quiet delight, as it spread itself in the shelter of the black birches.

Because the red sugar maple of the east has always been such a thrilling tree to me, I planted one of these. At first it seemed to suffer with our intense summer heat. It had purposely been placed in a sheltered spot with partial shade, but even there it languished. In October it flamed scarlet, but that may well have been a final farewell salute to an environment too tough to endure.

What we in our western valley may lack in colorful deciduous trees is more than made up for by our fiery native sumac. It thrives on even the driest gravel benches, where otherwise only sagebrush, greasewood and cactus can survive. I planted sumac in strategic places all around "Still Waters." Its luxuriant summer foliage and incandescent autumn colors are sheer joy—a delight to the eye and heart of any outdoorsman.

The last tree planted during our first season was a golden-needled larch from the high hills. Cheri and I made a special trip to the high country, just to pick one out. Tenderly we lifted it from its native ridge and bore it down beside the lake. It stands erect at the water's edge. If all goes well, its feathery form and golden needles will enhance "Still Waters" for a hundred years to come.

6
Mellow Moods

PERHAPS THE MOST pronounced and powerful impact that "Still Waters" made upon my spirit was in providing a sense of peace. Not that its atmosphere was still and static; it was not. But there lingered here an element of repose and harmony not often found in our busy world.

This peace was woven from many strands of the pulsing life about us. It came partly from our natural setting; partly from the other life forms that shared our lakeside world; partly from the kind neighbors and friends who came to call.

Never before had I lived in such close proximity and intimate contact with a mountain lake. Little did I realize its mellow moods would make such an enormous impact upon my soul. It was a moving and uplifting experience to be under its majestic spell.

This was true even when inside the cottage. Its expansive floor-to-ceiling windows gave the sensation that indoors and outdoors were one continuous whole. Often, as we sat at our meals or relaxed in the front room, I had the distinct impression of being one with the trees and shrubs, the lake and the hills that surrounded us. The feeling was one, not of human intrusion, but rather of having ourselves completely accepted and encircled by our natural surroundings.

There is something very special about such a setting. One *belongs,* in a unique and comforting way. And in this quiet acceptance lies great consolation. Put another way, it would be appropriate to say that it was not man who was imposing his dominant will on his surroundings, but rather had allowed himself to be enfolded and fully accepted into the natural community.

We of the highly sophisticated, hard, brittle, plastic Western world seldom sense this oneness with nature. We are too dedicated to material progress; to the use of mechanical power for imposing our will on the world; to speed and haste and great waste.

An African proverb that has comprised a large part of my lifelong philosophy is stated thus: *"Haraka, haraka, hana baraka,"* which in our idiom is, "Haste, haste, but no blessing."

The gentle tempo of the passing seasons at "Still Waters" reinforced this deep conviction. Some of my contemporaries may have raised their eyebrows and shaken their heads in disbelief at our simple lifestyle in that spot. But, for me, it became a quiet, serene backwater in a busy, boisterous world.

After all, there are certain values in life that money and material wealth can never purchase. Gold and silver, stocks and bonds, bank accounts and investment securities are not sufficient to assure peace of heart or serenity of spirit.

What price can be placed upon a life of simplicity, free from the fret and strain of trying to keep pace in a man-killing society? What will a person give in exchange for the quiet ecstasy of living gently in harmony with the seasons? What consolation can surpass that of the secure inner assurance that this indeed is my Father's world, in which He cares for me with intense personal interest?

At "Still Waters," we were constantly reminded that this caring was not confined or directed only toward us human beings. It embraced and enfolded the whole world around us. The trees and shrubs, with their foliage shining in the sun; the soft, sweet, fragrant grasses and flowers that flourished on our hills; the birds that built their nests and reared their young all around us; the insects that hummed in the sun and flitted across the lake; the wild deer and mountain sheep and mink and beavers and bears whose realm we shared; all reminded us that we were friends and neighbors. As the ancient Indians would say, we were all "brothers beneath the sun."

In this realization, we were back to basic beginnings. We delude ourselves if we believe our Father cares only for human beings. His assurance to us is otherwise. It is He who clothes the flowers of the field in great glory; He knows when a fledgling falls.

Sensations of this sort often engulfed my spirit as day drew to a close. Sitting in the soft afterglow of the setting sun, there were happy, mellow interludes in which to think long thoughts. Often, as the sun tinted the western sky with pastel shades of pink, mauve, rose and lavender, there swept over my spirit an acute awareness of the gracious presence of God's own winsome Spirit. Communion between us was very personal, very private, very profound.

This was one of the reasons we had searched so long to find "Still Waters." I longed for those times when I could be still and know God. In the tender hours of twilight and daybreak, this did in fact take place.

At dusk, the wind would die. The lake surface became a smooth sheet of shining translucence, which caught and mirrored the breathtaking beauty of the burning skies. In summer, these desert skies flame and burn with blazing banners of tattered clouds. From horizon to horizon, their glory fills the vault of heaven. The still waters of the lake double and intensify this spectacle, until one's whole being pulses with profound awe and adoration. Only God could paint the clouds, the hills, the valley and the lake with such splendid strokes of pigment. No two evenings, no two dawns, were ever identical. The Master is an artist of enormous and infinite diversity.

At dawn, the eastern sky above the rock ramparts often glowed gold. This same metallic tint would wash over the cliffs and ridges all around us. Often they looked as if cast in bronze, fresh from the sculptor's hand. The beauty and glory of their grandeur was reflected in the lake.

Not a leaf would stir; not a ripple would rise on the water. The whole world lay still—serene, breathless, yet majestic.

There would then sweep over my soul that sublime and stirring assurance: "This is the day the Lord has made. I will rejoice and be glad in it" (*see* Psalm 118:24 LB).

It was a moment to relish!

7
Rain in the Desert

YESTERDAY WAS ONE of those dry, desperate days that can make the desert a dread. The leaves on the trees hung limp and wilted, unmoved by any stray eddy of air. The grass, bleached and gaunt and brittle from too much sun, broke in bits under my desert boots. It lay crushed and shattered wherever touched by the hard hooves of deer that had dashed across it. I had followed three bucks that took shelter from the searing sun. They sought the dense thickets of alder and black birch beside the lake. But even there, every move they made was amplified by the crack and crackle of brittle branches and dry twigs.

The heated air of the valley was close, oppressive and stifling. No birds rose up to sing against the sky, which was empty of their sounds. Nor did any take pleasure in winging against the wind, for there was none. The whole desert realm lay still, impassive, weighted down with the heaviness of heat.

The sun itself, so often friendly and warm and welcome, was now a terror and torment. The intensity of its light drove every living thing to seek shelter in the shade. Its fierce rays scorched the skin and shriveled the body. Even a plunge in the lake provided only momentary relief.

As the long, slow hours of the afternoon wore away, I flung myself down in the dappled shade of a sturdy sumac that grew at the water's edge. Yet even there, the heat was so stifling, so smothering, that my breath came in short pants. My head throbbed with pressure. Even the ground beneath my body was too hot, too hard, too gaunt to provide any comfort. So I rose and wandered about, almost in a stupor, longing for some sign, some signal that the weather might break.

There seemed to be none.

The sunset, brilliant and dramatic with its multihued desert clouds, seemed to hold promise of more sun the next day. Slowly its fingers of fire quenched the last smoldering shafts of light, and the day died in a gray ash of cloud clinging to the westerly sky.

Almost with a sigh of despair, I resigned myself to the thought of another day of desperate heat and desiccation. What else could one do but accept the weather as it came, whether blazing like a furnace or chilling as a blizzard?

But just before bedtime, my eyes caught a glimpse of misty gold rising through the silhouetted saskatoons on the high bank behind the cabin. The moon was mounting the sky, shrouded in a peculiar halo of fine-spun light. It could spell only one thing: there was moisture in the atmosphere. Perhaps rain was in the offing.

It was the sign I had been seeking.

It was the slender hope of a change.

And in that hope, I fell asleep, weary with heat.

Long, long before break of day, when I usually awake, there was a stirring in the leaves of the trees outside my window. A breeze began to rustle the limp foliage. Leaves rattled against one another, and on the rising wind, I heard the rolling, tumbling sounds of distant thunder.

The rain was coming!

Soon odd drops began to spatter on the roof above my head. The cabin has no ceilings; it is open beamed. Only satin-smooth cedar boards with shingles over their top stand between me and the sky. So the increasing tempo of the descending raindrops was music to my soul.

This is an ancient sound—the sound of rain falling on leaves, on bark, on grass, on rocks and soil. It is perhaps one of the most soothing and reassuring sounds upon the planet. It speaks of refreshment, relief and life from death.

There in the darkness of the night, in the wetness of the rain, in the cooling of the air, there was comfort. All the world—the little world of this desert valley—rested in quiet repose. The refreshment of the rain came, bringing total relaxation.

All was well.

And in that knowledge, I rolled over and fell asleep again. My sleep was deep and sweet and strong.

In my subconscious mind, there was the music of moisture descending from above: a gift from God, my Father.

Several hours later, I awoke again. A diffused light filtered through the trees from an overcast sky. It was still raining, but very gently, quietly. The raindrops were barely audible on the deck outside. They scarcely dimpled the surface of the lake. Yet everywhere there was wetness, coolness and gladness.

Bird songs rang through the air with notes of crystal-clear beauty. The meadowlarks on the dry sagebrush benches flung their melodies into the morning light with gay abandon. The songs splintered themselves on the great bluffs and echoed off across the lake. Swallows swept over the lake in graceful arcs, calling cheerfully to their newly fledged broods to follow them in their swift flight. The orioles chattered happily as they moved from tree to tree in search of insects drowsy with dampness.

With the coming of the rain, shrubs and trees and grass and reeds glowed emerald green. All their tissues were taut and turgid with moisture. Even in the somber gray light, they shone wet and smooth and satiny, charged with fresh life from within. New vitality and dynamic vigor moved in every living thing.

I slipped quietly out the door. Standing alone, inhaling deeply of the exquisite fragrance of soil wet with rain, deep and profound gratitude welled up within me for such a joyous interlude.

The rain had come!

All of us together were singing thanks to God.

8
Tame Trout

OUR MOUNTAIN LAKE, though only about three miles long and three-quarters of a mile wide, is a native habitat to some thirty-odd species of fish. This may or may not constitute somewhat of a record for so small a body of water. Not being an ardent fisherman, my knowledge of such things is rather meager.

In part, the prolific abundance of fish in the lake may be explained by the diversity of its character. A rather large river flows into one end. There, mud and silt carried down from the mountains by spring freshets has formed rich alluvial mud flats and warm-water shallows. In places, the lake is scarcely deep enough to float a canoe.

In these shallows there is a luxuriant growth of bulrushes, water lilies and assorted aquatic plants that provide certain species with ideal feed. Here, too, insect populations proliferate, kept in control above the water by the swooping birds and bats, while below the surface, fish feed eagerly on the larvae and pupae of all sorts.

In other places, this same little lake is deep, dark and very chill. Just below its outlet there are two gorgeous and unique lagoons tucked away in a quiet curve of the hills. These lagoons have the appearance of twin volcanic craters. There the water is very deep, very cold, very blue and full of splendid deep-bodied bass.

We love to hike around these lagoons. They are much more impressive than any man-made lakes. Encircling their edges are steep banks of sandy desert soil. Acres of wildflowers flourish here in spring and summer. Solid banks of wild sunflowers blow in the hot breezes beneath the red-barked ponderosa pines. The effect is one of a gigantic park, adorned by the brilliant hues of the blue lagoons and the wash of gold on the desert benches, all interspersed with the rugged, rusty trunks of the veteran pines.

In autumn, the same setting is changed to brilliant reds and scarlets by the flaming banks of native sumac. All of it is too beautiful, too striking to be adequately portrayed by pen and paper.

But it is here that the bass and other lake fish feed along the shore and shelter in the dark shadows of the trees that overhang the banks.

In front of our own cottage there are some beautiful weed beds that grow in rich profusion. These bulrushes, which blow and bend in the wind, provide ideal habitat and cover for a wide array of birds and insects. Yet they also are a favorite feeding ground for the fish. Giant carp, perch and sunfish frequent the area. Their great splashes breaking the surface have always fascinated me. It does me great good to know there is a flourishing fish population in the lake.

From time to time, trout feed fiercely near the surface. In their great rushes, they burst through the barrier of water, breaking out into clear air, their shining bodies arched in glorious silver arcs. Spray flies in the glinting sunlight as they splash down again. Ripples radiate far across the smooth water, leaving widening rings to remind us of their presence.

Just how prolific and numerous the trout were we never fully realized until Cheri began to feed the fish. It all began with a dainty pair of spotted sunfish. They came into our tiny bay and began to stake out territory for their beds. Fiercely the little fish would attack and pursue any intruder. Steadily, day after day, they dug their beds, shed their eggs and sperm, then stood guard over their spawning ground.

Out of compassion and affection for the wee fish, Cheri began to scatter bread crumbs on the water. Her finny friends seemed glad of this unexpected bounty. But like so many things in life, one step soon led to another. One day, not only were the sunfish there, but also several small trout fingerlings. They, too, tasted the bread and loved it.

Not being an authority on fish behavior, I have no clear idea how the trout told their friends about the ready banquet of bread on our beach. But almost before we knew it, the first few fish soon increased to ten—then fifteen, twenty, up to thirty, then fifty or more—until I could no longer count their flashing, darting forms. At the last serious effort I made to take a census, there were well over seventy young trout swirling about beneath the surface.

Bread, it seemed to me, was not by any measurement the best food for fish. I gave the matter some serious thought and hit on the idea of providing our friends a high-protein food in the form of dog pellets. The results were utterly astounding. Their numbers increased even further, and the fish began to grow rapidly. In just a short time, they matured from slender fingerlings to fine, plump, pan-size trout.

It surprised us to see how quickly the trout learned to recognize our voices. They would come bursting to the surface whenever we walked out onto the rocks, calling to them or rattling the tin containing the pellets. To make sure all the fish would be fed, we scattered the food far and wide twice a day. This became a regular ritual, on which the trout thrived. It was also a novel experience for friends who came to visit us. Children, especially, were entranced and found endless delight in feeding our friends.

Deep down, I knew this happy arrangement would not last too long. The sharp eyes and keen senses of the loons, the grebes, the mergansers, soon alerted them to our concentration of trout. They came from all over the lake to raid this happy hunting ground. A smooth, slick dive, or a darting drive, a rapier thrust of their sharp beaks, and they would break water with a trout struggling between their mandibles.

But more than wild birds became aware of our trout. Fishermen in their canoes began to frequent our shore. It was a clear signal for our hand-feeding to end. I refused to have our friends betrayed. They would do much better foraging afar on their own.

It was another example of how unwittingly, even in good faith, our best actions and intentions can misfire. It was a case of members of the wildlife fraternity becoming overly dependent on, and therefore vulnerable to, human behavior.

As the season wore on and late summer moved into fall, some of the trout would swim past the big timber where I stretched out in the sun. These were just passing visits. Their silver sides would catch the slanting rays of the sun glancing down through the clear, cool water. In their swift, smooth action I sensed a gracious salute of acknowledgement to us, who had sent them off to such a strong start in life.

Not all of them had survived the fierce attacks of the winged hunters. And some, too, had been snared by the deception of the fishermen's flies alighting on the lake. Yet those that now remained were firm and fat and fit for winter weather. We were all friends together, still, and for that I was glad.

There would be trout rushing to the surface until freeze-up. There would be the splash of their rising to ripple the lake. There would be the dark, concentric, ever-growing circles of moving water where they fed. And for all their sights and sounds that enlivened our world together, I was glad and grateful.

To me, the fish and turtles, the mink and muskrats, the beavers and birds, the coyotes and bears, the deer and mountain sheep were all fellows of blood and bone and sinew, who reveled and rejoiced in our mountain realm. None of us dominated it or deprived the other of his share of it.

Each of us played our part in the finely strung web of life that enfolded us in a common joy of rich and hearty companionship. There was a sense of profound reverence and respect among us, each for the other. Our common ground and mutual interdependence guaranteed that none of us would abuse or exploit the other in greed or waste.

It has been ordained and ordered by our Father that we live in harmony with one another and with Him. It is possible to be at peace in life, and in very large and rich measure, we had found and fostered such serenity at "Still Waters."

9
August Wind

THERE ARE DAYS in mid-August that come winging in on the wind with mysterious magic. Like nature's notes of prophecy, they foretell the coming fall. They are not true summer days, even though by the calendar, autumn may still be more than a month away.

Yesterday was one of those out-of-season times—a pure Indian summer interlude injected into the very heart of August heat. And I loved it. It stirred my inner spirit and set my emotions in rhythm with its own wild freedom.

During the night a heavy downpour—unexpected and sudden, driven by a strong weather system off the Pacific—pounded the shingles. The falling drops splattered on leaves, bark, soil and stone in a steady murmur. All the earth sounds were stilled, but for the symphonic melody of a parched earth being soaked and scrubbed and sloshed with streaming rivulets of rain.

In the dim half-light of the damp dawn, wraiths of steamy vapor rose from the margin of the lake. They wavered among the graceful green wands of the bulrushes, betraying where underground springs of warm water bubbled below the surface of the lake. Spellbound, I watched a trio of playful mergansers dash and dart through this ghostlike scene, as if deliberately dramatizing its eerie atmosphere.

There was something very primitive, very poignant, yet delightfully arresting in the spectacle. Even the most artistic director of a film could not have staged the setting any more dramatically. The soft, cotton-wool-like mist moving formlessly among the swaying tule stems was a remarkable backdrop against which the excitable fish ducks put on their ecstatic performance.

Now one, then the other, then all three in unison would streak across the water like torpedoes, leaving wakes of white water behind them. In wild abandon, they would dive below the surface, then come bursting into view again.

Ecstatic with energy, they would stand erect, treading water with their short feet, flapping their stubby wings in self-applause. Somehow their whole show was an open, hearty invitation to any onlooker to "Come on in—the water is wonderful!"

This unplanned performance set the mood for the whole day. It was a thrill to be alive—aware—open to the powerful impulses of the earth.

As morning light touched the bold bluffs of Coyote Rock, the gaunt slabs of stone shone smooth and wet. At first the rock faces looked as though they had been sheathed in the first fall of early snow. In the deceptive light playing through the clouds and overcast, the shining stone appeared white and soft. But it was not; a glance through the binoculars revealed only stark stone shining, sheathed in wetness.

The powerful south wind that had pushed the storm in overnight continued unabated. It began to break up the cloud cover. Soon warm summer sunlight streamed down through the torn and tattered canopy. It left a dappled patchwork of light and shadows flung across the landscape—a landscape that glowed and pulsed.

As the last fragments of cloud were pushed across the brown bluffs to the east, blue skies of breathless beauty and clarity arched overhead. No longer could I resist the strong pull to slip outside and soak up the sun in my favorite spot. There would not be many more days like this before frost and snow and ice locked this little valley in winter's cold grip.

At the very water's edge, just a few inches above the granite boulders, I had wedged a giant driftwood timber. Where it came from is unknown. Seldom, in these days of laminated beams, does one ever see a great fir log like this. Cut from a single monarch of a tree, it is twenty-six feet long, a foot thick and eighteen inches wide. It is an ideal sunbathing deck where, like a smooth, contented seal, I stretch out to take the sun and listen to the lap of water on stone a few feet from my face.

It was here I rested and relaxed, reveling in the symphony of earth's music that surrounded me. Instead of abating, the August wind gathered force and energy in its fists. Blowing hard from the southwest quarter, it stirred the lake and churned up charging whitecaps.

For such a small lake in such a sheltered valley, surrounded by high hills and bold bluffs, it was exciting to see the wild action of the water. Driven strongly, the waves would run hard, climb to a rising peak, then cascade down in white foam that hissed in the wind. The wash of the waves, the splash of water on the boulders about me and the wind in the trees around combined to make music that thrilled me to the depths. It was a melody of ancient origin, but it struck responsive notes deep in the spirit of a simple man, stretched out beneath its beat.

There was something wild, untamed, untaught in that wind music. It was not contrived or manipulated by man. This was the sort of melody that had been played out upon the planet long before the earliest men had thought of a woodwind instrument as simple as a reed flute cut from the stem of some marsh grass.

But there was more, much more than the majestic music of God's own making that morning. There was exquisite beauty of wondrous proportions cupped in my valley world.

The wind-wrought surface of the lake shone like beaten silver. A million points of blinding light bounced and danced in a brilliant ballet of abandon. They glided and pirouetted across the sparkling stage in exciting performance. Perhaps not another soul had stopped to pause and take in the show.

For me, it was a stirring day. It had etched itself indelibly on my memory. This was a precious interlude lifted from time, to be stored sacredly in the vault of remembrance. Humbly I bowed in awe and gave thanks.

10
Friends on the Wing

LIVING AS CLOSE as we did to the lake and woods and wild hills around us, it was inevitable that some of our most intimate friends should be the birds. It is no small pleasure to have hundreds of birds of various species within a stone's throw of the windows. There was an intimacy—of sharing the same world of trees and water, cliffs and meadows—that is very rare.

For Cheri, in particular, the antics and behavior of the birds were a never-ending source of pleasure. She is an extremely acute and alert wildlife observer. The intense interest she displayed, often dashing from window to window to follow a bird's behavior, was often both joyful and hilarious to watch.

It was as if we had been admitted directly into the private lives of our feathered friends. Without fear or overshyness, they lived out their little lives in full view of our wondering eyes.

Those closest to us were a pair of beautiful barn swallows. With their shining plumage of gun-barrel blue and gun-stock brown, they circled the cottage in graceful swooping arcs. Quite obviously they were a young pair, mating for the first season. Their initial attempts to stick one of their mud-pellet nests to the cottage were clumsy and rather disastrous.

To help them out, I installed a small shelf just below the eaves and above one of the windows, where we could watch them. They accepted the site at once, and within a few days had a fresh nest, lined with feathers, ready for their brood to come.

They would be among the best of birds to control the mosquitoes. In fact, by midsummer there were literally scores of swallows swooping over the lake and around the water's edge. Any insect that dared to rise out of the tules or emerge from the shelter of the trees was promptly picked up in midflight.

The swallows' favorite perch was on our clothesline. Here they loved to sit and preen themselves, warbling contentedly. They are very vocal birds. Cheri would often stand at the open window, chattering to them in a happy exchange of mutual admiration. She kept me fully posted on the most recent and minute details of their activities.

In due course, the adults reared a strong and sturdy family of four fledglings. In just a few weeks, the young ones were swift of wing and sure of eyes. They would come sweeping through the garden, to settle on the clothesline when their wings grew weary. As summer moved on, they were joined by scores of other young fliers emerging from nests all around the lake. Besides the barn swallows, some of which had nests on neighbors' houses, there were tree swallows and cliff swallows. All of them combined obviously consumed thousands upon thousands of insects in any single day. Because of this, our own lives beside the lake were infinitely more pleasurable than they would have been if persecuted by hordes of mosquitoes, flies and gnats.

I was tremendously impressed with the calm courage of the swallows. Fearlessly they would attack larger predator birds that intruded on their territory. The magpies, crows and blue jays that dared to invade the environs of "Still Waters" were pursued in fierce flight, with the swallows sweeping down upon them like diving Stukas in deadly combat.

Another species of bird that brought flashing gaiety to our garden was the western Bullock's orioles. They are not only very colorful birds, adorned in beautiful black and gold plumage, but also very noisy. Their harsh cries and incessant calls, especially of the young, enlivened the woods and sang through the trees all the time they were with us.

Several pair nested within fifty yards of the cottage. Their intricate nests, woven from threads, string and slender stalks of grass, were suspended from the topmost branches of the native poplars. There they swung and swayed in the wind, appearing at a distance to be rather precarious, but close at hand revealing wondrous design of great strength.

I am fully aware that it is customary for the so-called scientific community to dismiss the extraordinary behavior of birds with the shrug of a shoulder and the all-encompassing word *instinct*. But for those of us who have lived in close intimacy with the wilds, this is just not good enough. Whence these so-called instincts? Whence these incredibly intricate and efficient behavior patterns, which so perfectly adapt a species to its particular environment? Whence the consummate skill, expertise and intelligence that enables individuals within the bird community to capitalize on and use the materials at hand to survive in its special setting?

Let me illustrate. One day Cheri hung a tattered piece of cloth to dry on the clothesline. Actually it was a duster with frayed edges. It had been there only a few hours when the orioles decided it would provide perfect nesting material. With great ingenuity and no little dexterity, they would fly down and cling to the cloth, tearing long threads out of the material with beak and claw.

This was an intricate process, and so I suggested that we cut strips of a softer material and hang them on the line for their benefit. Strange to say, it was a futile gesture. The orioles rejected the strips immediately. If they were to use man-made fabric to fashion their nests, it would have to be of their own choosing, unraveled by their own beaks and claws.

Again one must ask: Whence the intelligence to even know that cloth contained long, thin threads suited to their needs? Whence the capacity to ascertain that this material, even if obtained by great labor, surpassed grass in strength and durability? Whence the will and resolve to incorporate cloth, thread or string into a structure that ordinarily was fashioned only from plant fibers?

Obviously there is much more at work here than mere blind instinct. There is an element of thought, of deduction, of discovery, of determination that goes far beyond mere animal behavior. In all of it, we sensed a dimension of delightful supernatural design. It was not something merely acquired during the evolutionary process. It was evidence of our Father's care for His earth children.

By midsummer, the trees were literally alive with vigorous young orioles flitting and flashing through the foliage. They were pursuing all sorts of caterpillars, earwigs, ants and wood insects that flourished amid the labyrinth of twigs and leaves. It was a reassuring thought that the community of common birds all around us was so happily controlling the native insect population, which would otherwise have decimated the trees and shrubs that made our surroundings so beautiful.

As the seasons came and went, so did the birds. There was a steady succession of various species moving around us in gentle harmony with the length of day and time of year. Chickadees and nuthatches, warblers and juncos, robins and towhees—to name but half-a-dozen kinds—sang and whistled their way through the trees and brush in their tireless search for food for their families.

In all of this, we sensed the wondrous web of life, whose delicate strands embraced all of us. Indirectly and directly, we were all interdependent. The welfare and contentment of birds, forest, shrubs, and man himself were intertwined. Each of us was contributing something of value to the common good, while at the same time each derived that which was essential for his enjoyment and enduring existence.

This was one of those basic *beginnings* we had sought from the start in our search for "Still Waters." There was a fundamental feeling of harmony, repose and goodwill in all the natural life around us. None of us, whether birds, vegetation or man, were imposing ourselves upon another. Rather, the atmosphere around our home was one of quiet contentment. In this environment there was a natural balance, unmolested by crude or thoughtless behavior.

This may sound rather far-out and farfetched for those whose lives are lived in the labyrinth of a modern metropolis. But for us at "Still Waters," this was that unique and special ingredient that made our life there a quiet, gentle, unforgettable adventure.

11
The Little Stray

IT WAS A warm September morning, aglow with mellow sunlight and splashed by autumn colors. The birches were beginning to blaze, with bronze leaves fluttering in the wind. The sumacs on the hills flamed scarlet among the gray sage. A golden-breasted meadowlark filled the countryside with rippling notes of contentment that seemed to rise in joy to the blue, blue skies.

But all was not at peace. A sad and discordant sound suddenly came across the grassy glade of the vacant land north of us. From out of the wild tangle of trees and brush along the lake came a plaintive, sad, melancholy cry that sounded half-feline, half-human. It was a persistent, forlorn, pathetic sound, like someone lost and pleading for help.

My wife and I hurried to the edge of the underbrush. There a labyrinth of intertwined wild rosebushes, Oregon grape, snow berries and poison oak grew in wild profusion beneath the birches.

We could see a small, slim, shy animal coming through the undergrowth. The first glimpse or two made us think it might be a weasel. But when she broke out into the open sunlight, we saw it was a skinny, half-starved kitten. She was snow-white, like a weasel in winter dress. Only a smudge of dark fur between her eyes tinged the whiteness of her coat. She carried an enormous, fluffy, white tail, out of all proportion to her slim and shrunken body—now only skin and bones.

We called to her. Her response was to come bounding out of the bush. Her eyes—peculiar eyes, one brilliant blue, the other an orb of gold—flashed with fear and apprehension. At first she fled at our sight, but with patience and perseverance, Cheri was finally able to pick her up. Half-starved, having survived only on insects, the odd dead bird and wild berries, she was a pathetic little bundle of white fluff. Like thousands of other domestic pets, she had been dropped in the country, to fend for herself.

This callous abandonment of city-bred animals in the country is one of the cruel and heinous crimes of our much-vaunted modern society. Men and women who lack courage and compassion coldheartedly dump their feline and canine friends at the side of the road, then blithely drive away, leaving them to struggle for survival. This has become such a common practice by our populace that thousands of stray dogs and cats have to be destroyed every year by rangers, wardens and those who find them in their forlorn plight.

We picked up the kitten and carried her home to the cottage. It was almost like gathering up a bundle of cotton batten. The mere skeleton, with thin flesh stretched over her bony frame, was concealed only by the fluff of her white fur. At first it seemed she might not even survive. She was so emaciated that anything she tried to eat or drink only resulted in violent diarrhea. But Cheri had owned and cared for cats before, and her tender care began to pay off.

It quickly became apparent that this was no ordinary alley cat. She carried the royal blood of both Siamese and Persian aristocracy in her veins. In fact, she seemed to combine the best of both breeds in her unique makeup.

Having owned and trained only dogs all my life, it was a brand-new and rather unusual adventure to have a cat in the house. I had always been told that cats were arrogant, independent, proud and aloof. For that reason there had never been any great desire to have one share my life. But now there was really very little choice. This little white waif, of ghostlike appearance, had come into our care, and I was determined to see she would get a chance to enjoy her life with us at "Still Waters."

I soon christened her Oddy, because both her appearance and behavior were so odd. In time she began to recognize this name and would come when called by it.

Very quickly we discovered that she was an unusually alert and intelligent animal. She could be taught and trained as readily as any dog. What was even more impressive was her great and unbounded affection. She quickly dispelled all of my misgivings about the arrogant aloofness of cats. She showed beyond doubt that she was capable of reciprocating any love showered upon her.

She enjoyed our companionship and quickly made herself at home in our company. She loved to crawl up on our laps, purring so loudly the muted rumblings could be heard clear across the room. Sometimes she would stand on my lap, place her immaculate white front feet on my chest and reach up to touch noses. I guess this is the way a cat kisses. At any rate, she reveled in it so much she would tread my chest ecstatically, like someone kneading dough with deep delight.

Her behavior reminded me again and again of that of a dog. She would follow me around the garden. She loved to climb up on my back when I laid down in the sun for an afternoon siesta. She would be waiting on the lawn when we came home in the car, eager to greet us with a contented mew and bounds of delight at our approach. She snuggled down between us on the chesterfield when the day's work was done and we listened quietly to classical music in the evening.

Fine music seemed to have a special appeal to her. Often she would cock her head to one side and listen intently, like the dog with his ear to the gramophone on the old records. High notes on the flute or violin, or from a beautiful soprano voice, especially stirred her with pleasure. She would open her eyes wide, cock her ears and pay special attention, as though this was her favorite taste in symphonic fare.

Oddy, after her first few faltering days, soon began to blossom under our loving care. She started to put on weight rapidly. Her framed filled out, her fur began to glow and shine with well-being. And she took great pains to keep her coat immaculate.

She was a wild, free spirit, out-of-doors. She literally danced and tumbled about the grounds, like a windblown leaf. In two titanic leaps, she could bound up a tree with lightning alacrity. It was never a surprise to see her working her way across the slender branches above us with utter impunity. She never showed any fear of falling. And, unlike many cats, whatever she climbed she found equally easy to descend with great leaps and bounds, as if built of spring steel.

Her enormous agility and swiftness made her a formidable hunter. Besides all the food we lavished upon her, she augmented her diet with a steady toll of mice, shrews, moles and small birds she collected in the bush around us. It was a perfect place to hunt. She would steal through the undergrowth, her tail tip twitching with excitement, to pounce with intense speed upon her prey. Soon not a mouse was to be seen. She had made a clean sweep of the entire environs of the cottage. With winter approaching, this was a real benefit, for with freezing nights in the fall, the mice would soon move into the cottage, attracted by its warmth, shelter and fragrance of fresh food.

Contrary to much of what I had been told about cats, Oddy loved the water. She would spend hours working her way along the lake edge. The reflection of her own face in the mirrorlike surface fascinated her. She loved to dip her paws in the refreshing coolness, then shake them off vigorously. Often she sat entranced, watching the sunfish and small trout that swam past her only a few inches from her long, eagerly twitching white whiskers. How she would have loved to snatch one of these tasty morsels from the lake.

The wild ducks and geese also fascinated her. At dusk they would sometimes swim in close to shore, where she crouched, watching them intently. It was a mutual game that both ducks and cat seemed to enjoy. The ducks would swim as close as possible to her, as if enticing her to come out and play. They knew precisely how close they could come to her without being pounced upon. In convoylike formation, they would swim close, streaming past her, quacking in a provocative way that would start her blood boiling and her tail twitching.

When at last they had taunted her to extremity, they would turn tail, flip water in her face and leave her to fume in furious frustration.

But on balance, she did not lose all her games with birds. Morning after morning I would find scattered heaps of feathers strewn on the lawns where she had gorged herself on the warm flesh of a freshly caught bird. It soon became clear that she was a relentless hunter. If we wanted to enjoy the birds around "Still Waters," she would have to find another home.

This was a tough decision for us. Like so many things in life, there was no simple, single solution. Try as we might to discourage her from her death-dealing ways, she persisted in pursuing her prey. In so far as she could see, anything that moved was legitimate prey. It mattered not whether it wore fur or feathers—she would stalk it fiercely.

As it so happened, this really led to her ultimate undoing, for inevitably her own feminine presence soon led to visits from other cats much larger than herself. The nights of quietness would be shattered and splintered like broken glass with the awful screams of cats in combat. Oddy would arch her back, raise her hackles and defy any interloper to take another step onto her territory. She fought fiercely and courageously.

The final consequence was that some mornings she came to the door with blood upon her face, scratches upon her lips and a rumpled coat that betrayed fierce fights with others of her feline fraternity. We knew that sooner or later she would end up being pregnant or badly mauled by some belligerent visitor.

As it so happened, both came true. Oddy began to gain weight very quickly, so we suspected kittens were on the way. Her kittenish antics gave place to a much more placid and sedentary lifestyle. She would spend long hours stretched out in the most humanlike poses on the big armchair near my desk. It was hilarious to see her lying on her back, arms crossed, as if she were a little old man in his eighties, snoring up a storm.

Then one night she was severely mauled. A few days later, an enormous swelling developed on her back. It was so painful she would not let us touch her. Morose and ill, she simply dozed intermittently. She refused to eat or drink. Her eyes grew dull, and her energy drained away. There was only one thing to do; we had her put to rest for the sake of mercy.

Like a bright comet, this little white visitor had swept through our lives with gaiety and affection. She left behind a starry trail of happy memories. I was glad we had shared so freely of our affection. "'Tis better to have loved and lost, than never to have loved at all."

In the brief years of our human experience, some of us sense and *know* that our lives have been touched by the divine in diverse ways. Our heavenly Father does not limit Himself to human agencies to speak to His own.

In Psalm 19:1, the ancient bard wrote, without a moment's hesitation, "The heavens declare the glory of God; and the firmament sheweth his handywork."

And it is just as valid to say that there are occasions when He uses animals to minister to our deepest needs, just as He does with other human beings. Observe the comfort, cheer and companionship that comes to children and the very aged from their pets. The love and loyalty of dogs, cats, horses, and other domestic creatures sometimes puts human unpredictability to shame.

A very aged gentleman lives a few hundred yards down the lake from us. His twilight years are enriched and embroidered by the gentle stroll he takes every day with his faithful old Blackie. Together the two of them shuffle softly down our gravel road, soaking up sunshine, inhaling fresh air and exercising their aging joints. For both man and dog, it is the special interlude of the day.

In a similar manner, it is my conviction that Oddy was sent to us at a very special time in our lives, to share briefly a sorrowful interlude that weighed heavily on our spirits. It was in the sadness of difficult days that this gay-spirited cat came to us, like a gift of gaiety from God. Her warmth, her affection, her devotion, her fun, her hilarious humor, helped to ease us through a very trying time.

Often, as I romped with her in front of the fire or caressed her silky white coat as she lay on my lap, I knew this was no ordinary interlude. In His awareness and sensitivity to our special need, Oddy had been sent to minister to a man and woman in sorrow.

I would look down at her graceful, gentle white form and know she was like an "angel unawares" in our company.

12
Wild Waterfowl

THE LAKE THAT laps on the little sand beach at our doorstep is home to a myriad of waterfowl. It has, across the years, been established as a wildlife sanctuary. Here shotguns do not roar out death to the ducks and geese that flash across our skies. Nor do outboard motors disturb the gentle tranquility of the waters.

There is a wooded island at the lower end of the lake that has become the favorite nesting ground for the Canada geese. Safe from four-legged predators, the goslings can be assured of a safe launch into life. Last year some 400 geese were hatched on the lake. Day and night the wild cries of their coming and going filled the skies, to echo across the valley from ridge to ridge.

The Canada goose is an unusually wary and intelligent bird. The social behavior within any given flock is complex, tightly knit and fiercely maintained. The birds are exceedingly loyal to each other and to their young. The interrelationship of the birds is maintained by almost-continuous conversation, which I call "goose gossip."

It came as a distinct surprise to me to discover that the geese gabble and call to one another through the night. On bright moonlit nights, when the lake is a shimmering sheet of silver, their cries are a cacaphony that resounds through the valley with remarkable resonance. Again and again, their goose talk has awakened me from my sleep and drawn me to the window to watch their dark forms silhouetted against the silver sheen of the water.

Because of this, I suspect that geese sleep much more during the day than they do at night. With sentinels on guard, they slip their heads beneath their wings and rest undisturbed.

The size of the young broods of goslings is really astonishing; even more so when pairs combine in intimate clans for mutual protection and sharing of parental duties. It is for this reason that sometimes there may be as many as sixty or seventy bouncing balls of yellow fluff following in the wake of only two or three adults. They are guarded zealously and fearlessly. An angered pair of geese makes a formidable foe. Their flashing eyes, darting beaks and hammering wings will drive off most predators in short order.

The rapid rate at which the young geese mature is almost beyond belief. In the first few weeks, if feed and forage are plentiful, the goslings will actually more than double their weight every day. They relish short, green, tender grass and dandelions. In fact, adult geese are so addicted to dandelions that they will go great distances and risk real danger to dine on this unusual delicacy.

Two or three times, flocks of the geese decided to pay our little lawn a passing visit. Its emerald green grass was a tremendous temptation. In a matter of minutes, their sickle-sharp beaks had cut the grass to the ground, almost to the very roots. As if this was not enough, it seemed every one of the more than 200 geese that strutted about the place felt constrained to defecate on the lawn. The result can be well imagined.

When this had occurred several times, I decided enough was enough. In desperation, I stretched a long length of rope across the entrance to our little beach, about a foot above the water. From it we suspended slender strips of gaudy cloth. It looked exactly like a miniature farmer's fence erected in the lake. It worked like magic! For the remainder of the season, not a goose dared to trespass past it. So peace came again, while the geese gabbled happily just offshore in the weed beds where they loved to feed.

Learning to fly was a major milestone in the lives of the maturing juveniles. As they approached adulthood, they would expend enormous energy flapping their wings, treading water, trying to take off.

Sometimes they would stand on shore, stretch themselves full length, beat the air boisterously, then race along the beach, endeavoring to rise on the wind. It was all very stimulating, exciting and hilarious to watch. These experimental first flights were accompanied with exultant honking and ecstatic cries of delight. To finally break free and become fully airborne was a feat that called for tumultuous celebration.

Stretching, flapping, treading water, spray flying, rising above the lake in faltering first flights, they made the whole valley ring with their cries of conquest. They were on wing! They were away!

In very remarkable truth, this was so in more ways than one. For in just a few fleeting days, the entire lake suddenly seemed to be alive with long, wavering lines of geese flying just a few feet above its surface. Back and forth, up and down its length, they would beat their way. Night and day the sound of their practice flights upwind was carried to us on the shifting breezes.

Then suddenly a strange stillness descended on the scene. Almost overnight, most of the geese were gone. In response to an ancient urge, most of them left for faraway places on the prairies, where feed was more plentiful. The wise old adults had been there before. They knew all about the great grain fields, the open marshes, the potholes and the banqueting grounds of the stubble land.

Whence this wisdom? Whence the courage and stamina to vault the giant mountain ranges that reared their snowy ridges and rocky ramparts into the flyways of the birds? Whence the strength, in birds so young, to beat their wings against the winds with weary muscles and straining tendons, hour after hour, across uncharted forests, valleys, rivers and ranges?

There was a majestic mystery in these transmountain migrations. In that mystery I stood awed in quiet wonderment. This is my Father's world. He made it; He sustained it; He kept it; He cared; He knew if one fledgling fell along the way.

Besides the geese, there were numerous other waterfowl. Loons and grebes and ducks all nested along the shores, secreting their nests amid the tules or in the dense brush growing along the banks.

Of these, one pair of mallards especially interested us. The female was an unusual albino bird. She was courted ardently by several drakes. Finally one night, under the full moon, she was mated by a monstrous drake. Cheri watched the whole pageantry with intense excitement, reporting all the romantic details to me the next day.

In due course, the hen emerged from the bulrushes with nine ducklings in tow. She proved to be a most indulgent and alert parent. Her young ones flourished under her careful protection and by summer's end were even larger than she was. The family made a handsome flotilla as they dabbled about in front of the cottage.

It astonished us how nonchalantly these ducks faced rough weather on the lake. Even when stiff winds stirred the waves up into racing whitecaps, the little ones bounced about on the surface with ease and no apparent fear.

The ducks enjoyed coming into our tiny beach. There they would strut on the sand, gather gravel for their crops, then pause to preen their feathers in the warm morning sun. If perchance Oddy was around, they would drift just out of reach, then tantalize her to come after them with jeering quacks, as if to say, "Can't catch us—can't catch us!"

When autumn closed quietly over the countryside, the lake ducks were joined by other flights from farther north. The swift swish of their wings whistled through the still air. In the brilliant, brittle light of Indian summer, the flash of their forms shone silver and white against the blue of the lake, the blue of the misty hills, and the blue of the autumn sky.

Few artists have ever been able to fully capture the elemental rapture of this pristine pageantry on canvas. In part, this is because of the electric action, the scintillating sequence of massed bodies, in perfect formation, sweeping across the sky in wild glory.

Anyone who has stood alone at sunset or dawn, watching the evening and dawn flights of waterfowl, will know there is an aura of beauty and wonder here that no book can adequately capture. They are rich moments of ecstasy. They are magnificent intervals of time, which the passing years cannot erase from the memory.

This is but one of our Father's gracious gifts to us, His earth children. We are richer for the company of our feathered friends. We know it and, in humble, hearty contentment, give happy thanks.

One of my favorite birds on the lake is our neighbor the loon. Often quite a shy bird, those which nest in our area have become rather tame and less retiring in their habits. The loon is a large bird, beautifully adorned in brilliant black and white plumage of dramatic design. They are accomplished fishermen, of remarkable prowess in pursuing the trout and perch that share their watery world. They can dive to great depths and remain underwater for long periods of time.

There is a silken-smooth quality to a loon's movement in the water. There is a blending of body, plumage and fluidly flowing grace. When a loon dives, the water is scarcely stirred. The bird simply slides and glides out of sight in one smooth, subtle submersion. The same is true when he surfaces, scarcely rippling the water as his graceful form slips up out of the lake in a lovely arc.

Best of all, at least to me, is the long, lilting call of the loon. This cry carries across the lake in lonely, forlorn notes that spell *wilderness*. There is a wildness quality, a melancholy mood, a nostalgic note in this bird's unbridled call. It sends chills and thrills up my nerves. It spells out untamed places and untamed hours.

Being a son of the wilds, I find in it a bond and harmony with all things wild and wonderful.

13
Thanksgiving

IN CANADA, THANKSGIVING comes as a very festive occasion in the most mellow month of the year. October—with its blue hazy days, its glowing golden dress and its stillness after the stressful summer—provides a perfect setting for this winsome celebration.

This year, Thanksgiving was extra special.

We were sharing it with dear, dear friends, whose feet had traveled far—very far—down the twilight trail of life. Despite the many years that had come and gone across the horizons of their lives, they still stood straight, sturdy and shining in spirit. They were people of the land, who had laid out their lives in selfless love for the downtrodden, impoverished natives of Haiti.

But now they were back home. Like the hunter home from the hills, they relaxed quietly and contentedly in the knowledge and comfort of work well done.

Early in the day, Cheri began to busy herself about the kitchen. There was a turkey to stuff and truss. There were vegetables to prepare with care. Yellow yams (sweet potatoes), a staple food of the Haitian peasants and a favorite dish of our friends, would be baked and smothered in sweet, sugary sauce. A crisp, fresh salad, made from the overflowing abundance of garden vegetables given to us by generous friends and neighbors, would garnish the table.

To top off the meal, there was pumpkin pie to prepare. This would be relished with delicious tea, brewed from the clear, cold spring water that flowed into our cottage.

As Cheri sang about the house, filling its rooms with her happy tunes, I went to search for special firewood to fuel the fireplace. Perhaps, if I was fortunate, I would find some flaming fall foliage to decorate the big-beamed living room.

I did not have to go far. On a dry, sagebrush bench back of the cottage, I followed a trail that led up to the toe of a giant rock slide. Across the centuries, frost and sun, wind and weather had worked on the towering cliffs above, breaking off gigantic slabs of stone and shale. The tons of brown and gray rock thundering down the cliffs had sheared off several firs and pines, which had rooted themselves at random in this rugged terrain.

For uncounted seasons, the broken trees had lain shattered on the slopes. Exposed to the scorching desert sun and scarce winter snows, the wood had turned silver-gray with age. The soft layers decomposed slowly, leaving behind only the pitch-impregnated limbs and knots and roots. These made superb firewood.

Searching for old, bone-hard branches and pitchy pine knots is like searching for precious minerals. The prospector is stimulated and driven on by the dream of discovery. For in those fragments of fuel, as in some precious ore, there is locked up the enormous, painstaking processes of nature that took place long, long years ago.

I moved, almost in a spirit of reverence, across the broken boulders and tortured talus. Here and there, wedged in among the tumbled rocks, were gaunt, gray branches and scattered fragments of roots and knots, which would flame to life in our fireplace.

The accumulated energy of a hundred summer suns locked within the pitchy wood would be released in bursts of red, orange and blue flames. The pent-up power of solar heat would crack and burst its bonds as the silver-gray wood turned to glowing red coals, hot as the choicest of coal.

Carefully, I climbed about the base of the granite cliffs. Bit by bit I gathered up armfuls of the prized fuel. It was brittle and broke readily when hammered against a jagged stone. There was no need for either axe or saw. This was a simple hunting ritual, primitive as earliest man, done readily without recourse to tools of any sort.

As I gathered up the beautiful, broken, weathered wood, a sense of having stepped back in time swept over me. The ancient instinct of the race came over me. I was back to basics. The strength of my own muscles, the keenness of my own eyes, the bounty of the earth about me, were the guarantee of a good fire and good cheer.

The wood collected, I began to look about for some colorful foliage to decorate our rustic living room. My eye fell upon a distant flash of scarlet sumac. Most of the leaves had already fallen quietly among the dry bunch grass beneath the bushes. But here and there a few stray plants, growing in more-sheltered spots among the giant house-sized boulders, held their scarlet leaves in brave defiance of the elements. Sun and frost and vagrant breezes had not yet stripped their staghorn branches bare.

With great care, as painstakingly and precisely as if I were selecting exotic plants in an expensive florist shop, I chose several clusters of gay leaves. Their colors ranged from deep, rich scarlet hues to somber purple, from burnt orange to pale pink. They would make a handsome floral arrangement in any home.

As a final flourish, I plucked a few stalks of pungent rabbit brush, a desert plant whose brilliant golden sprays bloom at their best in late fall. Like the wild asters and goldenrod, these were the last salute of the long flowering season, which in this dry terrain stretches from late February to mid-October.

Happy in heart, singing in spirit, I bore my bounty home. As I opened the cottage door, the aroma of baking sweet potatoes and tender turkey tantalized my taste buds. It would be a delicious dinner, prepared with love and goodwill.

Sitting around the round wooden table that evening, all of us were engulfed in an atmosphere of warmth, love and gratitude to God, our Father. Out of His generosity and bounty, our lives had overflowed with good things and rich friendships. The sweet satisfaction of knowing that His great hand had been upon us, bestowing blessings beyond our desiring, humbled our hearts and drew us to Him in gratitude.

Cheri had placed a pretty candle in the center of the table. Its base was decorated with green sprigs of fragrant juniper. The gentle glow of the candlelight played upon the faces of our friends. They were people at peace. There was contentment there that came welling up from the inner depths of spirits in harmony with God, in harmony with each other and in harmony with us. It sparkled in their eyes and shone in their smiles.

When the feast was finished, we gathered around the fireplace. The silver-gray wood, which only an hour or two before lay bare and bleached upon the mountain, burst into blazing life. Its flames danced and played about the knots and burls, before leaping gaily up the chimney. Its warmth radiated into the room, warming the walls of cedar, enfolding us in "living" heat, unlike that produced by gas, electricity or oil.

Our friends reveled in its gaiety. They relaxed in its friendly atmosphere. At ease and joyous, we shared old stories and joined in hearty laughs, allowing the mellow memories of former times to engulf us in goodwill.

The old gentleman recalled how, as a young lad growing up on a Pennsylvania farm, he had gone to the hills in search of pine knots for their family fires. He, too, knew all about the magic and mystique of finding these pitch-laden prizes buried deep in the old pine woods.

As he recalled his boyhood escapades, a misty, wondrous light flooded his face. He was living youth again—the life of his boyhood days, with suntanned cheeks and bare feet. Never before had I seen him so handsome, so utterly alive, so wondrously well. It was as if forty summers had slipped from his shoulders. He stood strong again, erect and sturdy as a sapling of young manhood.

Cheri, in her generous, loving, gay way, offered to play a few pieces she was just learning on the organ. It was golden music, especially melodious because it was homemade with deep affection. The songs started the elderly lady's toes to tapping. Almost before we knew it, she offered to try a tune or two. In all her long years, her fingers had never touched an organ. But that Thanksgiving eve, there flowed from her heart and hands wondrous music of her own making. It was akin to a rebirth, a renewal, a recapturing of her gentle girlhood.

As time came for them to take their leave, I walked with them up the drive beneath the arching trees. There was a spring to their steps and a joy to their souls that refreshed my own spirit. We had shared and drunk deeply together from the deep delight of this day.

All of our hearts were aglow with true thanksgiving to God, our Father.

14
Beautiful Black Birches

Never lose an opportunity for seeing anything that is beautiful;
For beauty is God's handwriting—a wayside sacrament.
Welcome it in every fair face, in every fair sky, in every fair flower,
And thank God for it as a cup of His blessing.

—Ralph Waldo Emerson

LAST EVENING, AFTER a long, misty day of mountain rain, I looked out upon the lawn, and saw it lay carpeted in gold. Thousands upon uncounted thousands of tiny, shiny birch leaves, gilded with wetness, glistened on the green grass. Lying there in their myriads, they formed a wondrous irregular floral pattern, fashioned from tiny bits of life similar in design.

No two leaves, out of the millions that fell from the birch branches, were identical. Each was a unique structure of intricate complexity that now neared the end of its short-lived lifespan. For though the leaves no longer clung to the birch limbs, supporting the tree with their sustenance, the fabric of their flaming tissues would now begin to decompose upon the ground. Their cellular structure would contribute to the buildup of the rich black humus of the earth in which the black water birches thrived beside the lake.

For uncounted eons of time, the birches and poplars, the alders and willows, the red osier dogwoods and rose thickets, which flourished in the damp soil along the lakeshore, had made their annual contribution to its smooth, dark soil. Across the centuries, since the last giant glacier that carved this valley from granite rock had gone, the little trees had taken over soil building in this lovely spot.

As I cleared the virgin sod and spaded the loamy land for my garden this autumn, I could see in my mind's eye the long history of this gentle ground. Behind the gaunt blue ridges of receding ice lay a barren wasteland of glacial duff and rounded rocks. The finer till had been milled finer than any man-made mill could ever grind it, beneath the titanic raspings of ice shod with coarse teeth of fragmented rock imbedded in its blueness.

Century after century, in the brief, all-too-short summers of these northerly latitudes, stray seeds of dwarf arctic birch and northern willow had fallen upon the barren landscape. Here and there a hardy seedling of these pioneer trees—along with wild dwarf blueberries, mountain avens and some tough fireweed—took root in the rocky landscape.

Imperceptibly at first, but with increasing vigor, this persistent plant community began to clothe the bleak landscape with greenery in summer and brilliant color in autumn. The residue of their brief summer growth was quickly buried beneath long winters of snow, where it decayed. Slowly but steadily there was a buildup of thin soil, soon to be invaded by larger trees and more-luxuriant shrubs.

The eight or ten inches of velvet-smooth black soil that my shovel sliced through had taken ten thousand years to accumulate. Century upon century, there had gently accumulated layer upon layer of fallen leaves, dead twigs, decaying roots and shredded bark. Bacteria, soil organisms, insects, earthworms and fungi had found a fertile field in which to flourish. Each in its own quiet way contributed to the decomposition of the plant material. Each added the offscourings and residue of its own unique life force to the fabric of the earth.

In subsequent years, the dwarf vegetation was replaced and supplanted by larger and more-vigorous trees and shrubs. With the gradual advent of warmer seasons, earlier springs and fewer frosty days, the beautiful black birch, western poplars, mountain alders and red osier dogwood struck root in this sun-kissed valley.

To me, the graceful, slim-limbed western water birch, more commonly called the *black birch*, is one of our most beautiful mountain trees. It reminds me of the British name of endearment for their birches—"Lady of the Woods."

This tree is not attractive because of its scale or size. It has a most unusual growth form. Anywhere from six to twenty, or even more, slender trunks spring from a single root system. These dark, chocolate-colored stems radiate outwards at slanting angles from the center, each stretching toward the sun in a different direction. Where the tree is not cramped or constricted by competition from its fellow forest trees, it forms a striking vase shape.

The luxuriant black birch that dominates the front lawn of "Still Waters" is a classic example of this sturdy tree at its beautiful best.

Its glistening brown trunks tower upward and outward to some forty or fifty feet. Its intertwining slender limbs and branches form a majestic canopy, outspread to the sky like an enormous umbrella of greenery.

So dense is its growth of fine twigs and dainty, heart-shaped leaves, that chickadees, nuthatches and warblers can work their way through it without being seen. As they search its labyrinth of foliage for insects, only their chirping calls and the steady dropping of tree debris disclose their whereabouts. In summer these trees form a splendid shield against the hot desert sun. In their shadow, the grass lies green and moist and cool: a pleasant spot to sit quietly and listen to the wind play through the slender, drooping limbs that hang down in handsome, graceful pendants.

The black birch never grows big enough to provide logs for lumber. At best, a veteran will measure about one foot across at its base. But for fireplace fuel, this hardy tree has no rival. It burns hot and clean. Its glowing coals give off heat equal to the best of coal. And when the winter woodpile contains a goodly share of this wood, the happy woodsman knows he can count on a score of contented evenings before his open hearth.

With careful, loving husbandry, the black birch is a tree that will perpetuate itself almost indefinitely. If care is taken to remove only the largest and most mature trees from a clump, other young ones immediately spring up from the root system to replace them. The foliage of these tender new shoots is a delicate olive green, quite distinct from the darker side of the mature leaves.

The skilled woodsman with a kindly eye and understanding spirit will saw off the tree he cuts in such a way as not to mar the beauty of the younger stems that remain. I try to cut the trunk at an acute angle that blends in with the outward-growing tree form. And if the white wound is carefully painted over with dark-chocolate coating, it not only forestalls decay and insect invasion, but enables the tree to quickly heal over without distorting its elegant beauty.

Few are the trees found anywhere which lend so much beauty to lakeshore or stream side. They love water and are always found close to it—hence the name *water birch*. Their foliage, like fine filagree, is never found far from the sound of water, whether wavelets lapping on a sandy beach or the laughter of a stream tumbling over its stony course. Their long limbs sway in the wind, as if beating time to the water music about them.

In winter their intricate patterns of interlaced branches and twigs, shining black, stand out distinctly against the snow. In spring their hue changes to a ruddy, red glow as the rising sap swells the buds and streams through the slender twigs at the tips. In summer they are a gorgeous mass of greenery, pulsing and vibrant in the brittle sunlight. Their roots are deep in dampness; their heads are held proudly aloft. In autumn they glow like gold against the blue haze and clear skies of Indian-summer days.

It is then I go softly in search of the glistening mushrooms that grow about their base. And it is then I gather up huge armfuls of their bronze leaves to build my compost pile. To me, black birches are beautiful.

15
Mountain Glory

OUR LITTLE LAKE lies nestled among giant, rugged hills. In most countries they would be called mountains. They thrust their ragged ramparts, ridge upon rocky ridge, up to five-, six- and seven-thousand-foot heights.

Unlike some mountains, these rise one above the other in gigantic steps, one broken bench above the next. Colossal rock cliffs; breath-stopping canyons, cut through solid stone; bold bluffs of broken boulders; open, sweeping sagebrush flats; grassy slopes and thick-timbered ridges; all are interspersed in a wondrous variety of terrain.

Few places anywhere in the world offer such diversity of scenery and landscape in so small a compass. Within a radius of twenty miles of my cottage door, one can pass through the lush greenery of the lakeshore, with its marshes and alder thickets; into desert country, with cactus and greasewood; up to open parkland, where ponderosa pines and juniper predominate. Beyond this, the firs and jack pines begin to crowd the north slopes of the ridges. On the southern and western flanks, there are open bunch-grass slopes lying warm to the sun; while up on the very summit, there stand fine forests of larch and spruce.

With the approach of autumn, a gentle stillness steals over this high country. For weeks, it lies wrapped in the smoky blue haze of fall. Gradually frost and falling temperatures touch the trees. At first there is only the faintest hint of changing colors in the landscape. But as the days grow shorter, the flaming foliage intensifies its impact on the mountains. Before long, they begin to blaze with banners of golden glory.

Along the lake, birches turn from green to yellow to bronze. In the streambeds and damp draws, poplars are dressed with golden radiance. The vine maples and sumac are scarlet. But best of all, the mountain larches glow with golden light.

Of all our western forest trees, the larch is one of my favorites, only because of its autumn splendor. And few are the fall seasons that I fail to spend at least one day walking gently beneath their golden spires in the high country.

Unlike their eastern cousins—the lovely little tamaracks that struggle to survive in the sickly swamps and sloughs that have been left behind by the last ice age—the western larch can be a regal mountain monarch. There are larches within ten miles of my doorstep that thrust their great golden crowns two hundred feet into the sky. They stand solid and secure on huge, towering trunks, some of which are four to five feet through at the butt. In spite of their rather thin, fragile, rusty-red bark, some of them have withstood repeated forest fires across the long years of their rugged lives on the ridges.

This past week I set out on my annual pilgrimage to pay honor and respect to these grand giants. The morning light, streaming clear and uncluttered through their feathery foliage, was like fine-spun gold. The trees glowed with an incandescent light, which left the impression they were actually aflame with inner fire. Never had I been so deeply stirred by the living loveliness of the larches. They cloaked the high hills in golden glory. Giant gashes and splashes of vivid yellow ran among the green slopes and rock ridges in bold abandon.

I went to walk softly beneath some of the golden giants. Their glory had been strewn in profusion upon the ground. The forest floor was carpeted with their needles, which were turning bronze and brown.

Suddenly I happened upon an open forest glade in the very depths of a heavily forested draw. Momentarily, I could not believe what I saw. The first overwhelming impression was that I stood in a great cathedral. Several acres of open ground were covered with closely cropped green grass, where range cattle and deer had grazed. A silver stream ran through the meadow, and scattered around it stood gigantic larches, shining gold in the October sunshine.

For a few minutes, I could scarcely move or speak. I simply stood there, awestruck. It was a scene more superb than any man-made park could ever achieve. The open character of the clearing; the spacious openings between the towering columns; the brilliant contrast of the green sward, provided the perfect setting for viewing these mountain monarchs in all their majesty.

Not even the giant Douglas firs of the West Coast, the redwoods of California or the sequoias of the Sierras had touched or moved my spirit so deeply. As I stood silently in the clearing, it came home to me that some sturdy homesteader had once tried to hew out a home for himself in this peaceful paradise. Not a single old log or scrap of forest debris littered the ground. All of it had been cleared and leveled with loving care. Only here and there the forest giants, too large to cut down with an axe, had been left to grow into these great veterans.

One old stump, silver and gray with age, remained. It still bore axe marks, where a pioneer with muscles of steel and a hoping heart had homesteaded a spot for himself in the hills. Across the little stream, a hand-split log had been placed with care, to serve as a footbridge. Clover and grass seed had been sown and had taken root in the virgin soil. But since the time of its planting, it had been graced only by stray range cattle and wild mountain deer. They kept it neatly clipped, like a park tended by a loving caretaker.

As I walked softly across the green sward, I could hear the gentle gurgle of the little stream. It was suckled by mountain springs a short distance up the draw. A flock of pine siskins swarmed through the tops of the trees, sending down soft showers of golden needles. This fresh-fallen larch debris dappled the green grass in gay colors, like a plush floor covering.

None of this startling beauty had been expected. It swept over me in momentous wonderment. Few, few indeed were the human eyes that had ever set sight upon this spot. I was honored to be among the privileged people to set foot here.

It was with genuine reluctance that I finally turned to walk away from that serene spot. There lay upon my soul the inescapable awareness that I had glimpsed a fragment of mountain glory known to but a handful of mortals. Such moments are precious, rare and oftentimes very far apart. They are granted to us by God, as joyous reminders of His own wondrous character and dignity. He deals with us in such ways to make us understand a little of His loving care. His presence surrounds us on every side, yet how slow we are to sense and know: "Father, You are here."

As I came down off the mountain, a deep, upwelling sense of well-being engulfed me. Though it was late October, the sun was warm; its touch tanned my face and browned my bare arms. Not a single stray cloud hovered in the open skies, yet a heavy haze hung in the still autumn air. Distant hills and ridges lay swathed in multihued shades of blue. Those close at hand were almost blue-black, especially where the afternoon shadows slipped across the slopes. The distant ridges lay faint and almost pale, in pastel tones of blue and gray and misty turquoise.

There was a joyous sense of space and serenity to the mountain landscape. This was intensified by the vivid contrast of color that came from the drifts of larch trees running across the slopes. With the late afternoon sun shining through the fragile foliage, it looked like golden filagree. There were royal colors, blue and gold, spread across the landscape in wild and beautiful profusion.

The Master Artist, with deft strokes and delicate touches, had painted upon the canvas of my memory a scene that time would not erase. It was more perfect than any artist's landscape. It pulsed with light and life that had its origin within His own heart and mind.

I came home to "Still Waters" humbled in spirit, happy in heart, replete with bodily rejuvenation. The mountains had enriched me that day, and I was at peace.

16
McIntyre Canyon

LOOKING SOUTH FROM "Still Waters," across the clear-blue expanse of the lake, one sees the mighty mass of McIntyre Bluff. It is a gigantic rock prominence, sheered off on one side, leaving great vertical cliffs of granite that tower above the valley floor.

Legend has it that in one of the intertribal wars between the local Indians, a band of warriors was driven over the bluff in flight. They plunged to their awful deaths, crushed on the boulders lying at the base of the precipice. Even now, there are those who maintain that the mountain bears the resemblance of a bold Indian chief with prominent nose, protruding cheekbones and jutting jaw.

Geologists insist that the bluff was originally part of a natural glacial barrier that blocked the lower end of the valley. Its mass held back the melting glacial waters that flooded the entire valley into one enormous lake. Eventually, with warming weather and increasing runoff from melted snow on the encircling mountains, the original body of water burst its bounds. In a huge flooding, the initial dam of natural debris and glacial fill was washed away. Behind the flooding, only the gigantic bluff remained, as well as the interconnected chain of beautiful lakes that now adorn the valley.

On the other side of the valley, directly across from the bluff, is a remarkable small canyon. It is cut through solid stone, with sheer, winding walls, by an exquisite, clear-running mountain stream. This rather remarkable cleft in the rocks is called McIntyre Canyon. It is much less spectacular than the gigantic canyons of the southwestern United States, but it is still a spot of unusual vistas and mellow moods.

Access to it can be reached in just a few minutes from "Still Waters." Sometimes I work my way up the canyon from the valley below, or on the other hand explore it from the hills by climbing down through its steep-walled gorge.

The canyon is the sort of place one comes for hours of quiet contemplation and gentle reflection. It is not the sort of spot where chattering companions or noisy, ringing banter is in place.

Somehow, whenever I walk up through this defile, there lies upon my spirit a sense of the endless ages that water has been at work here, wearing away stone. This is no great, rushing river, like the Colorado that carved out the Grand Canyon. Instead it is a very modest mountain stream that tumbles from pool to pool in its laughing course through the hills.

In its passage across the centuries it has carved, chiseled and sculpted the gray stone into fantastic flowing formations. The swirling white water, streaming softly over and around the rocks, smooths and polishes their surfaces, to shining perfection. The grain of granite and veins of quartz that interlace their grayness lie exposed in wondrous beauty beneath the flowing water.

Out of the grim gauntness of the hills, a free-running stream has fashioned a masterpiece of exquisite beauty and splendor.

Sometimes I stand on the damp stone and reflect upon its exquisite character. I am reminded that, in similar manner, only the free flow of the river of God's own Spirit through my hard and stony life fashions it into something of beauty. Only the eternal impact of His presence produces a character of worth and loveliness.

In the stillness of this canyon, ferns and mosses flourish in the damp spots. Despite the dreadful desert heat, down in the deep and shadowed defiles there is coolness and dampness. Spray and mist and the steady evaporation of tumbling water from the stream insure the survival of water-loving plants. Their spores and seeds may have been borne here by birds in flight or by the vagrant mountain winds. No matter how, here they found favorable conditions to start life and establish themselves upon the cracked and weathered surface of the stone.

Throughout its length, the canyon is a shadowed gorge, yet also a natural garden. Besides mosses and lichens, there are banks of bracken, plus gnarled and twisted birches and poplars that have found a foothold in some fissure of the rock. There are beds of wild roses that glow pink in summer and red in fall, when their hips turn scarlet and their foliage flames like fire. There are sturdy firs and patient old ponderosa pines, whose horny roots have forced their strong fingers around the rough rocks, gripping them in a gnarled and viselike grasp. No rushing wind or flooding freshet can ever wrench them from their rocky handholds in the canyon world.

There is music in this canyon, too—wild music, mountain music—music not made by any human enterprise. It is the melodic strains of a stream singing over stone.

It is the muted notes of water murmuring in its gentle flow from pool to pool. It is the gaiety and rhythm of wavelets splashing on rocks, dancing on stage after stage of water-washed stone.

None of this is planned or programmed. It does not come stereotyped. The canyon music rises and falls in intensity with the passing of the seasons. In winter it is hushed and stilled by snow and ice. In spring it rises in tempo with flooding snow melt. In summer it sparkles and scintillates with sunshine. In autumn it is quiet and subdued, freshened by fall showers, but mellow with the blue mood of mountain haze and golden days.

As the hill breezes blow across the canyon country, they carry its song to any who will pause and listen. Sometimes the sound comes strongly, surely, stridently. The tumbling of water and thunder of its fall are trombones and drums sounding in the hills. On other occasions the faint, fine notes of a free-flowing stream are violins, whose high notes sing through the trees and reach for the sky through the narrow cleft above the canyon floor.

There are other notes here, too: the call of the rare canyon wren, who nests in the cliff face; the cry of the slate-gray water ouzel darting from pool to pool; the plaintive song of the song sparrow that echoes from the shadows and sets our spirits singing.

The canyon is a place of many moods and happy hours. It is a spot that reminds man that God, our Father, has been at work on the world a very long time. His work has been good and beautiful and sublime. Nor is it done yet.

17
Breaking Ground

WHEN LOOKING FOR a spot to settle, one of the essential attributes it had to possess was a patch of ground suitable for a garden. One of my dreams was to enjoy again the pleasure of producing and harvesting my own fresh, tender, homegrown vegetables.

For a number of years, while busily engaged with other responsibilities, there had not been either time or opportunity to enjoy gardening. Life in apartments and condominiums in a city setting deprives one of this delight. Urban residents may not realize it, but cement walls and asphalt streets have a way of isolating people from the healing impulse of trees and grass, fields and flowers. And in my inner soul there had always lingered the deep, persistent, at times painful longing for a bit of soil: A place where I could plant peas and beans; a spot where my own sun-kissed tomatoes and cucumbers could be plucked, just at their peak of ripened perfection, to provide heaping bowls of crisp, fresh salads.

Happily, "Still Waters" had some open ground, long ago roughly cleared, but never cultivated. The day we decided to buy the property, I had walked carefully over all of its tangled land. Young poplar saplings, wolf willows and mountain alders were springing up in wild abandon everywhere. Their roots ran in every direction, crisscrossing the woodland clearing in unchecked confusion. If left alone, in just a few more summer seasons the place would have reverted to native forest.

One of the first strenuous tasks I tackled was to chop out all this new growth. The piles of young shoots, along with weeds and other invading plants, were gathered up and burned in blazing pyres. There is something very primitive, very elemental, very much of the pioneer instinct in such work. It is intensely satisfying. It takes one back to beginnings. It is an inherent part of the ancient art of taking untamed land and turning it into a homestead; a place where a man decides to sink his roots a spell; a living monument to the end of his wandering days.

During the first summer, I kept the ground clean and clear with a mower. This was not easy. I did not want our tranquil setting disturbed unduly with the screaming sounds of a power mower, so the price to pay for peaceful days was to push an ancient hand mower over the rough ground. A kindly neighbor had freely and spontaneously offered to give me his old reel mower, if I would just take it away. It was exactly what I needed, not only to clip the grass short, but also to harden the muscles in my legs, arms and back.

In the early hours just after dawn, while the desert air was still cool, the ground would be mowed in gentle joy. The green grass glistened silver under the shining dampness of its dews. And my face and back glistened with drops of perspiration forced from the skin by the exertion of my body. Both the meadow and my muscles benefited from this morning exercise.

Every time I walked across the sward, I dreamed and planned just where the garden would grow best. I chose a corner where the slope of the ground faced south and west. Here the soil would be warmed to the utmost by the sun that arched across the valley from range to mountain range. It was a spot, too, with excellent drainage. Best of all, I knew, from planting some ornamental trees there in early spring, that its topsoil was deep and dark, rich with the accumulated humus of uncounted centuries.

But it would not be easy digging.

Again, I was determined to do the labor by hand.

I did not wish the roar of a tractor or tiller to disturb or desecrate the quiet calm and sensitive stillness of our Indian-summer days. Their quiet tranquility and still serenity were a special quality, which no modern machine was allowed to dispel.

It would be a tough task to turn this virgin sod. It had never been penetrated with the point of a sharp shovel. Its earth had never been turned to face the sun. No one had ever stuck a spade in this soil to plant a seed or grow a crop. In truth, this was to break new ground. And in that breaking there would be commingled sweat and joy.

It was late fall when I began to dig. It was a job that could never be done in a day, a week, ten days or even two weeks. For the better part of a month, my back would bend over this patch of dark earth. The warm autumn sunshine and the heavy labor of my own straining muscles would send little trickles of perspiration trickling across my forehead, face and forearms. Sweat would stand out on my shoulders, back and legs, bared to the blue skies. But it was hearty labor, done with all my heart. It was glad work, done with genuine gaiety. It was sweet toil, deeply satisfying to my spirit.

As my shovel plunged deep into the dark, mellow earth, it would encounter roots and rocks. An antique wheelbarrow, built of solid steel, with its iron wheel and accumulated coat of dried concrete, stood ever beside me. Again and again and again, I piled it high with stones and boulders wrenched from their sockets beneath the sod.

Some stones and rocks were so large and massive I could just barely roll them into the tray of the overturned barrow. Then, shoving and heaving with all my might, the wheelbarrow would be turned upright. Thus I hauled tons and tons of stone from the garden patch. The rocks were used to reinforce and enhance the lake frontage, where the lap of the waves tended to erode away the banks. So in truth I was accomplishing two tasks at once.

As day followed day of digging, the garden plot grew ever larger and more attractive. Black earth, mellow, friable and fertile, lay smooth and silky beneath the sun. It was free, too, of roots and stumps. For with fierce determination, I had torn the tangled mass of underground growth from the soil. The matted roots of snowberry, sumac and wild roses had been heaped in piles. These, too, would add fuel to the last fall fire that cleared the ground ready for spring seeding.

At last, one glorious October morning, the work was done. With enormous pleasure, I stood back to cast my eyes over the garden plot. Already I could see it flourishing with fruits and vegetables the coming summer.

Momentarily I paused and reflected. No doubt it was just as great a job for God, the Good Gardener, to produce His fruits in the little garden of my soul.

18
Gathering Wood

WHEN WE CAME to "Still Waters," one of our serious intentions was to become as self-sufficient as possible. This was to apply to not only the production of our own fruit and vegetables, but also our fuel requirements.

The little cottage, once it was properly insulated and winterized for cold weather, would be fairly simple to heat. It had only 440 square feet of floor space, every foot of which was used to maximum advantage. With the installation of our wood stove, which served as a combination cook stove, heater and open fireplace, the place could be kept as cosy and warm as a kitten's ear.

With continually escalating energy costs, it made good sense for us to try and supply our own heat from the wood we could salvage from the lake, as well as the fuel we could find in the nearby hills. In all of this, there was a decided degree of fun, excitement and pleasure. It is much more rewarding to gather one's own wood, with the expenditure of one's own energy, than merely to pay some public utility to provide it.

The heat and flames and fragrance from the fuel were doubly precious because of the little trips and happy hours outdoors spent in collecting it. As the old saying goes, cutting one's own wood warms you twice over: first in the sweat and labor of sawing and splitting, second, in the gentle radiation of its warmth in the living room.

Often, as I sat and listened to the splintering, crackling sounds of its burning, I was borne back again into the woods or along the lake, where it had been collected. On chill, clear, frosty nights, when the stars outside sparkled against the blackness of the desert darkness, the lively flames would leap and dance in a similar shimmering light. The energy of a hundred summer suns was released and radiated into the room to enliven the night.

The wood I retrieved from the lake was always somewhat of a

surprise. The lake itself was fringed with a mixed stand of mountain alder, willow, black birch and poplar. Some of these the beavers felled for food or material with which to construct their lodges. For one reason or another, pieces of these "beaver trees," as I called them, would break away from their original site, to be washed across the lake by wind and waves.

After almost every heavy blow from the northwest, a random collection of waterlogged wood was tossed up on our tiny gravel beach or caught in the tules along the shore. This bounty of free fuel always tickled my fancy. It was a bit like a fairy tale, to think my wood was being felled by my beaver friends, then ferried across the lake by the wind to be delivered free of charge at the front door.

A few days drying in the heat of our dry desert air, and this wood was ready for the saw and woodpile, where it hardened into first-class fuel. I enjoyed sawing up these slender poles. The physical exertion hardened my muscles and trimmed my body to that of a lithe young athlete.

There were occasional days when good-sized logs would come drifting down the river channel. How they got there was always a bit of a mystery. For a few days they would float around the lake, providing perfect perches for ducks, gulls, terns or crows that loved to alight on them. Eventually, when they came closer to the cottage, I would slip out in the canoe and tow them home for extra firewood. This was always a rather tricky little task, because it was easy to tip the canoe while taking the log in tow.

Other times, I would slip across the lake and find choice pieces of trees and logs that were lodged along the shore, stuck on sandbanks or caught in the bulrushes. These, too, would be loaded in the canoe to be carried home for fuel.

Perhaps even more exciting and pleasurable than these canoe excursions were the days I went to the hills for wood. The *wood days* were chosen with great care. Somehow one had to go in search of winter wood in just the right mood. There was something almost sacramental about it. It was a search for wood suitable to be sacrificed on the flames.

In these quests, I purposely avoided cutting any living, growing, vigorous tree that adorned the woods with its foliage and form.

Instead, I deliberately chose to gather what I could from trees or branches or upturned roots that lay upon the ground.

Loggers and fallers long ago had cut and slashed their wasteful way through the rough hills back of us. A tangle of twisted logging tracks and trails traversed the tough terrain. Here there were thousands of stumps to remind a man of the fine forests that had taken untold centuries to clothe these rugged ridges in glorious greenery. Many of the choicest trees were gone; still, sturdy second-generation conifers were taking their place. And in among these latter timber stands, there remained remnants of old, tough trees, which made fine fuel.

Often the prostrate trunks and limbs that still survived the long years of weathering were pieces of wood richly impregnated with saps and resins that prevented rot and decay. The wind-twisted trunks and rough, gnarled limbs turned silver-gray beneath summer sun and winter snow. When put to the flames, their pitchy fibers would burn with fierce heat and flashing flames, to leave behind a bed of glowing coals.

It was like prospecting for precious ore to go in search of such mountain-grown fuel. It was a real find to stumble on some prostrate old veteran, half-buried beneath the accumulated duff of fallen needles, cones and twigs of half a century. Protruding from the forest floor would be the hard, jagged old fir knots or twisted pine limbs that had turned hard as old bone.

Often these were so brittle with age that their wood could be readily broken by shattering them against a sharp stone. No need, even, for an axe or saw. All that was required to bear home a bountiful supply of beautiful bone-dry wood were sharp eyes, a knowing heart, and arms strong enough to gather up armfuls of the wondrous fuel.

This was conservation at ground level. This material, which otherwise would have wasted away and posed a fire threat to the forests, was used to maximum benefit and joy.

Occasionally I came across trees that had been blown down by the wind or overturned by recent road crews. They would lie not far from the open roads and tracks. Sometimes it would take a little extra work to clear a path to where they lay. Rocks and roots and the debris of broken branches would have to be removed so I could get at this treasure trove.

Last summer, I found a huge vine maple that had been overturned and torn from a creek bed by a caterpillar tractor making a new road. The multitrunked tree had ruthlessly been shoved out of the soil, then pushed aside, to wither away in the summer heat. It was a sad spectacle. Normally vine maples are little more than very sturdy shrubs. Seldom do they exceed twenty feet in height. Their main claim to fame is the gorgeous array of autumn colors that adorn their foliage. Some of these shrubby trees, rooted in the cliffs behind the cottage, carry leaves that vary in color from pale green to vibrant scarlet—all at the same time.

But this uprooted specimen was a huge vine maple. Its main trunk, nearly ten inches in diameter, was the largest I had ever seen in the species. Now it no longer could paint the hills with its fall colors. Like a soldier stricken in battle, it lay fallen and forlorn on the forest floor. Its life was done.

It took the better part of a whole morning to trim away its labyrinth of intertwined limbs, then cut it up into stove-length pieces. When I split up its creamy-white wood, which was tight-grained, I knew I had some of the finest fuel to come out of any forest. Its sawdust was fragrant, and its wood would burn with an intense, clear heat matching the best anthracite coal.

Almost with reverence and genuine tenderness, I took it home. As I stacked the clean, smooth-barked slabs in the sun, I knew I was storing away energy and warmth for many a winter evening. When the winds tore across the lake, shivered the birch branches above our roof and howled around the house, the vine maple would make up for all with its fierce, enduring flames, which would leap up the chimney, driving back the blizzard's chill.

19
Swans in the Mist

THERE IS A beautiful mountain river that cascades over a gnarled rock ridge several miles upstream from our lake. Its cold, clear waters rush and rumble through the broken gap cut in the stone by centuries of tumbling water. The shining spray and roaring white rapids are in vivid contrast to the blue stillness of the lake beyond and the sky above.

Farther down, its channel has been constricted by the industry of man. Its wild, native turbulence has been tamed. It runs softly, in still, smooth stretches between lush green fields of hay and grain. Here cattle graze quietly on the verdant meadows, their sleek red hides reflecting the warm sunlight like shimmering silk. It is a placid and pleasant setting, enhanced by the high hills and bold bluffs of brown rock that march down the flanks of the river's valley.

Gradually the ranchlands are replaced by marshlands. Here the river spreads itself into swampy mud flats, where bulrushes, blackbirds, herons, and a host of other marsh birds abound. This is where the Canada geese come with their fledglings in the spring. It is where the thump of the bittern and the shrill cries of the grebes echo across the tule beds. These are the ancient calls of the wild, which have been a part of this lake for ten thousand years.

In fall a peculiar phenomenon occurs over these reed beds and river mouth at dawn each day. Ghostlike plumes of snow-white mist begin to billow up above the surface of the stream. They are not stationary or still. Instead, the rising mists, like wild white horses rearing up in ranks of gleaming white, go galloping across the far side of the lake.

The clouds of phantom chargers are borne along strongly by the downdrafts of cool air coming off the high country. Manes tossing in the morning light, they sweep out across the lake, then lose themselves in the warmth and sunlight of the dry, desert air.

Into the white mists fly all sorts of birds, most of them winged visitors heading south. They come in hundreds, dark bodies bursting through the whiteness as they wing in from the north to rest briefly on the lake. Sometimes they simply vanish from view as the clouds of vapor engulf them. But through the white shrouds come their contented calls, as they feed eagerly on the rich weed beds.

Occasionally one or several pair of wild trumpeter swans come in to land on the lake. Of all our feathered friends, they are the most noble and regal. Their graceful forms and immaculate white plumage grace the blue waters in resplendent contrast. In ancient times, the trumpeters were reported to have nested in these marshes. But the advent of modern machinery and the cacophony of modern men gradually discouraged the shy birds from remaining on their traditional grounds. So at best they are here only a few short weeks in late fall.

The other morning I watched a pair wheel proudly over the lake. Even their flight was grand and stately. They moved in wondrous unison, like a pair of superb ballet dancers in a sublime *pas de deux*. Unhurried, unruffled—smoothly sailing across the stage of blue water, blue sky, brown hills and bronze reed beds—they soared effortlessly, sheathed in shining iridescence, their outstretched wings reflecting sunlight.

No ballet performance ever impressed me more. Their consummate natural artistry and gentle grace surpassed the loftiest passages from Tchaikovsky's *Swan Lake.*

With majestic beauty, they circled down into the mist, their flowing forms gradually melding into the enveloping whiteness. It was as if they had vanished into vapor, passing silently yet serenely from life into death.

It was a poignant pageantry. It had lasted but a few fleeting moments. It had been observed only by one man. But, as with so many of God's great gifts, the man was richer for having gladly received it.

20
Before Daybreak

AT FOUR IN the morning, on a clear, moonlit November night, the desert air can be crystal bright. The whole world lies sharp, still, etched with silver light. The stars pulse with intensity. The moon moves majestically across the night sky, appearing to drop steadily toward the western ridges. There is an awesome, wondrous breathlessness to the valley.

These are those still, sacred, special hours, in which the spirit of a man is moved upon by the Spirit of God. It was under desert skies like this that many of the divine revelations have come to the seers and prophets of all ages.

Only a random stray leaf, left here and there, hangs unmoving amid the delicate fretwork of the bare tree branches. Their lacelike intertwined twigs form a fragile pattern of black filagree against the mellow moonlight. Nothing stirs. Not a leaf trembles. Not a branch bends. Not a wavelet moves on the lake. Momentarily, the whole earth appears to be cast in priceless pewter.

There is an overpowering sensation of stillness: a quiet so acute that any sound of a passing vehicle would be an insolent intrusion. The drone of a distant plane would be a desecration. The clatter of man's clamorous civilization would be an imposition of discordant notes out of harmony with the spheres in space.

These quiet, morning moments are precious points in one man's brief life. Yet they are the essence of the eternal; for out of the endless, timeless immensity of eternity, God speaks softly, clearly and specifically to the waiting soul: "Be still and know that I am God." The words are poignant and appropriate. His own gracious Spirit is present, to commune with the heart quietly humbled by the breathless beauty about him. In such interludes, my soul is stilled, my spirit is at rest. All is well.

Amid the ebb and flow of the shifting tides of human history, these eternal values remain. No one can rob me of the stars. No man can deprive me of the moon's majestic mood. No crisis of civilization can completely eclipse the stillness of the desert night. These remain and endure. They are beyond the grasp of rapacious men, yet they are freely available to the most humble heart, which briefly but sincerely is open and responsive.

I have often sat alone beneath the stars and moon, wrapped in the wonder of their enchantment. Their soft and silver splendor spread across the earth is free for the taking. It is lavished with love across the landscape. It is spread with exquisite artistry upon rocks and grass, upon trees and water. Everywhere one turns, the light of the night glows gently. It makes the earth a magic sphere, suspended in space, shining with reflected light that may have taken ten thousand years to reach it from remote stars in the depths of distant space.

I cannot, with my finite mind and limited human perception, comprehend the enormity of eternity. Nor can I reach out to embrace the uncounted, unknown millions of stars, suns and galaxies of the universe. But I can bow my soul before the beauty of dawn, breaking now across the eastern ranges, and whisper softly, "Oh God, my Father, You are here; You are near; and You are very dear."

Inherently, in the fragile loveliness of this chill November morning, there is also present enormous integrity. For untold centuries, for millenia of unnumbered seasons, the steady rhythm of sun and moon, stars and planets has swung serenely across the skies. Men—simple men and wise men—have looked and longed and marveled at such majesty.

Man's puny pride, his arrogant intellect, his brazen bravado, have had no part in planning or programming this pageantry. It is strictly a divine production. Only God Himself could arrange such grandeur. It pulverizes petty pride.

For this I am glad.

It reassures: "*Thou, God,* changest not!"

All else may.

21
November Morning

NOVEMBER CAN BE bleak and bare and bitterly cold. But it can also be hauntingly beautiful in its melancholy muted tones, saddened by the last tattered leaves tumbling from the trees; the last forlorn flights of waterfowl leaving the icebound lakes; the last glimpse of gray ground, frozen like cast iron, waiting to be cloaked in winter white.

This was one of those mornings.

When I crawled out from beneath the warm wool comforter of the bed, I could feel a distinct bite in the air. There was a sharpness to its edge. I looked out across the lake, whose edges shone silver with a skim of fresh ice.

If I was to make one last canoe trip across the lake before final freeze-up, it would have to be now. A gigantic breakfast of cereal, toast, bacon and eggs, whose delicious fragrance filled the cottage, fortified me for the venture.

Taking my paddles, binoculars and axe, along with wool jacket, cap and gloves, I launched the canoe in our little sandy cove. The thin glaze of transparent ice crackled and splintered around the sleek green hull as I pushed off from the beach, breaking out into open water beyond.

Scarcely had I gotten out into the lake when a gusty wind came up. In just a few moments, it was moving the icy water in rolling waves. Its frosty edge cut my exposed face, making me set my jaw and grit my teeth in grim defiance of the worst it could do.

Fiercely, I dug the paddle into the stormy waters. I doggedly fought the wind that threatened to capsize the frail little craft, so fragile and easily flung about. My muscles had been hardened and honed by the summer's heavy work. Moving rocks, planting trees, mowing grass, digging virgin sod, splitting wood and mixing concrete had stripped away the softness and left me tough and trim.

Persistently, powerfully, patiently I plowed across the lake. No

November blow would hold me back from making the opposite shore. The icy water splashed against the prow. It slapped against the sides. It went swishing angrily beneath the thin belly of the canoe as I drove it against the wind. At last we came into the more quiet waters that lay in the lee of a long wooded point. There I could reduce the rate of my strokes and rest the paddle occasionally.

A last pair of belated mallards sprang up from the lake behind a clump of bulrushes, where they had been sheltered. Their explosion sent a spray of silver droplets shining into the sun, which was just lifting over the high hill. Necks outstretched, bodies straining with rapid upward wing beats, the two big birds climbed boldly above me. Suddenly they circled and sped down the valley, headed south for sunshine and warmer days. At that instant, I wished fervently that I too possessed the incredible freedom of uninhibited flight.

Gently the canoe edged its way along the sheltered shore. I finally found a small patch of sand on a bank beneath some aged black birch. Here I put its bow up on the shore, feeling glad to have found such a pleasant landing. Pulling it up well onto the sand, safe from wind and waves, I headed into the hills.

To my surprise, the wind gained in velocity. Angrily it gusted and howled around the giant walls of rock that towered above the lake. As they faced south, I had assumed they would be somewhat sheltered from the northern storms. Instead, the rushing air twisted and turned through the valley, bending the trees with its might, following the contour of the land like a hound hot on a trail.

Today there would be little relief anywhere from its onslaught. It gathered up the bleached, brown bundles of ripened knapweed and tumbleweed, tossing them across the benches, rolling them down the banks, scattering their sturdy seeds in every direction.

A stray raven, like a black bandit, also tumbled in the wind. His raucous cry swept along with him as he flapped through the forest and sought more-sheltered terrain.

I hugged the foot of the high cliffs, hoping to find a sun-warmed spot between the gray boulders that frost had forced off the mountain face. Steadily I worked my way up into higher ground.

My exertions made the warm air from my heaving lungs come out in white plumes that quickly vanished in the cold air. But the stiff climb kept me warm until I suddenly broke out into a little sheltered basin where all was still. Here there was a virtual sun trap, where the feeble November sun warmed the stone and tempered the air.

There was a sweet sensation of repose here. I pushed back my heavy wool cap and let the sun's rays caress my face. I pulled off my lined gloves and felt its feeble warmth on my gnarled and sun-browned hands. Here was stillness amid the storm, serenity amid severity. The contrast made it doubly precious.

Life is often like that. How little would most of us genuinely appreciate our Father's gracious gifts, were it not for the adversity of life's storms.

I had luxuriated in this gentle spot only a few moments when my ears detected the persistent, piping call of a canyon wren. The tiny brown bird, with its snowy-white bosom, flitted across the rock face above me. Erratically, he flew from crevasse to crevasse in the cliff, searching for insects with his long probing beak. Never for an instant did he relent in his chirping.

Much to my delight, he began to approach me. I stood as still as stone. Hugging the rocks, I endeavored to be as unmoving and inconspicuous as possible. Almost before I knew it, he was flitting over the rocks less than six feet from my face. It was my closest encounter with this beautiful and rather rare wren. He did not linger long in my company. Satisfied that he had searched the rocks around me well enough, he flew up the mountain, leaving me glad that I had come that morning, in spite of the weather.

Slowly I worked my way back through the forest. It was a comfort to tread softly on the deer trails beneath the big, red-barked ponderosa pines. Their long needles on the forest floor provided a cushioned path for my heavy hiking boots. Tramping woodland trails in silence has always been a balm to my wild and restless spirit. It does something to restore and refresh a man who quickly wearies of city streets and the noisy clangor of man's metropolitan world. The rush and confusion and tensions of the twentieth century strain us more than we know. For taut minds and tired nerves, a few miles of forest paths are a wondrous panacea.

I came across a gorgeous cluster of a dozen young junipers. They were growing vigorously in the shelter of a giant, dead fir. I marked the spot well in my memory, promising myself to return one spring day to dig one up for planting at "Still Waters." There its fine, feathery foliage would adorn one of the rockeries and gladden our hearts every time we looked out over the lake. It would be an enduring reminder of this November day.

Back at the canoe, I decided to load it with some of the sun-dried, bone-hard limbs of black birch that lay in profusion beneath the trees. The wood lying in the bottom of the frail craft would give greater stability in the choppy waters on my way home. Happily, the wind would be to my back, so it would be a swift crossing.

Out on the lake once more, the canoe sprang to life under the driving impulse of my powerful strokes. It literally surged ahead on each succeeding wave that the wind drove beneath it, like a charger champing on the bit. With the wind against my back and the sun on my face, we skimmed homeward toward the cottage in high spirits.

During the morning the wave action had fragmented the ice along the shore and in the tule beds. As we neared the beach, the sound of ten thousand tinkling ice bells rang through the chill, clean air. Fractured, broken, glasslike ice particles tinkled against one another and against the globes of ice that encircled each bulrush stem. Bending and blowing in the wind, they produced a symphony of sound delicately blending the innumerable sounds of a thousand ice bells in the breeze.

It was an exquisite homecoming. November was not all drab and bad. This had been a morning I would never forget, fashioned in exquisite beauty from wind and water, forest and frost.

22
Hike in the Hills

ONE OF THE great attractions of our gentle life at "Still Waters" consists of frequent hikes in the nearby hills. Few people are so fortunate that, within ten minutes of stepping out their front door, they can be in wild and untamed terrain. In our case, this high, broken country—with its sagebrush benches, giant broken-rock cliffs, open parklike forests and rugged hills—is ideal for hiking.

Part of its great magnetism also lies in the rich array of wildlife that is native to the area, both animals and birds. There is, as well, a wide diversity of trees, shrubs, grasses and flowers that lends interest to any ramble up the rock ridges. And, naturally, the broken character of the landscape, with its lakes and streams, provides wondrous long views of breathtaking beauty.

Any time that I set out on foot, a sandwich in my pocket and binoculars slung over my shoulder, it is with a keen sense of excitement and adventure. No two trips are ever the same, and it is surprising what new vignettes of wildlife or natural wonder will enliven my mountain rambles.

One autumn hike I took still lingers with limpid clarity in my memory. Most of the final tasks around the cottage had been cleared away. The garden was spaded and lay waiting for winter weather. The woodpile was piled high. All the trees were trimmed. The beach had been cleared and was freshly sanded. The road was graveled with crushed red shale from the hills. So all was well. There were free days now, to roam happily in the autumn sunshine.

I set out with a friend to climb the cliffs back of our bungalow. We had not hiked more than 400 yards when I spotted a select band of bighorn sheep. I say select, because among them were several superb rams. One of these was a monster—a big black male of magnificent proportions. Proudly he carried a commanding set of horns that were approaching full curl. Many a hunter would risk life and limb for such a trophy.

It surprised me to see such a splendid specimen so close to my cottage. How he had managed to elude the sportsmen for so many seasons was somewhat of a miracle, for every fall, these hills were hunted hard by hunters in quest of outstanding rams.

To my unbounded delight, the big black ram did not bolt. Instead, he sensed that the hunting season was over and he need fear no hurt from me. In any case, he was so intent on the ewes in his band that he scarcely gave us any notice.

It was a moving spectacle, to watch this superb specimen of his species move across the broken terrain with such proud and regal might. The easy, powerful, fluid strength of his enormous muscles rippled beneath his shining coat. Every step he took bespoke his majestic prowess. With exultant grace he would bound up and up, from boulder to boulder in great steel-spring leaps that looked so easy. Yet a man scrambling over that same ground would have to stretch and strain and struggle to even start to cross the rocky chasms.

With giant leaps, he would launch himself from ledge to ledge. Where I would hesitate to even look down because of the yawning chasms below, he would leap across lightly from toehold to toehold, his hooves finding sure footing in the tiniest irregularities of rock or unevenness of stone surface.

The quiet composure of the mighty ram; the calmness of his great yellow eyes; the obvious command of his presence; the sureness of his own superb strength, were all expressions of his wilderness realm. He was a pristine product of a tough and hardy species that had survived in this mountain terrain for uncounted centuries.

The enormous hazards of winter blizzards, raging forest fires, the predation of coyotes, cougars and bears, had been endured and overcome. The relentless pressures from hunters, disease and the inroads of ranchers' cattle on the bighorn range had been met and mastered. In spite of the worst that modern civilization, its men and machinery had done to his mountain realm, the great ram stood there as a symbol of wild majesty.

The sight made my blood race in my veins. It quickened and stirred my spirit. My heart pounded with primitive pleasure, and I confess that a choking lump began to rise in my throat.

This was more, much more than mere sentiment. It was an expression of profound and personal gratitude to God for the great privilege of having played a small part in the survival of these wild sheep.

Years and years ago, I had sensed that with increased development of this valley, the sheep range would be imperiled. This especially applied to the lower levels along the lakes, where they came for winter feed. Here the snow was less deep. Grass and shrubs on the lakeside benches, swept clear by winter winds, insured their survival.

Yet, as so often happens, no one in government seemed to share my personal concern. Homes began to be built along the lake. Campgrounds, orchards and roads began to occupy the grassy ground. Fences were erected, and steadily but surely the wild-sheep range was being constricted into an ever-diminishing size.

My apprehension was shared with other local wildlife lovers. A sufficiently aroused number of people banded together to form a local park-and-wildlife-preservation society. From time to time, I was invited to come and address this group. Some of the sessions were thrown open to the public. So it was that private contributions were collected to establish a fund, out of which land could be bought to increase the sanctity of the sheep range. Bit by bit, wild acreage was purchased, and the sheep were provided with adequate areas in which they could graze throughout the severe winter weather.

Little did I dream, in those far-off days, that it would later be my good fortune to have a home in the very heart of this sheep terrain. Little did I think that some of my happiest hikes would be across the hills I had helped to preserve for my wild friends of hoof, wing and claw. Little did I ever envisage the day when, with pounding heart and racing pulse, I would stand in silent wonderment, watching a superb ram standing on the skyline as a salute to my own service to him.

It is of such stuff that dreams and life's richest moments are made. There is a jewellike quality to such interludes. There comes a dazzling, shining, winsome awareness of having had a small share in an enterprise of enduring quality. I call it, in layman's language, having a part in our Father's majestic plans and purposes for the planet.

The bighorn ram, grand and regal in his demeanor that day, was not the only reward that came to my spirit. As I climbed higher along the cliff face, a gorgeous golden eagle sailed past me on outstretched wings, the wind of his passing whistling softly through his stiff flight feathers. He was coursing the cliffs and tumbled rock piles at their base for some sign of rabbits or marmots that might provide a meal. In a matter of moments, the great bird had come and gone, but I was richer for his passing.

As the sun began to drop down toward the blue ridges to the west, I turned toward home. The day would die quickly. Its hours had passed swiftly in the gentle company of my companions.

Striding down through the sagebrush and greasewood, I was suddenly startled by the unexpected explosion of a coyote from his bed beneath a bush. Evidently he had been sound asleep in his snug shelter when I burst in upon him. Crafty creature that he is, this coyote seemed to literally start out of his sleep running full speed, without having to become wide awake. In seconds he had zigzagged through the greasewood, put a rock ridge between himself and us, then melted from sight into the surrounding terrain. I was sure he was the same fellow who sometimes left his telltale tracks across my driveway.

In the gathering dusk we came across a covey of wild and noisy chukar partridges. Swiftly they scattered through the rocks and brush, calling to one another. Often I had thrilled to the haunting sounds of their cries from the cliffs. They were always a reminder that a bit of the wilds will survive and thrive, if given half a chance by man.

Trudging home, tired in muscle and tendon, my spirit was singing and gay. It had been a good day—a great day—a day to be remembered for its joy and splendor in the hills.

23
Neighbors

NO MAN, IF he wishes to be a truly joyous person, can live as an island of isolation. Even those of us who are by instinct independent individualists need neighbors and friends and kin to fully round out our lives. It is a poor person indeed whose days are not enriched by an interchange of love and kindness with his fellow human beings.

All of my life, it has been my wonderful good fortune to experience the warmth, affection and acceptance of good and kindly people. This is one of God's great gifts to me. It matters not where life's adventures have led; always there have been dear, bighearted, generous souls who took me into their circle of friendship.

This has been true whether my neighbors were tough-and-hardy ranchers and loggers; whether they were West Coast fishermen or native Indians; whether they were sophisticated scientists, bright intellectuals from the academic world; or whether they were the notorious Masai of the African plains. No matter what status or station a person's background may have been, always it has been possible to find those through whom the milk of human kindness, and God's own gracious love, flowed in full measure to enrich my own life.

When we moved to "Still Waters," I knew this would happen again, and it did. We were treated with a courtesy and kindness that touched me deeply. In fact, the interest, concern and genuine love shown by our neighbors remains as one of the bright, scintillating chapters of our experience there.

Harv was one of the men who helped us get started. He is one of those quiet, strong, gentle people who is ever ready and willing to lend a helping hand. Harv came down and built the cupboards in the cottage. Amid the pungent aroma of cedar sawdust, he sawed and shaped and fitted the fragrant lumber into beautiful built-in fixtures, where we could store clothes and books and boots and bedding.

He is a tall, strong, rawboned man, with a gentle smile and delightful sense of humor. Harv and I manage to take several tramps in the hills together every year. He loves the high country and wild places as fiercely as I do. All of our adventures together are replete with good cheer and lighthearted gaiety. Sometimes we go out to gather great loads of firewood in his big, battered truck. Never have I known a man who can ease a truck over such tough and impossible terrain as well as he can. He seems to literally love his vehicle up the most impossible places. And even though it is a machine built of nuts and bolts, steel and iron, it responds to his touch like a living being.

Harv is the one who came and helped me clear the site for my new toolshed. He can perform more work with a shovel in his big hands than any man I ever met. Rocks and boulders and roots were torn from the ground in short order under his tough hands, hands that can also tune an engine to run sweetly and serenely. He is a top mechanic, who can make iron and metal move when most of us would stand mocked by its malfunction.

Harv's dainty wife, Marie, is almost as tiny as he is tall. She is a vivacious, bubbling, enthusiastic soul. Her culinary skills are special. Any invitation to her home is a treat to superb cooking. Often she has shared her special pickles, preserves and meat with us.

In her kindness and thoughtfulness, she often offers Cheri rides to and from town. And when the two of them are together, I am reminded of a couple of happy schoolgirls away on some hilarious lark together.

Bill was a total stranger to us when we moved to "Still Waters." He and his wife, Phyl, owned the land adjoining ours. Both of them are people with a profound love for plants and trees and shrubs and flowers. Anything that grows also glows in their care. They have an innate instinct for making things grow. Their lot next to ours, though vacant and unoccupied, resembles a fine English park. Its elegant trees, its borders of beautiful evergreens, its flaming sumac and forsythia, are a never-ending source of pleasure to us.

At his own home, Bill has created a paradise of beauty out of a barren sagebrush gully. It is now considered one of the most delightful properties in the whole valley. He is a specialist in pruning and grafting and budding. His special hobby is collecting varieties of apple trees. Of these, he has some 132 sorts growing on his land. Roses are also his love. At one time, over 1,000 rosebushes graced his grounds. His big brown hands caress everything that grows in his soil.

Bill installed a new watering system on his lot next door. In bighearted generosity and thoughtfulness, he voluntarily offered to run a line to my lot, as well. He felt it would help to water the new garden I had dug and spaded with so much sweat and toil. It was a gracious gesture, a mark of a kindly neighbor.

Seldom did Bill ever come past our place without stopping in for a few moments of friendly conversation. Almost always he brought bags or baskets of fruits and vegetables from his own flourishing fields. Tomatoes, corn, peppers, peaches, potatoes and even peas that had been picked on his place were left on the step at our front door. Each gift was a token of this dear fellow's friendly spirit, reaching out to warm our own.

Then there was Richard. He came to our country from the heart of Old London Town. Like so many Englishmen, Dick brought with him a sense of humor, wit, and good cheer that nothing can suppress.

When first I met Dick, he was a bit of a skeptic. But all of that has been changed, as the love of God spread gently into his spirit. Dick has become a buoyant human being, filled and energized with irrepressible fun. He is a plumber, ever ready to repair a faulty water line or install a fixture that would flood out the rest of us.

Out of his own free will, Dick came down to make sure all the old, dilapidated pipes in our place would work at least half-decently. He crawled into the dark and dusty spaces where spiders spun their webs. He turned and twisted his agile frame into awkward corners under sinks and cupboards to couple pipes. Yet, all the time, there flowed from this fellow nothing but good cheer to enliven our days with his delightful wit.

When Cheri was ill, he and Cecile, his joyful wife, would pop in to bring gifts of baking and their own unique brand of get-well good humor. Even the most distraught patient could not help but chuckle with them. And, after all, laughter is the best medicine in all the world. When they left, there remained behind a legacy of love and warm affection.

Just down the road a wee way lived Tom. He was a spry man who, though well into his seventies, still built his own house, cut and split all his own wood, and dug his own garden.

Tom would loan me his truck whenever I needed this sort of transportation. He was glad to store certain precious boxes of films and slides in his cool basement. He was always glad to give any advice I sought that the long years of his own experience had bestowed upon him.

One of my own great and special joys was to attend a service at the little church where Tom worshiped. One morning this courageous, simple layman took the entire service for his fellow parishioners. He spoke happily, boldly, gladly of the great joy and fulfillment that Christ had brought into his life. When we walked out of that little chapel on the hill, I knew that our Father had been there, too, with a smile on His face.

Tom's vivacious wife, Vivian, often drops in with a bowl of strawberries, a bouquet of roses or several of the magnificent Spanish onions that she knows are my special favorite. Tom grows these to perfection on his little plot by the lake. They are sweet and delicious to the palate.

Olga and Carlyle are next-door neighbors: in fact, the only people whose house is adjacent to ours. Olga especially loves the soil, with the reverent intensity of one who realizes that it is upon the earth that all of us depend for our sustenance.

Olga digs and spades and plants and weeds and waters from dawn to dusk. The rattle of her shovel and the sound of her hoe at work on the stony ground of her garden are a constant reminder of her love of the land. She is burned brown as an oak plank with the desert sun. Her strong body and bright eyes are alive with vigor.

Often she slips over to "Still Waters" with cantaloupes, apricots, raspberries or vegetables. She always comes with good cheer. She, too, is full of fun, and we tease each other about the handsome house she and Carlyle are building. Carlyle has spared no pains to make it a fine home, built from concrete, giant bolted beams and great piles of lumber.

Another dear couple who live nearby are Abe and Helen. They have been friends for years, but now they are neighbors. They are sturdy, tough, kindhearted souls, whose industry and diligence have brought them nationwide recognition for their art in taxidermy.

Abe's work is well known from coast to coast on this continent. The birds and animals and hides and horns mounted in their shop grace the homes of outdoorsmen all over North America. But Abe is much more than just a taxidermist; he is also an ardent outdoorsman, and we have shared happy hours in the hills.

His workmanship can be seen everywhere in our little cottage. The exquisite quail lamp on my desk; the handsome elk-horn table in our front room; the mounted meadowlark on the wall; the gorgeous Grant's gazelle hide that Helen trimmed, are all reminders of this couple.

Last fall I asked Abe to make me a small ceiling chandelier from two pair of deer horns. He made a masterpiece of unusual beauty that hangs from our open-beamed ceiling. Like everything he does, it has upon it the mark of a master craftsman.

Abe has shown me where to get shale in the hills for my driveway. He has hauled loads of earth down to our place for building up the rockeries. He has helped me trim the trees that grow so profusely by the lake. He has been a generous, kind and caring friend.

All of these, and others, are people who, in their own individual ways, have injected an element of gaiety, adventure, warmth and enrichment into our lives. We are richer for them. In sincerity and honesty, we give thanks for all of them.

24
Flowers

FLOWERS HAVE ALWAYS been a special joy to me. This began with my earliest boyhood. With enormous enthusiasm and industry, my parents developed a gorgeous, parklike place for their home on what had been a barren, broken, rocky hilltop in the heart of Africa.

Our house literally stood in a gigantic garden of glowing color. Every sort of flower seemed to flourish and thrive under my parents' loving touch. Masses of bougainvillea and golden shower cascaded over the roof and porches of our home. Roses, cannas and iris of a hundred hues glowed in the garden. And in the house itself, almost every room was embellished with beautiful arrangements of cut flowers.

Because of this, no matter where life's travels have taken me ever since, flowers have attracted and drawn me strongly. It mattered not whether they were wild blossoms blowing in the breeze on some wild mountain meadow, or whether they were twelve perfect roses that came from a city florist.

The texture, fragrance, color and gaiety of flowers all hold a unique fascination. In the hills, in our home, or in my wife's beautiful blonde hair, they have always been a source of delight and joy.

Around "Still Waters," most of the terrain is tough, sunburned, desert benchland. Yet here wild flowers thrive and blossom in abundance. There are plants as formidable and hardy as greasewood, rabbit brush and spiny cactus. Each flowers in yellow profusion. Mock orange bushes thrive in the rocky draws and spread their delicious fragrance on the desert air. Entire hillsides are radiant with the gold of balsam root.

Some of the flowering plants are very tiny and fragile. The delicate rock rose, the scarlet bugler and wild phlox grow amid the tough bunch grass, gladdening the eye with their brilliance.

Thistles of various sorts thrive here. Their showy flowers,

abundant in nectar, provide a bouquet for bees and other insects that are drawn by their brilliance. From late February to mid-October, there is a steady succession of plants and shrubs lending their color to our valley world.

When we moved to "Still Waters," there were no flowers planted there to grace the grounds. The former owners had used skill in landscaping the property, but all of their plantings had been trees and ornamental shrubs. In themselves, these were singularly attractive, but I missed the brightness and cheer of color that flowers bring to any garden.

The first bush I planted was a handsome rhododendron. It was set right beside the lake, in the cool, broken shadows of the birch trees. It flourished in its newfound spot and glowed scarlet in early summer with its handsome red blooms.

A kind friend gave me a healthy plant of ragged robin. This was set in a sunny spot that would make it conspicuous for the hummingbirds. Before the season was over, the little winged acrobats would hover over its fragrant blooms, fighting fiercely for its sweet, pungent nectar.

We were also given a fine specimen of desert evening primrose. This showy plant provided endless interest, both to us and friends who came to visit. Every evening, just as the sun sank behind the western hills, two or three of its huge buds would begin to open. These buds were about the size of my smallest finger. Each was wrapped tightly in a sheath formed by the calyx. Almost as if in slow motion on a screen, each would begin to burst open before our eyes. In about three minutes, the full-bloom petals would unfurl as the calyx leaped open. Then, in striking beauty, the great golden flowers would be fully formed, thrust wide open, waiting for the night moths.

Children, especially, were amazed and excited by this evening performance. They would wait eagerly for the event. And if, perchance, they were fortunate enough to see the giant hummingbird moths come to feed on the flowers, their ecstasy knew no bounds. Gasps of delight and muffled shouts of enthusiasm would burst out in suppressed astonishment.

These showy flowers lasted only one night. When the hot

morning sun of the following day touched their petals, they faded and wilted. Only a single night were they available to be pollinated by the gray moths. These, with their acute sensors, would detect the primrose nectar on the night air. From afar, often more than a mile across the lake, they would come winging in, to do their crucial work in sustaining the species.

This intricate interaction of plants and insects was a ceaseless reminder to us of the wondrous interrelationship of the natural world around us. This interplay of diverse living organisms that were interdependent for survival and the perpetuation of the species was not something planned or programmed by the ingenuity of man or human intellect.

It might very well be asked which came first, the golden evening primrose or the great gray moth? Each contributed to the survival of the other. Each had its part in preserving the other. Each assured the other of the remarkable perpetuation of its kind.

Sometimes, in the face of such phenomena, my own spirit is stilled and silent. Here I stand in the presence of a phenomenon too complex and intricate and wondrous in design to be shrugged off with a toss of the shoulder. All of this is a remarkable part of my Father's world, arranged and programmed by Him with meticulous precision and beautiful harmony of design.

Besides the flowers that grew wild in the hills around us, many of which I often gathered and bore home for our own bouquets, there were those flowers brought to us by friends and neighbors.

Some of these dear people had beautiful gardens. From their profusion they plucked armfuls of roses, carnations, iris and lilies that were shared with us.

Audrey and Phyllis and Olga and Vivian and Cecile and Connie all came to our little cottage by the lake with arms full of fragrant flowers. There is something very special about receiving flowers from a friend. There is, bound up in the bouquet, much more than so many buds and blooms.

In those flowers is a sharing of beauty. There is a giving of one's own affection and love and warmth. There is an expression of kindness and caring. It is as if to say, in language no human words can fully express, "I'm fond of you. I care deeply about you. I wish to cheer your days. I want to brighten your home. I really love you."

The fragrance, the beauty, the aura of the flowers speak eloquently of the character and person of the donor. Just knowing and loving such people enriches our souls. And that has been the whole story of our life at "Still Waters."

Book III

Sea Edge

To
Those who love the sea edge and
sense God's presence there

Contents

"Sing unto the Lord a new song, and His praise from the end of the earth, ye that go down to the sea, . . ."

—Isaiah 42:10

1
My Bit of Beach

FROM THE FIRST hour that I strolled, barefooted, along the shimmering sands of this remote bit of beach I fell in love with it. It lay warm, secluded and peaceful at the base of rugged cliffs that had faced the surge of a thousand Pacific storms.

It was not an easy piece of coastline to find. Vague rumors had reached me from time to time that this stirring shoreline was a favorite wintering ground for scores of seabirds. I was told that seals and sea lions came here to rest on the rocks that stood out to sea. Reports came in that it was a choice location to watch the whales in their migration; schools of porpoises at play; pelicans diving for fish; and only once in a while, a solitary person taking a quiet stroll.

It had taken patience and endurance to discover the spot. I followed every road and scrambled down any cliff trail that led toward the ocean edge. Some trails came to empty dead ends. Even more were closed to public access. Then, at last, one sunny afternoon in early May I clambered down a steep, broken bank overgrown with wild beach peas and found my bit of beach.

Gulls, dressed in their immaculate white breeding plumage, wheeled in the wind. Their wild cries, so sharp and piercing, cut through the roar of the surf below them. Across the breakers came the harsh bark of sea lions challenging each other for their favorite ledge on the rough rocks at sea.

Flocks of sanderlings, flying in tight, flashing formations swept up and down the sands, their glinting wings reflecting the warm afternoon sun like shining mirrors of silver.

A profound sense of peace swept over me. It was every bit as real and palpable and strong as the incoming tide running across the golden sand. Here was intense inspiration of spirit, as tangible as the warm thermals rising against the sun-drenched ramparts of rock soaring above the beach. Everywhere there was beauty, splendor—the eternal impact of my Father's wondrous design conveyed to me in grandeur and loveliness.

At such moments—interludes of intense delight and keen spiritual perception—our inner souls long with exquisite yearning to know that somehow they shall endure. And little did I dream on that sun-splashed spring day, seven years ago, that in God's own good time, my permanent home would be perched on a height of land just a few hundred yards from this special spot.

Such is the gracious touch of God's hand upon our little lives. It is His generous pleasure to give us dreams. It is His unique habit to help us see those fond hopes come to exciting reality and heart-pounding fulfillment. This is all part of the exquisite wonder of knowing Him as a dear companion.

That first day of my discovery I little realized that this bit of beach would become one of the most familiar spots in all the world to me. I never anticipated that I would stroll along this sea edge hundreds of times in the years ahead. I could not envision the days without number that I, and only I, in company with Christ, would spend precious hours alone upon this sun-kissed strand.

But He did!

He knew all about the quiet hours in this place.

He saw the lessons I would learn from Him along this wave-washed shore.

He, and He alone, was aware how I would be nourished by each breath of so much space and light—such sharp, cool, clean air from the vastness of the ocean.

Here He would, through the sea and sand and sun and surf, disclose to my heart eternal principles that stirred me to the depths. Here I would understand some of the mystery of His ways with man. Here He would speak to me in terms a common man, like myself, could clearly grasp with acute perception.

From this bit of sea edge He has shown me, dramatically, tremendous truths in the form of ocean parables. These cameos of His own greatness are not mine alone to be hugged only to my heart. They are a legacy for all of us who have come to know and love Him.

Here they are shared in simple, precise word pictures. May they endure long after my footprints have left this lonely, lovely shore, to tread instead upon the eternal strand of a new eternity . . . far beyond my bit of beach . . . in the presence of His Person.

—"Song-o'-the-Surf"
10 December 1983, California

2
Ocean Majesty

THE OCEAN DRAWS me to itself with a powerful, yet gentle magnetism, calling to my soul with strains not always audible to the ear. It moves upon my spirit in magnificent majesty.

Though I have lived in close company with the ocean for many seasons, my awe has never waned—its wonder has never dimmed. Every time I step upon its shore, its broad expanse, sweeping away to the utmost horizons, captures my heart. I am caught up in the grandeur of its might—humbled, stirred and moved by its glory.

I am a man who must have space—wide expanses, long views and sweeping vistas—to thrive. These are as essential to my free spirit as is the wind to my lungs. I cannot be cramped in the narrow confines of man-made corridors fashioned from sterile concrete, cold steel or glinting glass.

Perhaps in part this is the result of my somewhat wild and untamed heritage: the wide expanses of the open sun-splashed African plains, the long vistas of distant hills dappled blue by moving cloud shadows, the great brooding mood of a realm not yet marred by man.

All of these have precise counterparts in the ocean expanse that sweeps away to the south on my bit of beach. Every time I approach the cliff top and hear the muted sounds of the sea at work on the beach below, a thrill of anticipation—eager, keen, and pulsing—surges through me. The trail winds down through a deep draw. Each step down provides an ever widening vista of the ocean spread out beneath the sky.

This path is really like a little pilgrimage.

It always ends at the same place—the sea edge.

Yet every new day is alive and fresh, and I am filled with anticipation.

It is this same vitality that is a large part of the ocean's magnetism, for it is not sterile. It is not cast in concrete. It is not fixed in place or arrested in action.

Everywhere I look there is motion, life, energy. The endless vitality of its environment engulfs me. I am surrounded with the vigor of its energy. The mighty movements of its tides, waves, sea currents and ocean breezes enfold me in their irresistible embrace.

This sea edge is a special world.

At best I can do no more than stand upon its shore and sense that I am but a minute particle of humanity on the edge of an ocean stretching around the globe. Its magnitude is beyond imagination. Its depth, its width, its length are beyond my measurement. Its power and dynamic action linked to moon, sun, stars and all the constellations of outer space are beyond my finite understanding. It is often a realm cast in dramatic light.

So I am stilled before its majesty.

My soul is silent in its presence.

There is assurance in its might.

Few, few indeed, are the mornings when I stroll along this shore that the ocean does not so impress me with its power, its glory and its majesty. I am humbled in its company. I am awed by its magnificence. Yet, wonder of wonders, I am also made glad to be with it.

For you see, strange as it may sound, though I was born and grew up hundreds of miles from the ocean, and was for years a stranger to it, I have come to love it. The ocean has drawn me to itself and won my total allegiance.

I really am an ocean lover.

In profound ways the sea has wooed my soul.

It has made me a part of its own life.

Just as much as the waves breaking on the smooth sand are an integral part of this wondrous world—or the gulls gliding along the cliff face, or the seals thrusting through the currents—so am I, as a solitary man, leaving the footprints of my small steps on the ocean edge.

All is passing. All is in motion. All is change—new every day, fresh in every way. None of it will stay. Only the ocean endures, eternal, unending in its movements.

So it is that these deep reflections and long thoughts move smoothly but surely into the realm of my spirit. In His own gracious and gentle way God has spoken to me more emphatically through parallels in the sea than any sermon in a sanctuary.

For to me, it seems, His majesty, His might, His splendor are as magnificent as any seascape. In quietness as I contemplate His character it equals and surpasses in grandeur anything known to man. The extent of His glory fills the earth.

As I am drawn to Him by the irresistible magnetism of His own greatness, there are pensive moments when in awe and wonder I sense that at best I can only really experience "the edge of His life." There is a dimension, at least in my earth life, in which He will never be known in all His magnificence. With my human fallibility and spiritual limitations I shall never fully comprehend the length or depth or breadth of His infinite, amazing love.

But, what joy, I still can touch the edge of His glory. I still am drawn into the intimacy of His presence. Coming softly to stand before His Majesty, I am moved by the touch of His life upon mine.

The innermost response of my spirit to His magnificent presence is, "O Lord, my Father, my Creator, my Most High God! You are here! All is well!"

Human language is strained to describe the sense of ecstasy, the upwelling of blessing, the surging tide of serenity that floods over my soul in such moments. This is an interaction between God and a common man made doubly precious because I was once a stranger to this One. I knew nothing of the inspiration of His Spirit. I was ignorant of and oblivious to the impact Christ's character could make on mine.

Just as the ocean sculpts and shapes my bit of beach with the rise and ebb of every tide, so there sweeps now across my soul the surging impulses of God's own gracious Spirit. The powerful current of the very life of Christ sweeps through my mind, my emotions, my will to do His own wondrous work.

Still I sense profoundly that I am, like my bit of beach, but a single soul on the bare edge of God's great love. But I am there—open, exposed, vulnerable, susceptible to every incoming surge of His Spirit, able to be altered, waiting to be worked upon, shaped and re-created daily by the impulse of His presence.

The beach does not shape itself!

It is a reflection of the movement of ten thousand ocean tides. It is the product of the ocean's might and power. It is the superb piece of artistic craftsmanship that emerges from the ocean's endless sculpting.

Nor am I a self-made man.

For there has played upon my life the eternal impact of the love of God in Christ which has shaped my character with eternal perseverance.

3
High Tide

NO TWO DAYS are ever exactly the same on my bit of beach. Part of its great appeal lies in the ever-changing appearances of its shoreline.

The subtle play of sunlight and shadow on the cliff faces alters their contours. Some mornings the rugged rocks seem softened by the muted pastel shades of the rising sun. They glow warm, golden, wrapped in sunshine and serenity.

Other days the same rock buttresses stand gray and forbidding in the fog and mist that swirls in off the sea. The shoreline looks almost black, dark with dampness, soaked with sea spray.

Always, always, always the ocean is at work on the land. Summer and winter, spring and autumn the changing tides rise and ebb shaping the character of the coast. Their force is utterly relentless—their power immeasurable—their titanic thrust untamed.

Great mysteries surround the majestic, awesome action of the tides. With incredible precision they move billions of tons of water from surface to surface upon the sea. They are the reflection of gigantic energy within the cosmos that knows no rest, that never slumbers, that never sleeps.

Hour after hour, year in and year out, for eons of time the tides have risen and fallen, then risen and fallen again upon this shore. They are a part of the fundamental creative forces set in motion by divine design to shape and sculpt the shore. Their work is never done. Their impact is ever there. Their polishing goes on toward perfection.

Amid all this constant action at the ocean edge, one of its most compelling interludes is the time of high tide. This is the hour when the beach appears to be its smallest. Trillions of tons of sea water have come surging into the seascape to flood into every cove and tide pool. Where before there had stood stretches of sand, reefs of rock or buttresses of basalt, now there shimmers the silver mantle of the sea.

The sea is everywhere. It flows with smooth swells over the rocks, over the inlets, over the accumulated debris deposited here by a thousand storms. The sea is bright, shining, like quicksilver running into every tiny crevice or rivulet that lies upon the shore.

All the ugliness of flotsam and jetsam cast up here by stormy gales is covered by the incoming sweep of the high tide. Every deformity, every gaunt and grim bit of junk that may have been deposited on this strand by the careless hand of man is hidden from view.

In its place there pulses back and forth the stirring sight of sparkling waves that break against the banks in a flashing spray of green and white water. Everywhere the ocean is moving logs, shifting stones, rearranging the contours of the shore. It will never be quite the same as it was before high fashioned. This is when, beneath the water's impact, eternal endless changes are wrought in wondrous ways.

This thrust and change brought to my bit of beach by extreme high tides has always thrilled me. The apparent enlargement of the ocean and corresponding contraction of the coast have portrayed to me a profound lesson in my life before God.

There just have to be times, when in His own gracious, irresistible concern, He comes flooding over my little life. There are occasions when the "high tide" of His powerful presence needs to inundate my soiled and shabby soul. There are days when more than anything else I must have that sublime sense of His Spirit sweeping into every secret cove and inlet of my life.

The world is so much with me. The careless hand of man, the cruel ways of our society, the thoughtless acts and omitted courtesies of my contemporaries leave a legacy of hurts and sorrow and wreckage in my life—the black rocks of rising anger, the hard jagged reefs of dark resentment, the flotsam and jetsam of ill will that clutter my character.

Only Christ can change all this. Only He can alter the contours of my disposition. Only He can displace the debris of my soul with the surging newness of His own person. There must be an exchange of His life for mine—of His desires for my, otherwise, selfish impulses.

It is He, who in the high tide of His relentless patience and perseverance, presses in upon my person.

I cannot, dare not, keep Him out. It is His eternal, sure incoming, as inexorable as the rising tide, that gives hope for covering all the corruption and defilement of my days.

Those of us who wish to be utterly honest with ourselves and with our Father know full well the need of His covering. We cry from the depths: "Who can cover my iniquities? Who can enfold me in righteousness? Who can fill me with the fullness of God?"

It is He and only He who can do this for us.

There is no one else.

And we must see this.

The beach does not cover itself.

It is covered by the sea.

The shore does not change itself.

It is shaped by the tides.

The sea edge does not diminish its own size.

The ocean does this as it sweeps in upon it.

The alterations and rearrangements of the coast are the eternal work of the eternal tides.

And in my life as one who lies open, exposed and receptive to the action of The Most High, it is He who will cover and conform me to His own pattern of ultimate perfection. He does not relent. He does not rest. He neither slumbers nor sleeps. It is He who is at work upon my soul and within my spirit both to will and to do according to His own grand designs.

The incoming of Christ by His sublime Spirit always changes the contours of our lives. Once we have been filled with all the fullness of His grace and goodness we are never the same again. His presence can inundate every crevice, can fill every corner of our convoluted lives.

Yes, there are days and there are times when only the high tide of God's overflowing goodness can put right all that is wrong within. Most remarkable, those looking on will know and sense the impact of His life on mine. For I am His bit of beach!

At high tide the surging ocean asserts itself with awesome power upon the open shore. Likewise in my life, the impact of God's pervasive Spirit, if allowed to do so, can move in majestic might upon my soul and spirit and body.

As the full weight of the sea currents change and shape the coast, so Christ, in control, recreates me as a man. He alters the contours of my character and conduct.

At full flood the tide turns the entire beach into a glistening expanse of water, brilliant as a sheet of beaten silver. And thus it is my Father enfolds my common life in the generous love and purity of His own perfection.

Little wonder John cried out from the depths of his yearning spirit: *"He must increase, but I must decrease!"* (John 3:30).

4
Breakers

YESTERDAY MORNING I stood at the edge of the cliffs and gazed up and down the coast. It was a spectacular scene of blue and white beauty. Though I have watched the winter breakers crash in thundering foam along this shore a thousand times, they still stir me to the depths.

From high vantage points atop the bluffs one can see up and down the length of the land for several miles in both directions. Here, in great bursting sheets of curling spume and white spray, the blue waters of the Pacific boil and roll against the beach.

The giant waves, spawned a thousand miles away in the uncharted depths of the ocean, have moved with enormous momentum across vast distances to come crashing on this coast. In a magnificent, surging, spilling, breaking action, ten million tons of water thunder on the sand. Approximately every six to sixteen seconds a fresh new breaker bursts into foam that rumbles and surges over the shore.

It is a sight as spectacular as any giant waterfall. For what the surf may lack in height it more than makes up for in extent. Its action is a thundering sea that spreads itself in wild display for miles along the continental ledge. Its untamed music is a song of splendor and glory, a song of the sea in motion, a song of the ocean at work upon the land.

Yet the outer grandeur of the breakers is not their only honor. For within the waves themselves there goes on a magnificent cleansing movement of the beach.

This inner action of the sea upon the shore is seldom understood by those who come here only casually. It is as if the curling foam, with countless flying fingers combs and scours the sand for any debris or silt that pollutes the shore. Caught up in the scrubbing, scouring, washing action of the rolling breakers every trace of the contamination is borne away into the sea itself.

As the waves wash across the sand and crash around the rocks, they run back in ceaseless motion carrying off the silt and mud that may have marred the shore. In wondrous ways the ocean currents carry this burden of sediment in suspension. Lifting it from the land, they finally lay it down in the remote depths of its own immensity. Thus the sea deposits the accumulated filth of the years in far-off ocean canyons.

It is a perpetual process. The poured out power of the breaking waves washes the beaches, yes, my bit of beach, with meticulous care. It is the life, the energy, the dynamic of the sea that spills out upon the shore to cleanse it from all its contamination.

Here a titanic interchange goes on endlessly. The ocean waters—clear, clean, fresh and pure—pour out upon the polluted sands. There they pick up the decaying debris, the bird feces, the fallen feathers, the flotsam and jetsam that would otherwise stain the shore. In their grasp the grime is gone, transported away into the ocean deeps. In place of the pollution there is left behind by the breakers shining sand and polished rocks.

So the breakers restore the beach, cleansing its shoreline and leaving the sea edge bathed in pristine purity.

Reflecting quietly upon this titanic transaction between sea and land, I have been deeply moved by the profound parallels that lie between my soul and God. As I meditate upon the majestic mysteries of His dealing with me I can clearly comprehend some similarities that have helped me understand the magnificence of His person, the magnitude of His intentions toward me.

For just as the ocean is ever at work breaking itself over my bit of beach, so my Father's unfathomable love is ever in action spilling out upon my sin-stained soul. Had He chosen, as well He might, to confine His compassion to Himself, I would never have known the cleansing, caring impact of His life on mine.

Like the breakers crashing every few seconds upon the shore, so His love comes sweeping over my soul from out of the eternal depths of His own infinite being. Over and over His life is broken on my behalf.

Christians, it seems to me, speak too glibly, too lightly, too flippantly of the cleansing blood of Christ. They treat it almost as a talisman that can be called upon in a moment of extremity.

It is more, much more than that! It is instead the eternal, everlasting, endless life and love of God Himself being poured out in unrelenting power upon us poor mortals. His majestic body broken on our behalf, spilled out in ten thousand times ten thousand actions of self-giving, self-sacrifice is for our cleansing—for our salvation.

Not until we, in awe, wonder, and humility, see the grandeur of His generosity that allows His pure life to surge over our pollution will we ever repent. Only then can we begin to grasp even a little of the wondrous work the breakers of His spilled-out love can effect in our experience.

Just as the sea absorbs into itself all the debris from the shore, bearing it away into the fathomless oblivion of its own depths, so Christ bears in His own person all the wrongs and ill will of our contaminated characters. He receives into His infinite forbearance all our wretched attitudes, our contorted decisions, our negative impulses. In their place He pours out His love, His care, His forgiveness upon us—new each day—wave upon wave.

The unique disclosure given to us by His own Spirit goes beyond even this, namely, that all of our sins and all of our iniquities are carried away into the depths of the sea of His forgiveness. Not only to be buried from view but also forgotten forever. Only God our Father could be so gracious. Only He could be so magnanimous. Only He could be so utterly astonishing.

In a word, to use the theological terminology of the New Testament, "He hath made him to be sin for us, who knew no sin; that we might be made the righteousness of God in him" (2 Corinthians 5:21). What an exchange!

There is enormous beauty in this transaction, a beauty that surpasses the breakers flinging themselves upon my bit of beach. There is also an eternal cleansing action in Christ's life laid down, spilled out upon my behalf to cleanse and purify me. That, too, transcends the eternal washing of the shore by the endless waves breaking over it.

The breakers make the beach beautiful both without and within. Likewise the outpouring of the love of God upon my life—the eternal, endless energy of His own person—purifies my character and beautifies my behavior.

The cleansing of the beach is one of the special secrets of the sea.

And the cleansing of my soul is one of the great mysteries of God's love for me—a love so great it stills my soul, it humbles my heart, it subdues my spirit.

5
Beauty on the Beach

AFTER EVERY STORM, after every high tide, after the powerful action of the combers that have cleansed the beach, there remains behind remarkable beauty. Not just the outward splendor of a wave-washed shore sparkling in the sun, but an intimate beauty of delicate design etched upon the sand, carved upon the cliffs.

This character of a coastline is ever changing. It never remains static. It does not become sterile and stale. Each new day makes a difference in its design. Every high tide alters its outline. Endlessly the sea edge is shaped into a myriad of fascinating seascapes.

Some days the shore, glistening like polished gold, has draped along its edge a delicate lacework of silver filigree. A thousand tiny wavelets moving on and across the sand, like a master-weaver's loom, fashion a blue and white embroidery on the beach. Its fabric flashes with the brilliant sequins of ten million bubbles that reflect the light as they burst into splinters in the surf.

The pattern of the spume that spreads itself upon the sand is of infinite, interacting fragments of white foam. It lasts but a few moments, caught briefly in intense beauty upon the eye of the onlooker. Then it is swept clean, carried away into the next incoming wave, to be replaced by another, equally arresting.

Everywhere there is action, motion, life and design. Picture upon picture is created in rapid succession on the shore. No two are identical, no two even appear similar. Each is a unique creation formed by the ebb and flow of the sea upon the sand. The shore is the master artist's canvas, the wavelets His sure, swift, brush strokes.

As the sea recedes on the falling tide it leaves behind a legacy of wondrous beauty. The tiny, hairlike rivulets of ocean water draining from the sand shape whole "forests" of little trees in the porcelainlike surface of the shore. Their design is as exquisite as any pattern hand painted upon the most precious bone china. The "tide trees" are always shown in winter garb, stripped of their leaves, bare, with bold trunks and smooth branches, drawn upon the still wet surface of the sand.

There are gorgeous undulations left upon the sea edge by the ebbing tide. The cutting, swirling, rhythmic movement of the ocean currents shapes the contours of the tide flats and sand dunes into smooth, soft curves that soothe the eye and still the soul. It seems almost an indiscretion to step upon their pristine perfection.

Here and there the dainty web of a crab's tracks or a sea bird's footprints only adds to the intensity of their lingering loveliness. Especially in late evening, or at early dawn, when the long low light accents their smooth forms into bas-relief, their beauty is so sharp, so stabbing, it almost pains.

Even the smoothing of stones, the polishing of rocks, the fashioning of driftwood by the oscillating action of the waves leaves one lost in wonder, awe and quiet gratitude for such gracious gifts from the sea. Everywhere one walks there is left the impress of the tides that work, often unseen, upon this bit of beach.

The high cliffs of sandstone, the rugged headlands of dark rock, the reefs and tide pools sculpted by the rasping thrust of a thousand storms are each a fine and splendid masterpiece. Each has been touched and transformed by the mighty power of the deep.

All of this beauty on the beach, all of these rare and delicate designs, all of the exquisite sea-edge forms are the fashioning of the tides. Every ocean current that swirls along the coast cuts and chisels as surely as any sculptor's tools. Every wave or wavelet washing against the land rasps and shapes with relentless artistry. Every ton of sea water pressing upon the beach compresses the shore into a special seascape.

So it is, too, with the impact of the presence and power of God Himself upon my soul.

It is the eternal persistence of His splendid Spirit that, working upon my mind, emotions and will, gently conforms them to His own wishes.

It is the compassion of Christ's love, the incoming waves of His wondrous grace that flood over me day upon day to submerge my spirit in Himself.

There, often unseen by the world, unrecognized by my contemporaries, unnoticed, even by my most intimate associates, He fashions me to the unique pattern of His special design for me. No two of us are ever exactly the same. Each is a "one-of-a-kind" creation shaped by the Master's hand.

In Christian circles it becomes increasingly common to hear the remark, "He is a beautiful person" or "She is a beautiful soul." It is really a carry-over into the church from a crass culture which exalts so-called "beautiful people"—a synonym for the sophisticated, wealthy, upper set of society.

Amongst God's people the definition of true beauty is not in terms of charm, charisma or the subtle flatteries of fashion, outward appearance or pride. It is, rather, beauty of behavior, loyalty of life, serenity of spirit.

These attributes of character and perfection of personality are seldom the sort to attract public acclaim. They are hardly the hallmark of those men and women adored by the world.

For, even of our Lord it was said, "He hath no form nor comeliness; and when we shall see him, there is no beauty that we should desire him. He is despised and rejected of men; a man of sorrows, and acquainted with grief . . ." (Isaiah 53:2, 3).

The world's estimation of "beauty," and God's evaluation of beauty in His people, are sometimes poles apart. And we must recognize that often the rugged character and sterling soul shaped under the formidable fashioning of the hand of God, beautiful to His eyes, may indeed be despised by our contemporaries.

Sometimes the most beautiful beach is the one which has endured the most severe storms. The most attractive sea edge has been exposed to the fiercest force of flood tides. The most spectacular seascapes are sculpted by the most sweeping wave action.

My very natural human reaction is to try to avoid the storms of life, to hide from the abrasive action of daily events, to retreat from the incoming impact of God's providential presence in my affairs.

But let me not!

As I recognize my Father's kind hands at work upon my life, I shall be quietly content to expose myself to Him. It is in the sure knowledge that He knows full well the best way to make me attractive to His eyes that I shall rest beneath His strong hands. In His presence I shall find peace. No matter what storms, trials or stress are brought to bear upon my soul I shall see them as His tools for shaping my character into a winsome piece of His workmanship.

Because He is here, active, patiently at work on me, *all is well!*

6
Healing Waters

FROM THE DAWN of human history men have been acutely aware of the healing properties of the seashore. Across the long centuries men and women, boys and girls have been sent to the sea for restoration of health, for rejuvenation of body.

To use an ancient British expression, "A few weeks by the sea will put it all right again." And so because of this amazing capacity to cure so many ills, the ocean edge has always been a favorite retreat for those who sought to restore their strength.

This has been true in my own life. At the rather early age of thirty-four I was invalided and sent back from Africa with less than six months to live. It was to the sun-drenched beaches of Vancouver Island I returned. There, as I lay on the sand, swam in the sea, strolled along the cliff edge, little by little strength, healing and vigor returned to me.

Now, well into my sixties, spared some thirty more years to serve my Master, I still refer to the seashore as "my health insurance." Few are the days that I do not spend an hour or two in solitude along the ocean edge.

The shore has an atmosphere of serenity, beauty, strength and invigoration that stimulates the whole of man. It is more, much more, than merely a balm for the body. As we shall see in subsequent chapters, it also has a profound impact upon our moral and spiritual lives. The sea can restore weary minds, strained emotions, flagging wills and aching hearts. But beyond all this, it can be that strong inspiration of God to lift our spirits, cleanse our conscience, and draw us to Himself.

Part of the reason that the sea possesses such potent healing properties is its content of a saline solution. It carries in suspension not only salt, but also a multitude of other trace minerals. Some of these rare substances are seldom found on land, yet they abound in the ocean.

The fact that the sea waters which wash over the coastline in a continuous scouring action are salty tends to sterilize and cleanse the shore. The salt actually counteracts decay of material that accumulates on the beach. It deters decomposition. It purifies and prevents undue putrefaction and pollution.

The result is that the beach is not only beautiful to behold, but it is also a lovely place to be. There is a fragrance, a pungent freshness, that permeates the air and quickens the senses. Part of this comes from the ozone off the sea.

There is a rich and abundant supply of oxygen in the breezes that blow in off the breakers. They are charged with moisture and trace elements that sweep in over the shore in potent stimulation.

The sea water itself is a marvelous healing agency. Cuts, wounds, abrasions, sores and skin blemishes are sterilized, cleansed and enabled to heal with great rapidity. Even injured joints and torn ligaments, if bathed in the sea, then exposed to the warm therapy of the sun, will mend in wondrous ways.

Just walking barefooted on the sand, letting the ocean waves play about one's feet and legs, is beneficial. The splash of sea water on the skin makes it throb and tingle with exquisite delight as the blood comes racing to the surface of the body.

Everywhere, in a hundred ways, the ocean waters heal.

Often, as I stroll along the shore, or sit quietly contemplating the grandeur of the deeps, the Spirit of God reminds me that similarly He is my great Healer. It is He who restores my soul. It is He who renews my spirit. It is He who imparts to my life the health and wholesomeness of His own character.

The unique disclosure given to us mortal men in God's Word is that at best we are corrupt. Our pride, our so-called self-righteousness, our perverseness are a pollution in the presence of the impeccable Person of Christ. There is a formidable force of decay and inner soul degeneracy within man.

Only the counteracting agency of the very life of God Himself can ever purge away our self-centeredness. Only the inner, sterilizing, sharp action of the self-sacrificing cross of Christ can eradicate my human corruption. Only the Spirit of God can enable me to see that my wrongs and wounds and selfish preoccupation can be corrected and healed by the touch of His life on mine. Only His love sweeping into my soul can sterilize it.

This healing, this wholeness, this wholesomeness, this "holiness" are all one and the same in God's estimation. They are simply synonymous in His view. If we are to know and relish His companionship, they are essential. Just as with the sea, there can be no restoration, no cleansing, no rejuvenation, no healing, no help, unless we are submerged beneath the overflowing fullness of His presence. We must lose ourselves in Him. We must allow His very attitudes, His disposition, His willingness for service, to inundate, touch and transform our lives, our hearts, our wills.

In Christian circles, this work of inner healing, this purification of our motives, this counteraction of God's generous love to our selfishness is sometimes called "the work of the cross" in the life of the believer.

It is just as dramatic as the action of the sea in sterilizing the shore to arrest putrefaction. It is the self-giving, self-sharing, self-sacrificing life of Christ that cuts diametrically across my selfish self-interests. It transcends the giant "I" in my soul, to pour itself out in service to God and man.

The cross in the life of God's person is more than a symbol of Calvary on the church steeple. It is more than an ornate crucifix on the church altar. It is more than a sentimental symbol of our Lord's awful agony.

The cross represents the judgment of divine justice upon sin and selfishness. It stands for the wide forgiveness of God's love and mercy extended to us in our pollution, declaring the depths to which Christ descended to restore, redeem and make us whole as His own people. This He achieved by laying down His life for us—pouring Himself out that we might be preserved and not perish in our own defilement.

This same purifying, redeeming, mighty work must proceed within my own life. Daily, in a discipline of total obedience to His will and wishes, my old, selfish life must be crossed out in conformity to His character. His Spirit must so submerge mine in and counteracting power and purity that my soul shall be set free from selfishness exactly as the beach is cleared of its corruption.

This healing action brings an inner holiness—a knowledge of the wholeness within of a wholesome spirit and a righteous soul at peace with God and with good will to men.

This release from my selfishness can come only from the constant impact of His life on mine. It is the result of the subjugation of my soul by His Spirit. It is the counteraction of my inner corruption by the purity of His presence, the cleansing of my character by His cross.

It is the outgrowth of the deliberate surrender of my will to His wishes with glad abandon. It is that which happens when I allow the fullness of His wondrous life to sweep over me as the sea sweeps over the shore.

The daily impact of His life on mine brings vigor and vitality. It insures health and holiness to all of life. It assures well-being.

7
Life from the Sea

LAST EVENING, JUST before sunset, I went alone, at low tide, to stroll along the sea edge. It was very nearly a zero tide, for it was the winter solstice. As I walked along the broad expanse of the beach, laid bare by the ebbing waters, I was again impressed with the abundance of sea life.

Everywhere I turned and looked there was life, life, life—not just the movement of the sea itself in the steady ripple of small wavelets breaking over sand bars, hidden reefs and exposed tide pools. But there was the equally vibrant, exciting abundance of marine mammals, sea birds scavenging the shore line, fish flashing in the current, and mollusks clinging to the rocks.

Two small neighbor boys, bare legged with tousled hair, were casting at the water's edge. As I paused to chat a moment one drew a beautiful sea bass from the foaming waves. It would provide a delectable dinner for him and his widowed mother. Even his dog was excited by the catch. In sheer animal joy he raced in circles on the sand as his young master gazed in youthful exuberance at the firm strong fish in his possession.

I strolled on, drawn by the startling black rock silhouettes that stood so stark against the silver sea. The setting sun, a burning crimson orb, began to glaze the world in a golden glow. It was as if amid the changing hues of sea and sky and shore, life, subtle and yet eternal, throbbed all around me.

A group of seals and sea lions, their smooth coats shining in the setting sun, moved about on the exposed rocks. Some swam smoothly in the current. A few fought for space on the rugged outcroppings of rock where they could stretch themselves with ease.

A flight of cormorants flew in from the far reaches of the channel. A score settled on the sharp pinnacle of a reef. Their jet black plumage and stiff erect stance made them appear as so many sedate clerics standing in stern consultation. Another flight came in to alight on the cliffs where they stretched their wings to catch the last warm rays of the winter sun.

Just off-shore pelicans and white-winged terns soared and dived beyond the breakers. They were taking small fish that surged to the surface of the sea in shining schools.

On the beach and in the tide pools there were innumerable tracks of crabs and sea worms, their coming and going marked by a fine-drawn series of minute indentations in the sand.

Every tide that rises here brings life in abundance. Microscopic plankton, one of the planet's greatest protein sources, abound in these rich waters. Seaweeds and ocean plant life of a hundred kinds flourish along this coast. They are all an intimate part of the wondrous web of life that thrives in the biota along my bit of beach.

Each is a gift from the sea. Each is a daily bestowal from the ocean deeps. Each is provided in innumerable abundance for all who will accept it.

As the afterglow dimmed gently along the shore I turned my steps toward home. I inhaled deeply of the pungent ozone on the evening breeze. With one long, last lingering view I watched the well-fed gulls preen themselves upon the sand. All was well and we were at peace.

In that brief evening interlude life—new life, fresh life—had come to me as well from the bounty of the sea. A new surge of well-being coursed through my bloodstream. A rich stimulus of inspiration swept into my soul. A profound sense of the presence of The Most High engulfed my spirit in quietude and serenity.

These are the abundant gifts of God our Father to us His earth children.

They come to us constantly . . . as continuously as the change of every tide, the shifting of every sea current. But they become ours only if we are there to absorb them into our little lives.

The bounties, mercies and benefits of the Lord are new every day. They are swept along the shores of our daily experience to replenish and renew our strength as God's people. The point is I must be there to partake of the life presented for my perpetuation.

The process is a dynamic, daily interaction of any living organism with its environment. Life proceeds and is preserved only so long as there is continuous correspondence between the individual body and the biota surrounding it. The day the creature ceases to draw and derive its life from its surroundings, it dies.

So it is whether it be a scallop, a fish, a sea bird or a seal. Each has life only by virtue of the fact it is feeding on the abundance supplied by the ocean around it.

Precisely the same principle applies to me—and others who claim to possess the life of God. He surrounds me on every side with the overwhelming abundance of His life. It is He who is the very environment in which I move and live and have my being. If I am to know His life, if I am to experience the energy of His presence, if I am to drink of the dynamic of His Spirit then it is imperative that daily I must draw upon His divine provisions.

Eternal life—everlasting life, endless life—is not some single, sterile, gift-wrapped package dropped down into my soul at a single point in time. This is a false and dreadful concept held by uncounted hosts of ill-informed Christians. Little wonder their experience of Christ is so sterile, so fossilized, so dead.

Life is a dynamic, daily interaction between an organism and its environment. As the organism enters directly into its life-giving surroundings, the energy of the biota, in turn, enters into it. Only then is there perpetuation of life.

This explains why our Lord, Jesus Christ, continually emphasized that for man to have life from above it was imperative to "eat of Him" and "drink of Him," daily! To "eat of Christ" is to come to Him every day in a deliberate act of faith, exercising our wills to expose and open our lives fully to the impulses of His Word and His Spirit. It is the entrance of His Word that gives us His life. For the words which He speaks to us, they become spirit and they become life to us as they are ingested and accepted.

"To drink of Christ" is to believe in Him implicitly. It is to assimilate His truth, His life, His spirit, His person by a deliberate function of quiet faith. We then proceed to comply with His commands, carry out His wishes, and cooperate with His intentions for us.

The net result is to find His very life surging in us and through us. We are in Christ. He is in us. We are energized by His Word, enlivened by His Spirit, and so made abundantly productive through our Father's bountiful grace.

The sea surrounds and engulfs every living form of life that is to be found along its coastline. The ocean brings life, energy, stimulation and vitality to every crustacean, every marine organism, every fish, every sea bird, every marine mammal. But each in turn, to survive and thrive in this watery world, must derive its life from the sea.

It is not enough to be surrounded by the great ocean waters. There is more to life in the sea than merely being swept to and fro in its changing tides. Each life form must be open, receptive, fully exposed to accept and absorb life and energy from the currents of the cosmos. Otherwise it becomes a shell or skeleton cast up on the shore.

So it is with the child of God.

Daily, hourly, momentarily Christ comes to us surrounding us with His Spirit. He brings to us in immeasurable abundance the resources needed for our eternal living. Yet there remains my responsibility to open myself to Him; to allow His Word ready entry to my mind, emotions and will; to permit His Spirit to invade my spirit, penetrating and vitalizing my intuition, conscience and communion with Him.

Only in this way—in stillness and quietude, in obedience and faith, in loving allegiance—can I ever know what it is to have His life, and have it more abundantly . . . now and forever.

Let my soul beware that, like some empty shell or sun-bleached skeleton, it be not cast away upon the sands of time—dead to Him, who comes to give me life.

Always, ever, I must be open, available totally to His incoming. Thus I thrive and flourish with His life.

8
Building Breakwaters

ROUGHLY TWELVE MILES away from my bit of beach, along the sun-washed coast, there lies a beautiful coastal town. It is nestled between the rugged ranges of the nearby mountains and the warm sand beaches of the Pacific.

Years ago it was decided a massive breakwater should be built out into the ocean. It was agreed by engineers and architects that such a structure could shelter small craft from the storms, providing safe haven for fishing boats and pleasure vessels.

What the planners appeared to overlook were the strong coastal currents of the sea that move relentlessly along this coast. These carry enormous loads of sand and silt in suspension as they course up and down the shore, season after season.

The result has been that despite enormous sums of money expended to build this impressive structure, the sea inexorably builds up a huge sand bar at the harbor mouth. So enormous are the loads of ocean-borne sand that by the end of the winter season the entrance to this haven is virtually sealed off. The result is that ships sheltering there are literally trapped, unable to set out to sea.

But building the breakwater has produced even more formidable problems. Cut off from the cleansing, sweeping action of the tides, the harbor becomes choked with silt, slime and dreadful sludge that settles upon the floor of this haven. On the surface it appears to be a serene and placid spot with the boats reflected in the mirror of the still waters.

Beneath that tranquil scene is a veritable cesspool of pollution and corruption.

Consequently every spring, at enormous cost and labor, huge, sea-going dredges are brought in to try to clear the harbor. The massive, noisy equipment is connected to huge lengths of rusting steel pipes that carry the black sludge down the coast and out to sea.

Week after week the giant diesel-driven pumps roar and thunder trying to draw the accumulated muck, mud, sand and sludge from the harbor. It spews out from the sewage pipes in a gushing stream of ink-black filth that contaminates the beaches and stains the lovely sea.

A dreadful stench of death and decay pervades the air. The ocean is so contaminated that for weeks no one can swim in its lovely waters. And even the beach itself is scarcely fit to set foot upon until with time it has again been cleansed and washed with the incoming tides.

But beyond all of this, the building of the breakwater has so altered the natural action and flow of the ocean currents that it affects other communities further along the coast. They are deprived of the sand which otherwise would wash up to rebuild their beautiful beaches. So, in places, after a severe "blow," the shoreline stands bare and gaunt, stripped down to boulders and rocks.

Not only does this endanger the property and homes of those who live along the shore, but it also puts them to great expense to try to save the beach. Massive truckloads of boulders, rock and stone are hauled in to try to shore up the banks. All sorts of elaborate sea walls are erected to try to provide protection from the ocean.

Yet the sea will not be held back. Year after year it presses in upon the coast, its coming as persistent as the tides.

Several years ago I used to live a short distance from the harbor. It was about a mile away, as the pelicans fly in a direct line along the water's edge. The annual ritual of dredging the harbor was regarded with disgust and revulsion by local residents. The pollution was appalling—the stench overpowering. The desecration of the beaches was disgusting.

Yet no lasting remedy has ever been found for the evils of the breakwater. No permanent solution has been devised for overcoming the defilement of the harbor. Nor is there any—for, in simple fact, man has shut out the sea! He has closed off the cleansing action of the ocean currents. He has excluded the healing, life-giving touch of the changing tides.

Often the powerful parallel so apparent in the hopeless quandary of the harbor has come home to my own spirit with tremendous force. For we human beings build our "breakwaters" against God. We erect our barriers to keep out the strong currents of Christ's life that come flowing toward us. We devise elaborate schemes and structures to hold back the impact of His Holy Spirit upon our souls.

The tragic, terrible truth is that most men and women do not want their lives left open, exposed, vulnerable to the impact of God's life upon them. They much prefer to build their snug little harbors of selfish self-interest where, they imagine, they are safe and secure in the storms of life.

The double tragedy is that what on the surface may appear to be so serene, below the surface is dark with defilement. What at first glance looks so desirable and successful, on closer examination proves to be rotten and corrupt with unspeakable pollution and insoluble problems.

During the years in which I served as a lay pastor it startled me to see how many people, even within the church, went to such great lengths to keep God out of their lives. They had built formidable breakwaters around themselves lest He come flooding into their experience.

In ignorance they had erected barriers of unbelief against Him. In fear they had fashioned bulwarks of anxiety and apprehension against Christ. In hostility and defiance they built barricades of belligerence against His Spirit.

Often these breakwaters against the incoming tides of God's grace, mercy and compassion were erected against the church, against other Christians, against God's Good News, or against the convicting action of God's Spirit. The general attitude was: "Keep out of my life."

Somehow, strange to say, many people do not seem to mind encircling a bit of the sea of God's grace in such a way that it provides them with a so-called "safe haven." They rather enjoy having a snug little sense of security within the shelter of some formal, rigid religiosity. Even the idea of the encircling wall of creed is enough to cut off the full impact of the incoming life of Christ. The social functions of church fellowship are a sufficient barrier to preclude the powerful presence of God's Spirit flooding the soul with character-changing force.

So on the surface such lives often appear respectable, proper and secure. Yet within, there lies the awful silt of sin, the sediment of selfishness, the sludge of a corrupt character.

There are as many ways to build breakwaters against God as human ingenuity can devise. There are scores of excuses that can be brought up to keep out Christ, to resist His Spirit.

The ultimate decision is mine as to what will be done with my bit of beach.

My life can be a bright, open expanse of beauty, joy and vigor for the honor of God. Or it can degenerate into a self-centered, constricted little character that is dead and corrupt with its own selfish preoccupation.

The former will be a joy to Christ and a blessing to every life that touches it. The latter will be a grief to God's gracious Spirit, a bane to those who seek shelter behind such artificial barriers.

9
Sea Walls and Sand Castles

THOUGH MY BIT of beach is still rather remote and somewhat sheltered from the pressure of people, here and there I encounter the remnants of human activity. Like almost all beaches around the world, it bears its burden of industrial and commercial debris. These are much less conspicuous here than on many coasts. Some visitors have even remarked that it remains one of the loveliest shores they have ever seen.

Yet, at the foot of the sea cliffs, where the path to the beach descends to the sands, there are shattered, broken fragments of sea walls and concrete buttresses. These were elaborate engineering attempts, made in former times, to try to restrict the relentless action of the tides and storms that crashed against the bluffs.

Lying prostrate, pathetic, half buried in the sand are seaworn walls of brick and concrete blocks. Toppled and torn from their original sites, they lie all askew, washed over by the waves, looking like so many fallen gods. In actual fact, they are just that, for it was in the hapless protection of these pathetic structures that previous home owners had placed implicit trust.

But the battering of a thousand storms, the pounding of ten thousand tides, the eternal erosion of the ocean currents have all combined to reduce them to rubble. Now the cement, reinforcing steel, bricks, wire, tangled pipes and broken mortar stand in wild disarray as silent reminders of how absurd it is to try to keep the sea at bay. Even the most ingenious sea walls eventually crash down to collapse in broken wreckage.

All is for nought. All is but passing. All is change!

The very first home we were shown for sale on this coast was threatened by the collapsing cliffs on which it was built. We loved the location but dared not risk living there. Two years ago the owner spent some $50,000.00 trying to barricade the bluffs with an enormous wall of gigantic concrete bags. Still the tides surge over and around the wall. The cliffs collapse beneath the pounding shock of the surf.

Today the lovely house stands in awful peril, only a few feet from the edge of the precipice. In time, it is bound to collapse and crash to the beach below.

What happens in such horrendous terms to oceanfront homes also occurs with regular frequency to the charming sand castles built by children on summer holidays—not that many youngsters come to this beach. But the few who do, love to erect their ornate castles behind their high sea walls and deeply dug moats.

As I stroll along the sands I occasionally come across these crumbling works of happy childhood dreams. The surge of the waves, the tumbling of the surf, and in a few swift strokes all the labor is swept away into oblivion. At best there are left behind only a few seashells used to adorn the castle or a collection of smooth stones put in place to protect the walls.

Pausing to watch the action of the waves, washing either over the wreckage of sea walls or the crumbling ruins of a small sand castle, a profound sense of pathos sweeps over me. I cannot seem to ignore them. It is impossible for me to pass them lightly.

They speak to me in terms so clear and emphatic, my attention is always arrested. For here, before my gaze, in sharp, stabbing severity stand parables of spiritual truth.

You simply cannot stop the sea. It is relentless. It is irresistible!

For me, as a man now moving gently through the lovely twilight years of life, the remnants of sea walls and sand castles always bring up poignant memories. The gracious Spirit of Christ always uses them to remind me of my own perilous past. At the same time, however, He also quietly reminds me how in spite of my own dream castles, my own strong will, so stubborn in resisting Him, He has preserved my life to this point in time.

All of us build our sand castles on the sands of time. All of us dream our little dreams of what we shall do with our lives. We dig our deep moats around those very private ambitions. We carefully erect our walls of self-protection to surround our elaborate aspirations. We shape and mold our decisions and personal choices into castles of self-interest and self-gratification.

Most of us do this happily, blithely in our youth. We behave as though there were only time, lots of time, and us. There seem to be so many years ahead, so many seasons to carry out our schemes, so many days to do our thing. We forget so soon that God is even there; and though He is, He seems as remote as the moon that turns the beach to silver at night.

Yes, not only do we plan and build and scheme and work to erect our sand castles, we also forget that the tides of time and the power of God's presence are as inexorable as the ocean tides rising in response to the gravitational pull of the moon.

For in the full flood of high tide—under the rising surge of the incoming surf, beneath the sweeping course of the ocean currents the castle—the walls, the moats, the work of our dreams—will disappear . . . lost in oblivion.

Such is the end of those aims and ambitions built in thoughtless, careless abandon without reckoning on the power of God. Beautiful but for a day, they are swept away into nothing.

And so there comes to my spirit again and again the ancient eternal question. "Where and on what are you building your hopes?"

Is it on sand, or is it on the rock of God Himself?

What happens to sand castles takes longer with stout sea walls. Yet the same basic principles are at work.

For years and years I was building a strong sea wall of self-defense against God. It was not shaped from concrete and reinforcing steel. Instead it was fashioned from the formidable, tough, unyielding rigidity of my own self-will. It was so stubborn and determined it withstood the stresses and strains of countless storms.

I was very sure my strong will was as secure as any sea wall. It would keep the incoming tides of my Father's pervasive presence from invading my privacy. It would restrain the waves of His love and concern from washing into my life. It would exclude the impact of His Spirit upon the inner sanctum of my spirit.

For some of us it takes years for the eternal tides of Christ's coming, and coming, and coming again, to finally break down the last tough barrier of our resistance. It takes the eternal perseverance of our Father to demolish the hardness of our hearts. It takes the sweeping waves of His Spirit to finally surge over the strong bulwarks of our souls.

Then and only then, lying broken before Him—contrite in spirit, shattered in soul, repentant in genuine remorse—do we see clearly how we built our lives oblivious to His power, patience and perseverance.

Often, all there remains of our best laid schemes is wreckage.

All of it is a grim reminder: "Let your life, your character, your career be built always in the intense awareness, *'O God, You are here, I cannot keep You out.'*"

Ultimately, always, He will have the last word!

10
Updrafts

ALMOST EVERY MORNING that I stroll down to the shoreline I am impressed by the warm updrafts of ocean air rising against the cliffs. It is a phenomenon peculiar to this stretch of coast.

Because these beaches, unlike most of the west coast, face south they are warmed by the sun all day. Even in winter the layer of marine air lying just over my bit of beach is trapped against the high bluffs soaring above the sands and rocks at their base.

The result is to produce an unusual hothouse effect. Here temperatures are several degrees higher than anywhere else. The proximity of the open Pacific with its moderate temperatures, combined with the reflected heat from the sun-kissed cliff faces, warms the air to produce an environment of pleasant softness.

Here the sea breezes move gently above the surface of the ocean. They caress the coast as they eddy over the sun-warmed sands. Then in steady, even updrafts they rise against the bluffs with the constant pressure of their thermal currents.

So constant are these updrafts that daring young men and women who enjoy hang-gliding can ride the updrafts for hours and hours at a time. They soar above the ocean breakers as if suspended in space.

More impressive even than the human fliers are the birds that ride the thermals. Sea gulls, pelicans, hawks and lesser shore birds soar on the ocean updrafts with remarkable beauty and grace of flight. Their movements on wing are as graceful in motion as any ballerina floating across the stage of a theater.

The soaring of the sea birds has always impressed me. Not only is the essential beauty of their bodies and wings stretched out against the blue sky impressive, but so also is the remarkable ease with which they sail upward in silence and grace.

There is, beyond their beauty, a sense of pure power that presses upon them, bearing them higher and higher. There is an incredible exhilaration in their mounting up against the backdrop of clouds and open sky. There is a glad, free, uninhibited joy in their flight patterns.

They are a glorious expression of airborne artistry. The intricate circles and lines they cut against the sky are every bit as arresting as the most detailed and perfect figures carved by a classical figure skater on a sheet of ice. In every action there is precision, energy and superb performance.

Yet, the invisible, incredible secret to it all is the rising thermals lifting, suspending, moving them in the air.

One thing I have always noticed is that none of the birds ever attempt to soar when there is a downpour of rain, cold downdrafts of air in inversion, or gusty gales battering the bluffs.

At such times, with complete acquiescence to the change in climate, they simply settle quietly on the beach. There standing sedately on the sands or perched safely on some cliff-top tree, the birds gently preen themselves. They fluff their feathers into perfect position. Then they rest their wing muscles. Some even sleep briefly in utter contentment.

They are not exercised or excited because they cannot soar against the stormy skies. Knowing the sun will shine again, they simply rest quietly. They wait patiently for the rising updrafts that will bear them aloft once more.

Across the long years of my life, God's Spirit has taught me some unforgettable truths from watching birds in flight. During quiet walks along the sea edge Christ has brought home to my innermost spirit powerful parallels learned from the ocean updrafts. My Father has used the splendor of soaring birds to show me something of His own wondrous faithfulness.

For the birds along the beach, and for me as a man, life has all sorts of weather. Just because I am a child of God does not exempt me from the downdrafts of disaster, the cross currents of calamity, or the dark, rainy, dreary days of distress. These are as much a part of the warp and woof of life's tapestry as are the sun-filled days, brisk with warm sea breezes.

The climate may be fair or foul. The winds of change may be offshore or onshore. The days may be bright or bleak.

But the ocean is always there. Its presence and its power are ever at work, seen or unseen. And ultimately its influence is beneficial and beautiful.

The birds know this. But most of us human beings forget the faithfulness of our Father. Quietly, calmly, the birds adjust their behavior to the changing pattern of their surroundings. We humans, however, fight and buck the setbacks of our surroundings. We fret and worry over the fortunes and misfortunes of our little lives. We insist on trying to soar and sail away into the heights when we should just sit still and wait upon the wind of God's Spirit to lift and guide us.

Most of us modern Christians know precious little about waiting patiently for the Lord. We prefer to use our own high-powered technology to be on an "eternal high."

Our preachers, teachers and effervescent evangelists would lead us to believe that we can always live high in the sky, soaring against the sun. Not so. This is not God's design. Nor does He arrange our affairs that way.

We are bound to have our days of rain, our times of tears, our hours of disappointment. There are bound to be blustery storms of testing, counter air-currents of frustration and nights of darkness.

But through them all, in them all, our Father is always there. He does not desert us. He does not abandon us. He is at work in the environment of our lives, persistent in pressing in upon us in ways we do not always see, much less understand.

In these difficult, grievous, heavy times He expects that we shall simply settle down quietly upon the shore of His great grace and wait patiently for Him. He does not call us to beat our way with flashing wings and spent bodies against the storms of life. He does not ask us to fight the adverse winds in fury.

He simply tells us that those who wait upon the Lord, who wait for the weather to change, who wait for Him to alter the environment, will mount up with wings refreshed. They shall fly and not grow weary, borne aloft on the fresh updrafts of His faithfulness.

For, our Father is true to His children. Just as the sun will shine again after the storms have swept my beach, so the rising power of Christ's presence will again warm the shore of my soul. The uplifting wind of His Spirit will once more bear up my spirit. Again I shall soar in strength and beauty.

There are days to rest quietly, waiting gently on the sand. There are days to rise up and ride the surging updrafts of His presence that carry me aloft into the clouds of His joyous delight and exhilaration.

11
Solitude by the Sea

WE LIVE IN a noisy, crowded, busy world. At least most people do. Jammed and crushed into the "pressure-cooker" crucibles of our contemporary cities and towns, millions of human beings know little about solitude and stillness.

The thunder of traffic twenty-four hours a day, the rumble and roar of aircraft overhead, the cacophony of loud music, blatant advertising and high-powered programs in the media invade the sanctuary of our homes.

Relentlessly the presence and pressures of other people make their impact upon us. Our bodies grow weary from the constant assault of noise, commotion and tension. Heart attacks, insomnia, ulcers and irritability are part of the price paid for such physical abuse.

Often men and women suffer enormous anxieties and stress in mind and emotions because of the constant tensions of our twentieth-century society. Without realizing it their nervous systems and mental stability are strained to the breaking point. Some eventually do succumb. Mental institutions, psychiatric hospitals and offices that claim to cure the condition are crowded with pathetic patients.

In the realm of man's spirit the devastation wrought by our much vaunted modern way of life is beyond measure. People are so driven and mesmerized by materialism they become slaves to insatiable desires. A thousand false voices call to them to find fulfillment in the transient, tempting pursuits of time. They are assailed by perverted propaganda which would have them believe leisure, pleasure and treasure of an affluent society will satisfy their spirits. But they do not!

Man was made for a greater good than all of these. He was made for God. And he will never find rest of soul, serenity of spirit, until he finds that repose in stillness and quietness in company with Christ.

It is for this reason, more than any other mentioned in this book, that my hours on my bit of beach are so treasured. There in the solitude afforded to me at the sea edge I constantly discover a dimension of divine serenity that is a balm to my spirit, a deep therapy to my soul.

Because of the terrain along the coast, the hills and mountains run down to the ocean. There the tides have carved out high cliffs. At the base of these bold, light-colored bluffs lie the beaches. Strolling along the shore one is shut away from all the noise and clamor of civilization and commerce on the benches of land above the beach.

Only occasionally is there even a house in view. Here and there perhaps the rooftop of a cottage perched at the cliff edge can be seen. There are no roads, no cars, no noisy vehicles—simply the ocean, the sound of the surf, the cries of the sea birds and occasionally, on blustery days, the wind gusting across the cliffs.

Here there is remarkable solitude. There is a sense of stillness greater and more majestic than mere silence. It is the hush and quietness of a small fragment of the planet still in its pristine state. It is the solace of a bit of beach not yet polluted or ravaged by the grasping hand of man.

Strolling on this ocean strand I sense that I am alone, yet not alone, one solitary man moving quietly, gently in awe before The Most High. It is not that I have earned or deserve the privilege of such precious privacy. But rather it is the fundamental fact that I discipline myself to take the time to seek the stillness of this shore. It is there for others to share. Yet few will ever deliberately seek solitude.

Many are afraid to be alone with their thoughts. They are intimidated by the idea of spending several hours in stillness, allowing God's Spirit time to speak to them.

I have been ridiculed, both privately and in public, by those detractors who insist that the measurement of a man's usefulness is how busy he is. It is the unwritten rule of our contemporary society, both within the church and outside it, that our effectiveness is directly proportional to how much we are on the go—for God, or man.

The truth is, our Father calls us, at times, to come apart and be still before Him. Christ calls us to commune with Him in meditation and quiet contemplation of His character. The Holy Spirit calls us to serenity and rest so that we may be sensitive to His wishes.

Of course it can be argued that different people can find their privacy and seclusion in different places. There are all kinds of so-called "prayer closets." It is inevitable that there must be. The important point is, that each of us who claim to be God's children need quietude alone with Him.

For me, the ultimate in solitude is often found on the wave-washed shore, several hundred yards from my front door. There I go with a towel in hand to spread on the sand or rocks; a small well-worn Bible; or a good book; and a spirit of eager anticipation ready to listen, eager to respond to the impulses of Christ's Spirit.

Nor does He disappoint me.

For it is there we meet in quiet communion, one with another.

Being alone on the beach has some remarkable advantages not apparent to the stranger. There are no interruptions in these precious interludes—no telephones, no doorbells, no mail delivery, no one calling for attention, no neighbors' dogs, or police sirens, or roaring motorcycles, or raucous radio noises.

Peace pervades the shore.

The song of the surf fills the air.

A sublime, intense sense of God's presence is everywhere.

In this arresting atmosphere I feel wonderfully free—open before my Father, relaxed in communion with Christ, uplifted by His wondrous Spirit.

As He speaks to my spirit, there is often an audible response on my part. In such a setting I can give thanks aloud. If so impelled I can hum a hymn or sing a song of joyous praise and exultation in the greatness of my God.

The gulls don't mind my melodies. Sometimes a seal will raise his head above the surf to see whence the sounds come. Occasionally the ground squirrels scrambling along the cliff face will stop to whistle in the wind at my singing.

But we are all sharing this sea edge as friends together. Great and small our Father formed us all. This is a fragment of the firmament that we revel in and rejoice over with endless gratitude.

Not all the hours at the sea edge pass in glad praise.

There are times of tears. There are sessions of intense intercession when a solitary soul pleads with His God for a world gone awry. There are acute moments of pain when deep remorse and genuine repentance are wrung out from a broken heart and contrite spirit that has grieved Christ's Spirit.

Yet for me, such encounters are more profound, more purifying, more redemptive than any service in a sanctuary.

The whole earth and sea and sky are pervaded with the presence of The Most High. Everywhere I turn there is impressed upon my still spirit the power of His majesty. Awed, amazed, stirred to the utmost depths, I stand silent, alone, serene.

A man has met his God.

A soul has been refreshed.

All is well, for God is here. Emmanuel!

12
Sea Wind

THE SEA WIND has a special tang to it unlike any other wind found anywhere else in the world. There is a unique, stimulating pungency to ocean breezes that stirs the senses profoundly.

There are few people indeed who do not respond with an element of excitement to the invigoration of the fresh air that moves strongly at the sea edge. It stirs the blood, refreshes the lungs, and sharpens the senses.

The sea winds along our Pacific coast, except for an occasional winter storm, come with beautiful regularity. As the southern sun warms the adjoining land during the day, ocean breezes begin to build up, blowing in over the shore from the open sea. This constant, steady flow of marine air tempers the heat of the land. It bestows a balmy, equitable climate in which plant life flourishes and human beings take great delight.

The breezes bend the fronds of the palms, rustling the slender segments of their graceful leaves like so many muted Spanish castanets. The lap of the waves, the song of the surf, the cries of the sea birds are caught up and carried ashore on the wings of the sea wind.

More than all of this, however, is the soothing, cool, therapeutic touch of the wind on one's face and arms, back, legs and entire body when bared to it. It is as if the moving air enfolds me in its embrace and holds me gently in its arms.

The ocean air caresses the cheek, massages muscles, and leaves the surface of the skin tingling with a special sensation of exhilaration and general well-being.

Because my bit of beach lies open, fully exposed to the great expanses of the South Pacific, the prevailing winds that blow across it come from afar. Some of them were spawned far out to sea. They come ashore with utter freshness, total cleanliness. They have never been contaminated with industrial pollution.

The air moving around me in my morning walks is sharp, clear and wondrously wholesome. It is charged with ozone from the ocean, brisk and clean with the pungency of the sea itself.

To inhale deeply is to sense the surge of pure drafts of air entering my lungs. The high level of oxygen in the sea wind provides a powerful impulse to my whole body. My lungs pick up the oxygen rapidly to transmit it to my bloodstream. It courses through my whole circulatory system, cleansing the liver, quickening the body metabolism, stimulating the brain.

To breathe deeply of the ocean breezes is to be tremendously invigorated. It is to be fully alive, to sense the strength and vitality of the ocean itself entering my whole being.

There is something very arresting about these air movements which is reassuring. They come fresh every day. They are inexhaustible. Though not visible, they are enormously apparent. They exert a constant impact on anyone or anything exposed to them . . . they do not diminish!

Most important, not only does the sea wind surround me on every side, it actually fills my whole being within as I open myself to receive its rejuvenation. It runs its finger through my hair; it kisses my cheek with its touch; it caresses me in tenderness; it stirs me with energy and vitality as it surges into my body.

It makes me strong and fit, alive and energetic.

Little wonder that I love to walk in the wind.

Little marvel that I relish its touch on my senses.

Little surprise that I open myself to breathe it deeply.

All of which is a vigorous response to the wind's gentle, yet persistent impress on my life. I come to love it. I relish its vitality. I revel in its invisible presence.

It is exactly the same with the wind of the gracious Spirit of God. He is everywhere present around me, though unseen to my physical eyes. His power and energy pervade the earth. His benefits enfold me on every side. His mercy and compassion come to me fresh and new every day. And if allowed to, He will enter my life, there to do His own dramatic work as surely as the sea breezes that blow along my beach.

The Word of the Lord is very specific, very precise, very clear about our life in His Spirit. He urges us again and again to walk in the Spirit. He emphasizes the need for us to be in the Spirit. He points out that we must open ourselves to His incoming. He must have entrance into our daily experience. He is the inspiration for our spirits, the stimulation for our souls, the quickening for our bodies. We are to be invaded and filled with His presence.

There is nothing magical or mystical about this. The sad tragedy is that too many Christians have made it such. They have cast a cloud of confusion over the otherwise lovely and beautiful work of God's Spirit in the midst of His people.

He comes to us constantly from out of the very depths of the greatness of God. He is ever present with us, surrounding us on every side with the wonder of His own Person. Though invisible as the sea winds He exerts His own enormous power upon the earth. He is constantly available to us. But to enjoy the dynamic of His vitality it is essential to open ourselves fully to His influence.

This takes time. It takes time to be made wholesome. It takes time to expose ourselves to the incoming of God's Spirit. It takes time to become holy as He is, the Holy Spirit of the Most High. It takes time to be still before Him and to be sensitive to His impulses and wishes.

Just as the wind off the sea is here, moving, flowing, blowing about the beach, so the wind of God's Spirit is very much at work in the world, moving mightily around us on every side.

The essential question for the Christian is, am I aware of His presence? Do I really appreciate the fact that His energy, His power, His vitality, His influence, His benefits are freely available to me?

Most of us know very little about walking in the Spirit. We are seldom energized by the reality of His presence at work upon us. We are so bundled up in the impedimenta of our human trappings that He is seldom given a chance to touch us at all. We are so insulated from His impact upon us by our preoccupation with our personal priorities, we know nothing of the stimulus that comes when we stand stripped and exposed before Him.

It takes a certain element of self-discipline to get out of a cozy home and take a tramp in the wind. It calls for courage to throw off the coat and open the shirt to let the cool breeze play upon the chest. It demands some discipline to inhale deeply of the sharp wind off the sea, to sense its vitality race through the veins and quicken the pulse. But it is worth it all to be fully alive.

So it is with the Spirit of God. He comes constantly to renew and refresh. He comes to encourage and invigorate. He comes to impart to us the resources of the Resurrected One.

It is in Him that we find energy, power, vitality, the very dynamic for positive living . . . today.

The wind and ocean air which I inhaled yesterday will not do for today. The breezes which refreshed me last week will not so refresh me this morning. The surge of oxygen that cleansed and energized my body metabolism about a month ago will not suffice for my work this afternoon.

I must be refreshed, rejuvenated, requickened, yes, refilled each day. There is no other way. The supply and source is inexhaustible. The movement and flow is eternal. The dynamic energy never diminishes.

All that is required is that I expose and open myself before Him to be totally available to His personal impact upon me today. To so live—sensitive to His presence, aware of His wishes, obedient and open to His will—is to be filled and stimulated by His Spirit . . . now and on into eternity.

13
Place of Peace

MY BIT OF sea edge is a special place of peace. This strip of shoreline, that runs like a slender ribbon of sand and rock between the ocean and the land bluffs, is a small world of precious tranquillity.

On this beach of shining sand and golden rocks there rests an atmosphere of quiet repose and gentle contentment shaped by the sea. It is akin to the seclusion found in the upthrust alpine meadows of a great mountain range untrammeled by man.

My place of peace, though so close to the clamor of civilization, still remains uniquely apart from it. The high ramparts of the ocean cliffs stand guard against the commotion and conflict of the discordant sounds of human industry. The thunder of traffic, the wail of sirens, the roar of trains and planes, the bustle of business scarcely intrude here at all.

If they do, even briefly, their noise is muted by the sound of the surf, the cries of the sea birds, the song of the sea winds. Caught up in the offshore breezes, the intruding disturbances are carried away quickly into the immensity of the ocean. Peace returns and quietude prevails.

It is the atmosphere of repose that draws me here again and again. Enfolded in the endless, eternal action of wind, waves, tides and currents, the beach breathes serenity and strength. It is a quality of life ever harder to find in our crowded world.

This sea edge is a unique spot of seclusion and privacy. It is a place where a person can go to sit lost in thought, or take long walks thinking eternal thoughts, or repose in the sanctum of quiet communion with his Creator.

One does not have to be a saint, recluse or mystic to partake of this environment. For it casts its special spell upon the most common of us common people. From barelegged boys sitting on the wave-battered black rocks, staring out to sea, dreaming dreams, to elderly gentlemen strolling softly in the sunset of their days, there emanates the contentment found in the quiet company of the ocean.

This tranquillity settles down into the soul and spirit as softly as a sea bird settles down upon the shore. There the gulls and terns and curlews and pelicans rest on the sand, preening their immaculate plumage in peace. The beauty of their bodies, reflected in the mirror surface of the wet and shining shore, is etched in soft shades of gray, brown and ivory white.

The warmth of the sun, the softness of the sea air, the drift of haze and sea mist wrap this bit of beach in folds of quietude. It is a spot to come with a good book, with a thick terry towel, and an hour or two to stretch the body and stretch the soul and "extend one's spirit" to meet one's Maker in quiet communion.

Even the birds on the sand, the ground squirrels sunning themselves on the banks of clay, the seals stretched contentedly on the rocks revel in the peace of this place. Here there is respite from the rush and fury of the struggle to survive. Here there is privacy to withdraw from the pressures and rivalry of foraging for food. Here there is relaxation from the rub of life's stresses and strains.

The hours spent in peace here are hours of healing. They are interludes of serenity for the soul, times for making one whole in the world of fragmentation and bruising abuse. The moments slip away softly, their motion as smooth as the murmuring movements of the sea, caressing the conscience, mending the mind, stilling the spirit.

Not only do the southern sun, the pungent sea air, the tingling ocean water turn the body a lovely golden brown, but they also turn the soul into a citadel of contented serenity with the spirit ensconced in quiet rest.

The sea edge is in very tangible truth one of God's great gifts to His earth children—not just exclusively for man, but also for all his brothers of paw, wing, flipper or shell. It is a place to be shared, relished, cherished and preserved. For here one can find wholeness, soundness, health and beauty amid a troubled world.

There are those who rather naively insist that our Father can be found only in the formal and sometimes rather august surroundings of a man-made sanctuary. But my contention is that He is more often met in the majestic amphitheater of His own wondrous creation. He cannot be confined to structures of steel, concrete and glass devised and erected by the efforts of man.

He comes softly to meet the soul open to receive Him upon a stretch of sand, along some leaf-strewn forest trail, across a summer meadow deep in sun-splashed daisies, or on a storm-blasted mountain ridge.

Yes, our God is everywhere present in His universe—even in our bustling canyons of brick and iron that roar with the thunder of our vaunted technology. He is even in our ghettos of grime, and in our luxury condominiums crammed with their ceaseless sound and fury.

The problem is most people will not take either the time or trouble to find their "place of peace." They cannot be bothered to seek an oasis of serenity in the desert of their drab days. They have never discovered the healing stillness of some quiet spot where they can meet God and know Him in gentle meditation.

Crowded, pressured, driven, desperate, they rush on and on!

It takes time to draw aside from the society of man.

It takes time to enter deliberately into the presence of God.

It takes time to commune with Christ as friend.

For some people such time is simply not available. They feel it is wasted, thrown away, spent for naught. They would prefer to expend it on something much more stirring and exciting—like a football game, a soap opera, or perhaps even the fluctuations of the stock market.

There is a certain discipline of soul, a setting of the will, a determination of spirit required to meet with God's Spirit in a place of peace. It calls for much more than merely feeling like it. It demands a deliberate act of faith that in such a spot I shall meet my God. Such meetings are not encounters arranged by the church, denomination, or assembly of God's people to which I belong. Rather they are a private rendezvous planned purposely, carried out quietly, between me and my Father.

For when I truly am fond of Him, such personal interludes are extremely precious. They are encounters in which Christ communes with me in the very depths of my being. Through His Word and by His Spirit His presence becomes every bit as tangible to my soul and spirit as the touch of the sun on my cheek, the caress of the sea wind on my face, the refreshment of the ocean on my body.

Most of us know very little indeed about opening ourselves to the incoming peace of the presence of The Most High. Rarely do we expose our minds, our emotions, our wills fully to the influence of His Holy Person. We seldom dare to invite the living Lord to search our spirits, cleanse our conscience, enliven our intuition, so bringing us into close communion with Himself—the Christ of eternity, the One who loves us so profoundly. But when we do, we find peace—His peace—for He speaks peace to us.

Peace that passes our human comprehension is not a quality of life which excludes us from the stresses and strains of human society. It is not a sheltered withdrawal from the wrongs that rack our world. Nor is it a cloistered existence in which we are cut off from the calamities and conflicts of our generation.

The place of peace to which God our Father calls us is that intimate inner acquaintance with Himself whereby we come to know so assuredly: "O Father, You are here! All is well!" This is the personal, private encounter with Christ which brings serenity amid the storms of life. It is the pervading influence of His own Spirit, so profound He speaks peace even in the midst of earth's most formidable pressures.

The peace He provides is not such as the world supplies. His peace is of eternal duration. It is as timeless as the tides that shape the sea edge and form my bit of beach. In His peace my soul finds strength, my days find deep delight.

14
Sound of the Surf

AS I SIT at my desk writing, long, long before dawn ever tints the eastern horizon with gold, I can clearly hear the voice of the surf on my bit of beach. Some days it is muted and soft like a distant whisper. Other times it is distinct, sharp and emphatic with the clear notes of an ocean orchestra. Occasionally it thunders and booms with the roar of giant breakers bursting like artillery shells against the bluffs.

The sea has many sounds. It speaks in a wide range of accents to those of us who live near it and have come to love its voice. The notes played upon this strip of shore are some of the most sublime music of divine design composed in the cosmos.

The songs of the sea, the murmuring of streams, the running notes of rivers, the thundering of waterfalls, the soft melody of lakes lapping on a shore, the fine music of a fountain flowing over its rocks are all fluid sounds produced by water in motion. In this music of the ages there lies remarkable therapy for the whole of man . . . body, soul and spirit.

Running water, whether in waves, ripples, cascades or simple oscillation, brings with it a balm to weary bodies—a repose to high-strung souls and a quiet serenity to the human spirit.

Primitive men knew this instinctively. They sought solace and strength and inspiration from the voice of the waters. They spoke in awe and reverence of the singing streams and thundering seas. They came often to the water's edge not just for refreshment but also for the rejuvenation that the water music provided.

For me as a man, a great part of the pure pleasure derived from the sea edge is the loveliness of its sounds. For those not attuned to its music, unaccustomed to its rhythms, there may appear at first a restlessness to its beat upon the beach. But with further acquaintance and increasing intimacy the beach lover comes to know every nuance of the ocean sound, to enjoy the variations of its voice, to respond to the stimulus of its song.

In fact, a large part of the unalloyed fascination of the shore is the symphonic variation of the melodies played upon it. There are days when the sea, under a brittle blue summer sky, barely whispers in soft notes of tiny wavelets caressing the sand . . . like the gentle tones of a violin string section. Other days there is the steady beat of breakers pounding the rocks like drums in the distance. Then there are times when with thundering notes there are the trumpet sounds of great waves rolling in from the deeps—the crash of their breaking on the beach, the clash of cymbals in the hands of the celestial music maker.

In all of this I find enormous stimulation, splendor and joy. The sound of the surf speaks to me at the greatest depths of my being. It is ever there, ever present, ever pervasive. Even though my thoughts and emotions may be preoccupied with other interests and activities, in the background there persists the eternal song of the sea.

Whether my hours on the beach are taken up with reading a book, enjoying a brisk stroll, lost in quiet prayer or simply stretched in the sun thinking long thoughts, the ocean music surrounds and enfolds me with its melodies. It is superior to any stereo sound. It comes to me clearly with the utmost fidelity, untarnished by human technology.

In a word, a large part of the wonder of this music from the deep is that it is there free for the listener. There is no charge for admission. There is no limit to how long one cares to stay and enjoy it. It has neither beginning nor end. Freely it is given, freely it may be received. One can come heavy in heart, downcast in soul, weary in spirit, yet go away renewed. Often after a quiet interlude by the sea my steps turn toward home revitalized and invigorated by the music of the morning. As it sweeps over me in wave upon wave of inspiration, hope and uplift, my spirit and soul are energized by the eternal music of the spheres. My whole person is at peace with the benediction of God, my Father's, blessing.

He chooses to speak to us earthlings in various ways. His thoughts and intentions toward me as His child are clearly articulated in many modes. We speak freely of "hearing His voice" and being attuned to His purposes. The Scriptures are replete with references to the songs of love that come to the bride from the Beloved. There is the sound of the Shepherd communing with His sheep.

In music of as many moods as that produced by the ocean upon the shore, God's gracious Spirit plays upon the shore of my soul. Sometimes He speaks to me in the softest whispers. It may be a gentle suggestion from His Word, the kindly remark of a caring friend, the refrain from a song, the momentary impact of an exquisite sunset or the serenity of a star-studded night.

In that fleeting, sublime instant, my spirit, quietly responsive to Christ's presence, is sensitive to His voice. I sense acutely I have heard from Him. He is here. All is well. The music of His companionship cheers me. The melody of His good will assures me He is near. He has spoken to my spirit.

On other occasions His Spirit, through His Word, comes to me with great force and profound conviction. He speaks loudly, clearly. As pervasive and powerful as the ocean is upon my bit of beach, so equally is the presence and power of Christ in the life of His intimate companions. There come times in the life of the earnest Christian when all of his experiences are under the influence and touch of the Master. It is God, the very God, who, at work upon his life, produces music not of his making.

The shore does not compose the melodies played out upon its strand. The sea does! The shore does not shape the sounds of the surf. The ocean does! The beach is but the amplifier from which there emerges the score of the Maestro.

So it is with me. If there is to emerge from my brief and fleeting sojourn here any music of eternal worth, it must be of my Master's making. My spirit attuned to His can reverberate with the rhythms of eternity. My soul in resonant response to His voice can reflect the joyous music of my God. Out of the innermost depths of my being can come melodies arranged and scored in the sanctuary of The Most High.

As eternal as the surge of the sea, so is the ever moving melody of the love of God my Father flowing over me. As soothing as the sound of the surf, so is the quiet assurance that sweeps over my soul that Christ is my constant companion, speaking peace to my spirit. As inspiring and thrilling as the thunder of the breakers on the beach, so is the strong surge of God's Spirit breaking in upon my life. In a hundred places, in a score of ways, He is ever pressing in upon me to inspire with great joy in songs of praise.

Yes, yes! There are grand and splendid sounds on the shore of my sea edge. But there can be music and melodies just as glorious and wondrous played on the strand of my life. It is freely available if I will but give Him the time.

15
Bluffs and Cliffs

IN SEVERAL OF of the earlier chapters of this book passing reference was made to the rock bluffs and sandstone cliffs along my bit of beach. In large part they are what contribute to its striking character. They give this part of the coast a strength and seclusion that makes it very special in nature.

Many mornings, even in the worst of winter weather, I am profoundly impressed with the dramatic change in climate as I descend the trail that winds down the cliffs. It is like stepping down into the warmth of a solarium. The sunshine, soft as it may be with the winter sun low on the horizon, is trapped by the cliffs and reflected back upon the beach.

This solar heat combined with the thermal warmth of the ocean itself creates a remarkable micro-climate along the foot of the cliffs. Here temperatures may be as much as twenty degrees warmer than up on the windswept meadows above the beach. The imposing bluffs break the force of breezes blowing from the high mountains to the north. So the shore becomes a secret Shangri-la for men and wildlife who seek its pleasant sanctuary.

Here flocks of sea birds, gulls, pelicans, curlews and sandpipers come to rest on the sands. Some of them, weary with their long migratory flights up and down the Pacific flyway, pause here to rest their wings and preen their plumage.

Here red-tailed hawks, kestrels and even crows ride the thermals and forage for food along the bluffs. Herons and egrets soar on the warm winds rising along the cliffs, their snow white wings sharp against the blue sky.

At low tide the sea-washed sand, smooth as a piece of ancient pewter, damp with shining sea water, reflects the grandeur of the bluffs as in a mirror. Their golden, tawny faces and rugged gray ramparts appear doubly impressive when viewed from the sea edge. Somehow they look so massive, so stalwart, so eternal, so enduring.

But in reality they are not!

The forces of weathering are ever at work on them.

Their character is one of constant change.

The pounding of the surf, the crash of giant waves, the working of the wind, the rivulets of winter rain, the lashing of seasonal storms off the sea, the variation of temperatures from day to night—all erode, sculpt and shape the character of the cliffs.

Some of these bold bluffs may have withstood ten thousand storms. But then one day a giant fault will appear in the cliff face. In time a thundering avalanche of rock, soil, and debris will crash to the foot of the rampart. Rocks, rubble and scattered stone will lie shattered on the sand.

It takes time and hundreds of tides to wear this material away. The running of the sea currents, the rasping of the sand, the softening of the sea water will do their unceasing work to beautify the beach again. For the cliffs, like the sand, are in eternal flux. They know only endless change. They are at best the passing reflection of an ever-changing seascape.

Yet, in a wondrous way, this is all a part of the eternal fascination of the sea edge. There is nothing static or sterile about it. Subject to the action of the ocean it is being altered from strength to strength, from glory to glory, from character to character. It is not stale, but stimulating.

Often as I wander quietly along the foot of the seacliffs I am reminded vividly that my own life is just like they are. My own character is just as subject to change. There really is nothing about my person which cannot be altered by the passing of the seasons.

There are, it seems to me in moments of quiet reflection, areas of our lives where we seem to be very similar to sand on the shore. Our minds and emotions are easily moved, played upon, and shaped readily by the current of events and circumstances God arranges around us.

The influence of people, the impact of the beauty of the natural world, the care and affection of family and friends, the attention of our associates, the flow of time and study and knowledge shape our thoughts and mold our emotions rather easily.

But standing in sharp and solid contrast, like the bluffs above the beach, there tower over our lives the strong, formidable bulwarks of our tough wills. The hard rock of our apparently invulnerable volition is like a bastion of basalt against the storms of life.

Of course I can only speak with authenticity about this inner bastion of the will from my own personal perspective. Yet, from what I have observed in the lives of others, it appears to hold equally true for them as well. For ultimately, man's volition, tough and hard as it may appear, is subject to change under the impact of God's presence and the circumstances of change which Christ can arrange in our careers.

It is the man whose spirit has been shaped by the weathering wind of God's Spirit; whose hard heart has been broken by the breaking power of our Father's love; whose tough will has been altered by the touch of the Master's hand, who becomes a beautiful character.

He may be as rough and rugged as the rock ramparts rising at the sea edge on my bit of beach. He may seem as scarred and chiselled by the work of the world as are the cliffs by the attrition of wind and water. He may appear as worn and twisted by the conflicts and storms of life as the bluffs above the beach. But despite it all, there is a striking dignity, a strong serenity, a tender warmth to the fortitude sculpted in his face by a thousand storms.

There will be faults and cracks in the character of the man who has withstood the endless stresses of many changing tides. But under the great, good hand of God, each mark, each line, each change in the contour of his character will but enhance its appeal. It is under the shaping, chiselling forces of life's varied experiences that Christ can sculpt us into magnificent masterpieces if we will but let Him. These are the well-worn tools of His trade for turning out beautiful souls. His Spirit can work wonders on the rough stone of our tough wills, bringing them into lovely conformity to His own will.

It is this sort of person, who, standing tall, despite the worst weather, reflects back something of the warmth and wholesomeness of Christ. As the sandstone cliffs with open face to the southern sun create their own marvelous mini-climate on the coast, so the man open to the impact of the "Sun of Righteousness" reflects something of God's love to a weary world around him.

There is a warmth, an appeal, a quiet serenity in the presence of such a person. Constantly there goes on a change, a transformation, a transition from glory to glory, from character to character as the gracious Spirit of God moves upon a submissive spirit.

In the shaping of such a life others find a place of peace, an oasis of repose. It is in the work, the words, the silent influence of such a person attuned to the will of God that men and women, boys and girls, animals and even plants will thrive and flourish.

The strong people, the sturdy souls, the quietly contented characters whose impact goes on without their realizing it, are ever a benediction to both God and man in the world. Even long after they are gone, changed and transformed into the enduring dimension of eternity, their gracious, glowing endowments will remain to enrich our lives.

It has been my rare privilege to walk softly in company with some such souls. They have done me every bit as much good as the bluffs along my beach. Through their words, by their friendship, in their letters and writing, from their memoirs, God has used their characters to touch and change my own.

These have been the reflectors of His grace and goodness to me. I am rich for having known them. My earnest prayer and ardent hope is that I, in turn, may have been a bulwark of strength and assurance to others who sought solace in my company.

16
Winter Weather

ON THE COAST of southern California, where I live, pleasant weather prevails most of the year. In fact, our short strip of shoreline, running roughly east and west for about thirty miles, is one of the few areas in North America blessed with a true Mediterranean climate. Here the sun shines, at least for several hours, most days of the year. And, very rarely does this bit of beach remain wrapped in rain and dampness more than a day or two at a time.

Still, occasional winter storms surge out of the Pacific. Freighted with dark clouds bearing warm subtropical moisture they move in over the coastal mountains, powered by oceanic pressure systems. The rain pours down in heavy deluges that send sheets of water streaming across the countryside.

Very quickly the excess flood waters gather in every stream, creek and river bed. Many of these are dry, sun-drenched trenches most of the year. But now they are suddenly filled with cascading, rumbling flows of silt-laden water. They pick up soil, sand, debris and driftwood that is carried down to the ocean in flooding torrents.

Suddenly the sea is stained brown and red with the river silt. The ocean, under leaden gray skies, surges onto the shore, driven by the wind, in dark waves laden with mud and debris from the land. Along the line of high tide a windrow of broken wood, logs, planks and tangled branches litters the shore.

Rivulets of stained water cascade off the cliffs. They carve sharp, ragged wounds in the face of the bluffs. The rain streams down from the black sky in sheets. The low dark clouds rumble with thunder. The sea roars!

The sound of the surf storming against the shoreline can be heard like a distant roll of drums in the distance. Even under the pall of the heavy overcast, the ocean still bursts into white breakers that appear almost ghostlike and ominous in the stormy darkness. Sometimes the cross-currents running in the sea are so strong the waves crash across each other moving in different directions at the same time.

The thunderous action of the combers clawing at the beach will strip away the sand, laying bare the shore bed of rock and rubble. The howling of the wind; the churning of the sea; the tangle of driftwood and shattered seaweed tossed up by the tides; the bleak, gaunt barrenness of the coast during such a storm leave the impression of utter desolation.

Those not familiar with my bit of sea edge are often dismayed by the spectacle of damage during a heavy "blow." Yet, always I am reassured that the beach will not long remain battered and bruised. Its beauty will be restored. The ocean will bring back the sand. The silt and mud and debris will be borne away into the ocean's canyon deeps. The sun will break through the clouds again. And in the place of winter's turmoil, there will be repose and rest once more.

Promise of this often comes with a beautiful rainbow. I recall vividly one evening going down to walk on the storm-battered beach. It had been a most difficult day, dark not only because of the howling storm, but also dreary because of painful reverses in other areas of life. It seemed I had never seen the beach in such disarray, stripped of its lovely sand, strewn with storm wreckage. It exactly matched the melancholy mood of my own inner spirit, grieved and torn with trouble.

I stumbled over the wet stones, hunching my back against the gale; grimly I pulled the big wool sweater tight around my chest; I uttered a silent prayer of relief and respite. "O Father, reassure me You are here!"

In a matter of moments an exquisite, brilliant, glowing rainbow began to arch over the beach. One end was anchored on the dark brooding bluffs. The other stood strongly amid the surging black and white breakers in the sea. Arched over the agony of a storm-stripped beach with its broken piles of shattered driftwood and scattered flotsam shone the wondrous colors of the most beautiful rainbow I had ever seen.

Their intensity was so pronounced they pulsed with glowing light, caught from the low rays of the sun breaking through the dark overcast of the clouds. Suddenly in a blaze of golden glory the whole coast and ocean edge was awash in a glow of burnished light. I was too moved in spirit to keep walking. Awestruck I stood alone, still and beyond words on the storm-ravaged shore.

Wave upon wave of enormous emotion swept through my soul. Impulse upon impulse of powerful reassurance inundated my spirit. In the splendor of the rainbow I sensed again the eternal, enduring goodness of my God. In the blaze of light from the setting sun I saw acutely the changeless character of Christ. Like Noah of old, after the dreadful ordeal of the flood, I sensed again the presence and promise of the almighty Spirit of the Eternal God: *"I am here. All is well. Fear not."*

Gently, softly, the rainbow began to fade. Ever so slowly that evening the last faint colors drained from the scene. The afterglow of the setting sun seemed to linger longer than usual. Everywhere there was peace.

In utter rest and with total composure I again began to stroll along the shore a short distance. Then in quiet repose I turned my steps toward home, refreshed in spirit, at peace in my mind.

Tomorrow the sun would warm these shores again. Tomorrow the ocean current would bring back the sand. Tomorrow the curling waves would cleanse away the filth, covering the ravages of the storm. Tomorrow this sea edge would sparkle with fresh brilliance.

Life for God's child is like that. Just because we belong to Him, does not exempt us from the dark storms and heavy weather of life. We must, and can, expect that in the short sojourn of our brief years here there will be some gales of adversity, some "blows" off the open seas of our days.

But the stirring truth remains that for those of us who know and love Him, our Father is always there with us. As the ancient prophet Nahum declared so boldly: "The Lord hath His way in the whirlwind and in the storm, and the clouds are the dust of His feet" (1:3).

He is ever active in our affairs. He is ever reliable in arranging the circumstances of our lives behind the scenes. He is ever near us moving on our behalf to bring about changes that are intended for our good. In the darkest hours we find Him closest.

The storms of life come and go. The winter weather is but for a short season. The dark squalls and gusting winds are passing phenomena. When they are gone, the rainbow of God's blessing and reassurance reminds us of His presence. The unique peace which He alone can provide for His people pervades our spirits. And the rest He promises us endures as our legacy. All of us have winter weather. We face those formidable interludes in life when everything looks dark and depressing. We all have times when our days are strewn with the apparent wreckage of wrong choices and derelict decisions. The best of men and women know what it is to be stripped down to the bedrock of sheer survival.

Yet amid all such storms what a consolation to know our Father has His strong hand upon us for our own good. What an assurance to recognize that Christ can be counted on to control the final outcome of our apparent calamities. What a strength to see His gracious Spirit bring great glory and beauty out of what to us may have seemed only disastrous!

Tomorrow is always His. It belongs to Him.

He can make it mine as well!

17
Winter Rains and Beach Flowers

THE SOUTHERN CALIFORNIA coast is world renowned for its glorious sunshine. Its beautiful beaches are a mecca for millions who love the sea and enjoy the surf. Near the metropolitan centers, homes and harbor structures crowd the shoreline. Concrete, steel, glass and brick dominate the landscape. The shore remains not much more than a strip of sand betwixt sea and land.

But where I live, the coast is still very much as it was when the first Spanish explorers set foot upon its shores. There are meadows of native grass and wildflowers that flourish along the beach. Here and there clusters of California sycamores and oaks march down the canyons to the sea, while along the cliffs a scattering of native plants and shrubs grace the bluffs casting a network of fragile growth over the ever-eroding land formations.

I have always been astonished at just how hardy and persistent these coastal wildflowers are. For though the climate may seem soft and gentle, in reality, where they are rooted on the abrupt beach bluffs, it is tough and stern. There are some seasons when, apart from fog and ocean mist, they never receive a drop of rain for months on end. The surface of the soil is heated to high temperatures and the earth bakes hard as a brick road.

In fact, one type of soil, common to this area, is a rich black clay known throughout the Southwest as "adobe." In the long summer droughts it becomes as tough as concrete and as durable as rock. Yet under the touch of winter rain it becomes soft, plastic, soaked with a massive amount of moisture like a great sponge.

It is the warm sea showers of our winter season that bring about such a spectacular transformation of the coastal terrain. The brown, golden hills of summer that stretch down to the sea like a blanket of bronze become an emerald green. This mantle of grass pulses with a green glory which no words can adequately describe.

It is of such shining intensity and serene iridescence that after a warm winter rain it seems more like a dream than reality.

Often as I move along the shore it appears so utterly beautiful, so completely perfect, so exquisitely lovely that it is akin to walking across a painted stage setting. On one side the blue Pacific stretches away to the horizon. Along its fringe of beach, the rolling surf lays a lacework of immaculate white across the golden sand. On the other side, the shoreline itself undulates above the brown, buckskin cliffs in a gorgeous carpet of green grass and blowing wildflowers.

The wildflowers come in many hues and shades. There are brilliant beach peas of flaming pink. I have gathered some of their seed and planted them in my own garden. What a show they made, spreading out into huge clumps of bursting blooms. The tough and hardy ice plants, turgid with the winter rain, burst into colors as varied as a rainbow. There are yellows, reds, purples and pinks, some of them so prolific they appear as rugs of flowers flung at random over the cliffs and rocks.

Wild golden mustard, purple and blue clumps of ceanothus, native pinks, and a whole host of less spectacular plants burst into color along the sea edge. Their survival is assured by the coming of the winter rains. Their perpetuation from season to season is guaranteed by the moisture sweeping in off the sea.

Though many of the species germinate and take root in the toughest terrain, somehow they thrive there to grow and blossom in glorious abundance. Despite the ravages of long months of summer sun and the inroads of wild rabbits, ground squirrels, pocket gophers and moles that tunnel and burrow around their roots, the native vegetation emerges each spring to clothe the seascape in beauty.

It is as if nothing can deter the wildflowers from bursting into bloom. They are made that way. They simply will have their day!

Yesterday was one of those days. This has been an unusual year. For more than eleven weeks, all through the winter months, there has been virtually no rain, no storms, no winter moisture. The whole earth lay parched, thirsty, dry and barren. I went early to a small rise overlooking the coast and there, stretched in the shade of a scrubby, wind-bent oak, reflected on how drought had ravaged the land in the days of Elijah.

Like him, after his great conquest on Carmel, I lay prostrate on the crest of the hill, casting my eyes out to sea. The sky seemed as if made of brass. Only heat haze drifted across the drought-stricken scene. In quiet confidence I bowed my face to the ground and pled earnestly, "O Father, refresh us again with a rain from the sea." It was a simple, single sentence prayer, spoken from the depths of a common man's spirit.

By evening great, gray banks of clouds began to move in off the ocean. They were being pushed toward shore by strong winds from the sea. As darkness descended, I went outside to stand in the gathering storm and I could feel the first drops of moisture falling on my face. Within a few hours thunder rumbled along the coast. Lighting flashed over the waves. Then the rain fell in torrents.

What a sweet sound!

What a refreshing for the earth!

What a renewal for all things living!

At dawn the storm had passed. The clouds had crossed the coastal mountains. The last filaments of their white veils vanished beyond the crest of the rock ranges. But behind their going the whole earth pulsed fresh, washed, cleansed, shining and brilliant. Every leaf, every blade of grass, every bit of bark throbbed with life, life, life. Rain had come! The earth was restored!

It is precisely the same with my soul. There have to be those interludes in life when there sweeps over my mind, my thoughts, my emotions, my sensitivities, my disposition, my will the refreshing effulgence of the living presence of God's gracious Spirit. He simply must come as surely and as strongly as any winter storm from the ocean deeps. He must sweep over my spirit from out of the wondrous depths of my Father's boundless love.

Christ, when He was here amongst us in human guise, put it to us plainly. He encouraged us to seek, to knock, to ask. He assured us His warm and gentle Spirit would be bestowed on those who longed for His refreshing (Luke 11). Most of us are too timid, too shy, too hesitant to try.

But if we are to blossom where we are planted, then it is

essential that we be watered where we are rooted. So many lives are like "adobe clay," hard as stone, tough as concrete, unyielding as a rock until touched by His grace.

Out of such unpromising materials our Father can produce a splendid show of colorful blooms. With the touch of His Spirit and the refreshing rain of His presence, our rugged, rocky souls can blossom like my bit of beach after the advent of our warm winter rains.

18
Sea Birds

SEA BIRDS ARE one of the most fascinating, as well as beautiful, creatures of our coastline. Not only are they an integral part of the seascape all year, but the sound of their cries rings over the beach in wild melodies that match the music of the surf.

It so happens that because of the great diversity of terrain along this ocean edge, it provides a wide variety of habitat suited to many species of birds. Both land and sea birds intermingle along the shore. For here the mountains meet the sea. Foothills run their sun-warmed feet into the surf. Creeks, streams and seasonal water courses create lagoons and salt water marshes where birds abound. Open meadows, deep in wild grass and brush, with a scattering of native trees, run along the shoreline. High cliffs and lofty bluffs provide updrafts upon which raptors love to soar in search of rodents and insects.

It is almost impossible to stroll along my bit of beach without encountering a score of feathered friends. Some, like the gulls, cormorants, terns and pelicans, skim softly just above the waves. They wheel and circle and cry in the wind. Some days when wild weather is in the offing they will soar high into the sky, mere specks in the wind, cutting silent circles against the gathering clouds.

If shoals of herring or anchovies are running in the current, flocks of sea birds follow them in wild excitement. Plunging, diving, circling and splashing into the sea with wild abandon, the birds feed on the silver hordes with incredible frenzy. In great flocks they come winging in from the channel islands to feast on the ocean bounty. Then, at last, replete with fresh fish they settle softly on the shore.

There are mornings when I have counted well over a thousand gulls in a single flock resting on the wet sand where the tide recedes. Their gorgeous white and gray plumage is mirrored in the reflecting surface of the shore. Their vast number of multicolored shapes lie like a beautiful quilt of gray and white flung at random across the beach.

Intermingled among the gulls are somber pelicans standing silently in stately dignity. Here and there are a few pairs of curlews, yellowlegs or whimbrels preening themselves in the morning sunshine. Everywhere there is an aura of peace, serenity and well-being amongst the birds.

As I approach, they lift off gently into the breeze, circle softly around me to alight again on the sand behind my back. In front of me there are often energetic, erratic little flocks of sanderlings and sandpipers. With exciting energy and flying feet they feed tirelessly between the waves that wash across the shore.

If startled or alarmed, the shining birds flash away from the surf, skim over the waves, banking and wheeling with breath-taking precision. The movement of their tiny forms in perfect formation reflects the light in brilliant colors from shining silver to pure white or beaten pewter. To watch them fly in such marvelous, intricate patterns without confusion or collision is to be thrilled and stimulated with pure pleasure.

The same sensation comes to me as I follow the fairylike flight of the delicate terns that skim above the sea. Their lightness, their brightness, their beautiful swift wingbeats above the water rivet my attention with breathless exhilaration. It is almost as if they are angels of light hovering over the shore.

No two species of birds have precisely the same life pattern. Their movements on the sand, their search for sustenance from the sea, their flight formation, their form and rate of wingbeat, their cries in the ocean wind are all different and engaging. Each has found its own niche here in the complex pattern of ocean life. Each brings to the beach its own unique beauty and inspiration. Each enlivens and enriches my days along the shore.

Often as I watch the birds I am deeply impressed with the concept that they are as much an integral part of the shore as sand or sea or shell or stone. It may be at times they are only transients, visitors, moving up and down the Pacific flyway from the Arctic to South America. Still they are a part of the pulsing ebb and flow of the sea life that surrounds me. They are in constant motion as much as the surge of the surf or the wind over the water.

They are in truth one of the beautiful bonuses so richly bequeathed upon all of us who love the shore and spend a part of our lives there.

It is exactly the same in our life with the Lord. Often, so often, I am profoundly impressed by the beauty of the bountiful bonuses He brings to my days. I can never be sure what sudden shining surprises He will inject into my experience.

Like the birds on the beach, there are those times when their numbers are so great I am overwhelmed with the impact of their presence. I cannot help but pause and stand in awe, overwhelmed by the myriads of wings soaring against the sky or smoothly burnished bodies resting quietly on the sand. There are birds on every side—birds above, birds around me, birds before my feet.

So it is with life. There are days when the marvelous blessings of my Father come winging in upon me in such abundance I can scarcely comprehend the outpouring of His generosity. There are days when in awe and wonder I can only lift my heart in praise, my spirit in adoration, for all the bounties He bestows upon the beach of my life.

The benefits come from far and near. Some are letters, phone calls, messages from friends in the family of God that stir my spirit, quicken my pulse, inspire my outlook. Others are close at hand—the loveliness of the land, green hills after the rain, warm earth after the storm, sunshine through the clouds, the beauty of the flowers, the voice of a friend, the smile of a stranger, the companionship of a dear one.

Like the birds along the beach each is designed and ordered of God to enrich my days and enliven my world. They are gifts from the sea. They come at no cost. They charge no fee. They are there, free, for the one who will pause to receive their uplift and inspiration.

Other days on the beach are not as replete and full with birds. Still there are always some there. It may take a little time to find a solitary curlew or a single tern. But they are to be found. And in the spread of a mottled pair of wings with gorgeous tan feathers or in a single flash of white wings over the waves there lies enormous inspiration.

The best of blessings do not always come in crowds.

There are those still, quiet moments when alone in gentle communion with Christ I sense and see the momentary glory of His person. The intense nearness of His Spirit as soft, yet sublime, as any tern on wing, moves my spirit. And again I know, "O Father, You are here! I have been enriched by Your beautiful bonuses."

As with the lone and sometimes solitary sea birds on the beach, there are times when we must search and seek for the bonus blessings of our God.

Yesterday I went to walk along on the shore. In mid-winter it appeared desolate, empty and forlorn. Its mood exactly matched the melancholy of my own emotions. I had been seriously ill for several weeks. Strength was slow to return. Responsibilities and work were falling far behind, overwhelming me with their pressures.

As I strolled alone along the sand, suddenly my attention was arrested by a magnificent snow-white heron soaring on the thermals above the beach. Herons seldom do this. Usually their flight is slow, ponderous and heavy. Yet this beautiful bird sailed in utter serenity, scarcely moving a wing, gliding in rhythmic circles against the brilliant blue sky. Finally it soared down to settle sedately on the crown of a wind-tossed Monterey cypress clinging to the cliffs.

At once my spirit was inspired. My emotions were moved. My whole being was galvanized by the splendor and glory of this sight.

Out of the silence, out of the stillness, out of the serenity of that moment my Father spoke to me in accents only His: "My son, you are not forgotten. I am here to help, to heal, to lift you above the burdens of life!"

I needed no more. I had seen a vision of beauty. My life had been enriched by the bounty of my Father's bonus.

At dawn today, with renewed strength I got up and began to write this chapter. It was the first solid, fresh work done in long weeks of weakness.

Yes, our Father is ever faithful. But there are days when we must seek and search to find the presence of His person. Then, when we do, what a delight!

We are set free, free, free, as any bird on wing against the blue.

19
Broken Rocks and Smooth Stones

ONE OF MY favorite beach hikes takes me roughly two miles along the shoreline. The trail winds over a variety of coastal terrain. There is a steep path that first leads down an eroded coulee where a small seep of water trickles down the cliffs to the sea. Here a beautiful warm sand beach arches against the clay cliffs in a soft, half-moon bay.

Beyond the bay a bold headland of sandstone formation juts out into the sea. It is rugged, with wind-chiseled caves underlying the shelves of stone. Native ice plants and wild shrubs cascade over its rough features. Often, under the weathering of Pacific storms, giant slabs of the sandstone formation crash down on the boulders below.

Here bit by bit the huge rocks are rolled and tumbled in the high surf until their surfaces are smooth as satin. It is not easy to hike across these rock piles. Their character is never constant. Every "big blow" and every extreme high tide shifts the stones, rearranging their positions in the pile.

Once past this point, the sea edge trail runs out onto wide shelves of gray rock that lie open to the sea. In spots, these slabs of smooth bedrock appear as eternal as the sea itself. But they are not. The relentless battering of the surf, the sledgehammer impact of a thousand storms, the hydraulic compression of mountainous waves crack the rock and shatter the stone.

Bit by bit, week by week, year after year the fortresslike formations are slowly reduced to rubble. One spot in particular, swept clean by the sea, is a favorite spot of mine to spread a towel and stretch out in the sun after a brisk swim. Here I lie alone to relax and read. Yet I am ever aware that the rock around me is constantly changing.

Hairline cracks appear in its surface. With the rush and thrust of incoming tides the fissures open wider under the weight and pressure of the sea. Fragments of rock are broken from the bedrock.

Then in time these boulders are shattered and tumbled in the ocean until reduced to small smooth stones.

Passing these outcrops of rock and smooth shelves of stone, the beach trail leads on to yet another gorgeous stretch of sand. Scattered here and there along its upper edge are windrows of small stones and exquisite, multicolored pebbles shaped by the sea. Many of these little stones are of delicate hue and attractive shape. Some are so beautiful in texture and color that they make lovely jewelry.

I have picked up translucent agates and snow-white stones of such perfection that they made lovely pendants my wife delighted to wear.

A short distance down this great sweeping beach that extends for several miles along the coast stands a group of giant conglomerate boulders. They are as huge as a cluster of haystacks. They stand like giant sentinels on the sand, their rugged character chiseled and sculpted by the surf that beats against them.

They, too, are gradually being broken by the sea. They, too, are slowly being shattered into smaller pieces. They, too, one day, will be reduced to small smooth stones that lie wet and lustrous, shining upon the sand.

Then someone will pick up a piece and bear it home as a special treasure gathered between the tides.

These small smooth stones are not something to be hoarded and gathered only for one's self. They are bits of beauty to be displayed upon a window ledge, to be shared with friends, to be passed on with happiness to children who come to visit in our home.

In His own special way God has often spoken to me distinctly through the stones on my bit of beach. In their beauty and attractiveness I have been made to see that some of the choicest treasures in life come to us through a long history of hardship.

Small shining stones are not shaped in a day. They are not formed in a single storm. They do not emerge to lie shining in the sun from the turbulence of one night's tide.

They are the end product of a long and painful process that has gone on for countless years and scores of stormy seasons. Small smooth stones once stood as sturdy rock ridges or rugged bedrock.

Broken and battered by countless thundering seas, they have been shaped to ultimate perfection in the rolling mills of tide and surf. Their smooth surface emerges from the rugged rasping of sand, the grinding of gravel in the rock tumbler of the tides.

Our lives, too, are like that. It takes the hard and sometimes shattering events of life to break our hard hearts. It takes calamities and losses to crack and fracture our bold, brave facade. It takes the surge of sorrows, the grinding of grief to shatter our proud spirits, our tough, hard wills.

Most of us don't want to be broken in the storms of life. We much prefer to protect our personalities from the stresses and strains of our days. We would rather, much rather, be tough and rugged and self-assured than contrite before Christ, repentant in soul before His Spirit.

No, as the rocks resist the action of the sea that surrounds them, so we resist the movement of our God who enfolds us in His encircling care. We see the impact of His presence upon us as something shattering, painful and at times very unpleasant.

Many of us would like to avoid the mills of God. We are tempted to ask Him to deliver us from the upsetting, tumbling tides of time that knock off our rough corners and shape us to His design. We plead for release from the discipline of difficulties, the rub of routine responsibilities, the polish that comes from long perseverance.

We are a restless generation. We of the West want and insist on instant results. We demand a quick-fix. We look for shortcuts and immediate results. We are quite sure we can be a rough slab of stone today and a polished gemstone tomorrow.

But God's ways and our ways are not the same. His patience is persistent. His work is meticulous. His years know no end. His perception of time is that one day is as a thousand years and a thousand years as but a single day.

The shattering of rock, the smoothing of stone, the polishing of a jewel in the sea requires eons of time. Can I then expect the breaking of my hard heart, the smoothing of my spirit, the shaping of my character as it is conformed to His own to be any less time-consuming?

If it takes fifty years to fashion a gemstone on the shore, can it not be understood that it will take a lifetime for my character to be made into the likeness of Christ?

The tides of time—the endless surf of changing circumstances, the tumbling of unexpected events, the eternal pressure of His presence, the washing of His Word that sweeps over my soul, the stimulation and surge of His Spirit, the polish of His mercy and kindness and love—will leave me lying contented, smooth, and shining in the glory of His Sun.

This all takes time.
This all takes care.
This all occurs in the ocean of His providence
for me as His person.

And because of it all, one day He will see fit to pick me up off the sands of time. He will bear me away home with Him as a special treasure. For I shall be one who has been fashioned under His watchful eye to be one of His small, smooth stones, a jewel of great worth in His estimation.

What good cheer this is for the child of God!

20
Shells along the Shore

SEASHELLS HAVE PLAYED a rather unusual role in our home. In a strong yet gentle way they are a constant reminder to us of the sea we love so much. They speak of the summer sands, of low tides, of roaring surfs, of quiet interludes in company with the ocean edge.

The moment one enters our front door, it is to see a gorgeous twisted driftwood root surrounded by shells. There are shells of all sorts adorning the window ledges. Shells of spectacular shape and color are on display amongst our bookshelves. A small basket of minute shells stands on a beautiful burl table. Its contents are reserved for children who visit us and wish to bear home a choice gift from the sea in their hot little hands.

It is the sharing of shells which has come to mean so much to us. My wife has fashioned exquisite pendants from choice shells which she gives to her friends on special occasions. Often when I return from a stroll along the shore I will bear in my well-worn pockets a lovely specimen or two for her. At the sight of them her warm brown eyes glow with pleasure and a winsome smile steals across her features. "*Just for me!*" she murmurs happily.

All of this may sound rather ordinary to the reader, and it would be if we lived where seashells are abundant. But on my bit of beach they are not. Here at our edge of the sea the crash and roll of the surf is so constant, the grinding and tumbling of the waves so tremendous, that few shells survive intact. Most are shattered.

For me "shell hunting" means just that. There are often days when not a single unbroken specimen can be found anywhere on the sand. Of those which remain undamaged only the thickest, heaviest and toughest seem able to endure the grinding of the ocean mills.

Scattered here and there in sheltering crevices amongst the rocks one can sometimes come across a lovely shell. Half buried in the gravel, sheltered a bit by the surrounding stones, some of the more frail and delicate specimens do survive the breaking of the surf that roars around them.

Perhaps it is because of their comparative scarcity on our coast that the shells cast up on our shore seem of special worth. It is because they are rather rare that they seem to possess a special value out of all proportion to their appearance. For many of them lack the ornate shapes or exotic colors of shells gathered in warmer waters.

Still, for me, finding fine shells remains a happy fascination that has never diminished across the years. Somehow they are one of the beautiful bonuses that come to us from the bounty of the sea. They are gifts bestowed freely for the taking.

As I pick up a shell, wash the clinging sand from its surface, and feel its form between my fingers it elicits awe and admiration from within. The special shape, the delicate designs in its surface, the smooth flow of its convolutions, the exquisite hues of its colors, the sheer loveliness of its form command my attention and draw from my spirit genuine gratitude.

All of this happens the moment I pause in mid-step to stoop down and pick up the treasure from between the tides.

It takes time to do this.

It takes some thought as well.

It takes attention to what the sea is offering.

All of life is like that. Everywhere, scattered here and there along the shore of our lives the tides of time cast up their quota of beautiful bonuses. They may not all be obvious. Some will be less than spectacular. Yet scattered along the strand of our ordinary days it is possible to find precious gifts from God.

There is an old hymn that used to be sung in our sanctuaries much more than it is today. Entitled "Take Time to Be Holy," its theme is that a person who would be whole and wholesome in life has to take the time to be alone with the Lord. There have to be intimate interludes with Christ in which He can convey His life and character to us.

It takes time to look for the special little gifts His gracious Spirit sees fit to bestow upon us in the common round of our daily lives. Like shells upon the sand, they may not always be obvious. They may not be so large we just stumble over them. It may take time and effort and thought to find them. But it can become a habit for us to be constantly on the lookout for bits of divine loveliness and natural beauty all about. There is such a thing as God's child learning to look for the exquisite touch of his Father's hand and heart in the world around him.

It was a veteran missionary working amid the awful poverty, squalor and degradation of India's poor who taught his children early, "Learn to look. Observe quietly. Think long thoughts. Find what is beautiful. Give humble thanks. Recall it to mind often. Refresh your soul in the gentle stream of our Father's bounty!"

To do this is to live with an attitude of gratitude. It is to discover fragments of loveliness in the most ordinary events of life. It is to search and seek and seize every evidence of bonuses bestowed by the gentle hands of our loving Father.

We of the affluent twentieth century have had our sensibilities seared, our appreciation jaded, by the easy overabundance of our days. Few, few amongst us know anything of the humble art of a lowly heart that can find inspiration in the soaring flight of a gull or the exquisite shape of a shell or the song of the surf.

We of the West have, by our crude and crass culture, become so conditioned to look for the sensational and spectacular in our experience that we miss seeing the stars while looking at our spacecraft. We know so little of the sublime, because we are so attuned to the clash and crash of our civilization. We prefer crowds and mass displays to the enrichment of soul or uplift of spirit that can come to the person prepared to spend a few moments alone in company with Christ.

The Lord is not confined to the pages of Holy Writ.
He is not to be found only in our solemn sanctuaries.
He is not restricted to liturgy or creed.
He is everywhere at work in our weary old world.
He is to be met in a thousand disguises.
His touch is to be found at every turn of the trail.

The point is I must be attuned in spirit, receptive in soul, alert in attitude, to detect the impact of His presence upon my path.

The bonuses of my Father are everywhere about me, scattered at random, freely, like shells upon the shore. But it demands time, thought, attention and perseverance to discover their sheltered spot, their hidden secret places.

Life can be profoundly rich without being pretentious. It can be filled with overflowing vigor if we but pause to relish the fragrance of the breezes that blow across our strand. It can provide an abundance of joy and humor and good will if we seize the seashells scattered along the sands of our times to bear them home to be shared with others. It can be wholesome, hearty, yes, even holy, when we take the time to spend quiet interludes in company with our Father.

Human spirituality does not consist only of creeds, churches, biblical knowledge or good deeds. It is made up as well from the humble art of learning to see and find the impress of my Father's hand in all the land. It is woven into the warp and woof of our little lives by sweet associations in the company of Christ, who cares about sparrows, lilies, and shells from the sea. Human spirituality comes to us afresh every day by His gracious Spirit who touches us with the impress of wind and surf and sea and sky and a thousand glorious sunsets over the shining shore of our days! All for free! All for the taking!

If we will but pause in mid-stride to pick up the treasures of our God from between the tides of time we can become richer in spirit than we ever dreamed.

21
Sunrise and Sunset

FOR OCEAN LOVERS, sunrise and sunset are perhaps the most poignant interludes of the entire day. These hushed hours bring to the beach a unique aura of splendor and stillness that speak to the innermost spirit of man. They are moments in which often all sense of time is temporarily set aside, to be replaced by awe, wonder and quiet reflection that extends into eternity.

This is especially true of sunrise over the sea. For in this hour of early dawn the shore lies stripped of all human life. The clash and clamor of all human intrusion is stilled. The feverish activity of modern man is absent.

Peace pervades the realm of sea, sky and shore.

Slowly the eastern sky turns from gray to gold, to burning red. The low light casts the coast into sharp silhouettes. Headlands, hills, trees, rocks and birds along the beach stand sharp against the light, cast in brittle black.

The long slender fingers of early dawn reach out from the central palm of the rising sun to stretch themselves across sea and sand. The whole seascape is caught up and wrapped in a golden glow.

If there are random clouds above the horizon they will burn bright with changing colors of crimson, purple and yellow.

A peculiar hush lies heavy over the shore. The sand is swept clean by the overnight tides. And all the world lies fresh, burnished, new as if for the first time it came clean and fresh from the Creator's hand. And in fact it has!

For in truth no two dawns are ever identical.

Nor are the advents of any two days the same.

Each bears a beauty uniquely its own. Each comes with freshness for a new beginning. Each carries the capacity for great adventure, stirring events.

Likewise it is in my humble, quiet walk with God. The imprint made upon the sands of time this dawn are unlike those ever made before.

There stretches before me a strand of eternity upon which may be etched designs of divine inspiration.

It is as clean, clear and uncluttered as any stretch of beach unmarked by the tread of man.

No one has passed this way before.

No one has lived in this moment in this special spot before this time.

No one has left any mark upon this hour.

The dawn announces a new day. It ushers in an untrammeled way. It waits to hear what God will say.

So I am handed a fresh scroll of unfolding time.

What will be inscribed upon it? What designs shall I draw upon the parchment of its hour? What mark or message will be left here of eternal worth and lasting merit?

Every dawn breaks anew upon my soul with the promise that today can be cherished. It is a special treasure of time entrusted to me for the Master's use. It is not bestowed to be squandered in languid living, rather it is received to be emblazoned with impulses and actions of His design.

He is the author and originator of those lasting impressions of divine love, which through my humble hands and lowly heart can decorate this day. Under the gentle stimulus of His winsome Spirit, the spotless scroll of this strand of time can be embroidered with blessings as beautiful as the lacework of white foam on the beach at break of day.

It may be but a fleeting smile, a gracious gesture, a tender thought, yet it leaves an imprint for all of eternity. For in every action there lies a shaping power that changes character for all of time. So in the dawn of each new day comes the chance to be conformed ever more closely to the character of Christ.

It is in the sum total of ten thousand new days—in the accumulated impact of uncounted new sunrises, in the exquisite beauty of unnumbered dawns—that my life can be changed from glory to glory, from character to character, by the pristine splendor of the Spirit of the living Lord who surrounds me with His effulgence.

For just as my soul is stirred and stimulated by the rising of the sun, so, too, my spirit is inspired and quickened by the splendor of the Son of God, whom the psalmist calls the Sun of Glory.

He rises with great healing in His majesty. He rises amongst us bringing new hope for every day. He rises to shed over us mercies and bounties of blessings that are new every morning.

In the acute awareness of all this, life becomes much more than a mere march of time across the calendar. In company with Christ each dawn comes as the beginning of a new chapter in the pageantry of my days.

What is inscribed upon that chapter depends upon the intense sensitivity of my spirit to His. It comes from the willingness of my will to comply with my Father's wishes. It can be beautiful if He is allowed to be the author of my work.

Gradually as the sun moves in grandeur across the sky, the hours of the day are flooded with light, warmed with pleasure. Then slowly as evening descends the burning orb of fire settles softly into the sea, as though settling down gently for the night.

The brilliant banners of tattered clouds, tinged with intense red, rose and pulsing scarlet hues, remind us that the day is done. What has been done has been done!

There can be no replay of this day, except in fleeting memory. There can be no rewriting of the script etched upon these hours. With the indelible ink of eternity there has been inscribed upon the page of this eternal sheet of time either something of value, or only what is vain.

Sunset is an hour for quiet reflection. It is the particle of time poised briefly for a brief review of what was done this day. The afterglow closes the chapter, putting a period to the writing of my journal.

Eventide is the time for taking stock of how the day was spent. It calls briefly for a serious evaluation of the manner of my conduct. It speaks softly of work well done, of progress made, of the touch of God's hand upon my life.

It must be hard indeed for skeptics, atheists and agnostics to view sunrises and sunsets. The splendor of their glory, the beauty of their colors, the intensity of their inspiration that comes from our Father's loving heart, are to the unbeliever nothing more than mere chemical and physical responses to external stimuli. No wonder their world is so bleak, their despair so deep, their future so forlorn.

But for God's child sunrise and sunset are very special. They are intense interludes of quiet communion with the living Christ. They are moments of majesty in which our Father displays His love and might. They are scenes of spiritual exaltation to which His glorious Spirit lifts us to wondrous heights of pure joy in His presence.

Again and again across the passing seasons of my years, sunrises and sunsets have induced me to think long thoughts about God, eternity, the brevity of my little life, the coming of Christ, the guidance of His Spirit along the shores of time.

Often I reflect upon the beauty of sea and sky and sand. Amid the musings of my spirit I realize that at best such glory is but a tiny glimpse, a fleeting foretaste of the wondrous splendor that awaits the children of God. What joy Christ sets before us! What intense and exciting hope He gives us! What tremendous longing He instills in our spirits for that realm where He will be the source of all light!

So dawn follows darkness. Sunset follows day. Our short sojourn here is marked off in the steady rhythm of the seasons, tides, moons and sunsets. Each is a beautiful reminder—"O my Father, You are nigh! Your glory fills the whole earth! All is well with my soul! In Your presence there is joy forevermore!"

Book IV

Sky Edge

Mountaintop Meditations

In memory
of
Harvie
One of the finest companions
who
ever tramped a mountain trail
with me

Contents

A Note of Gratitude

THIS BOOK HAS emerged from the agony and anguish shared with friends who faced great suffering and sorrow. For nearly two years we have tramped the trail of tears with various families who faced death with fortitude and faith. Only the presence of Christ could overcome the pain and pathos. To Him I give genuine gratitude for His grace and His strength to accomplish this work amid such adversity.

I am deeply thankful to my wife Ursula for sharing the sadness, even to tears, that brought this book to life. It is no light thing to enter fully into the suffering of others. Yet it is the noble service to which the Master calls us.

My Friend

He was tall and slim,
rugged as a cedar snag.
With great, strong hands,
quick to serve, ready to help
those of us in need.

He bore a gentle spirit,
free from guile or pomp.
His was a humble heart,
with a simple, quiet trust
in Christ our Living Lord.

We tramped the hills together.
We roamed the ridges free.
His eyes aglow with peace,
his face alight with fun,
for we were in his "realm."

He loved the lofty hills.
He loved the singing streams.
We shared their splendor often;
we revelled in their strength.
No need for more than these.

Enough to be his friend.

A tribute to Harvie Murfitt

1
The Birth of This Book

THIS BOOK, *Sky Edge,* is a collection of simple parables drawn from my adventures at the edge of the sky—on the high mountains I love so fiercely. It is intended as a companion piece to *Sea Edge,* written in the same style, produced in a similar format.

At the time *Sea Edge* was being created it was thought we would live by the ocean edge for the rest of our days. But it was not meant to be. Our Father had other plans for us. It became clear that we should return to the high, dry, vigorous climate of the interior, intermountain region of the west. So once again our "home terrain" was one of rolling rangeland nestled amid lofty mountain ranges that reached to the edge of the sky.

In His gracious, gentle way our Father had prepared a place for us. It is a cheerful, cozy, warm cedar chalet whose massive windows look out over a splendid landscape of rugged ranges, rolling hills and a small, shining mountain lake. It is a very serene setting. Here we can hear the call of the Stellar Jays and the soaring hawks. At night the winsome wilderness call of the coyotes carries across the valley. We are surrounded with pines that sing in the wind, and shrubs of native origin that bear their own abundance of wild fruit.

A short, vigorous hike of only a few minutes takes me into terrain as primitive and untamed as it was when only the Indians hunted these hills. High snow-capped peaks stand on the perimeter of our mountain realm. Their melting snows feed sparkling streams. These in turn nurture mountain meadows and eventually shining lakes.

Within a radius of twelve miles of my front door can be found unspoiled mountain habitat that shelters bears, deer, mountain sheep, cougars, marmots, coyotes and a dozen other species of mammals. Here, too, is a variety of upland terrain that attracts scores of various bird species. Every sort of winged visitor spends part of the year in this upland realm, from the regal Golden Eagles that nest on our granite cliffs to the swift Barn Swallows that built beneath our eaves; from the great flocks of Canada Geese that nest in our lakes to the Mountain Bluebirds that adorn our high rangeland.

More than all of this, our high country is also a region of remarkable repose. Not that it is remote and inaccessible. That simply is not so. For not far away there are highways, towns, an airport and most of the other commercial activity that is characteristic of modern society. It just happens that where we live is a sheltered mountain valley that has remained almost untouched and untrammeled by modern man. And we feel fortunate indeed to savor its serenity for as long as our Father may desire.

In recent months I have relished mountain interludes of unusual uplift and inspiration. Never did I dream that such adventures would be mine so late in life. From the perspective of my advanced age they are doubly precious, both for their spiritual uplift, as well as their physical and mental stimulation.

This book is an earnest endeavor to share with the reader some of the stirring eternal truths which God, by His Spirit, has made so vivid and vital to me. He has always spoken to people of His choosing in the solitude of mountains. So it is appropriate that He should do so again.

It is not surprising that the Most High met with people like Noah, Abraham, Moses, Elijah and others in the high places. Even our Lord Jesus Christ often communed with His Father on the hill slopes and chose to reveal some of His greatest truths to His followers while on the mountains.

Like the sea, mountains often convey to us mortals the impression of immense durability. Yet they are subject to constant change. Weathering and erosion change their appearance. Still our Father uses them to speak emphatically to us earth children in flashes of spiritual insight.

Life in the high country can be most stimulating. The slopes challenge our strength, test our muscles, harden our bodies. The sweeping vistas and serene solitude energize our minds, quicken our souls and toughen our resolve. The grandeur and glory of the lofty peaks with star-studded skies sharpen our spirits and stir us to contemplate deeply the supreme issues of life.

It is in the quiet interludes on some remote ridge against the edge of the sky that God's eternal Spirit can speak with stunning clarity. There away from the crush and commotion of our culture He, Christ, God very God, can commune with us at great depths. In the stillness and solitude of the hills and valleys it is possible to know our Father and understand His eternal intentions for us.

Modern people, living amid the mayhem of our giant metropolitan centers, have been cut off from the wholesome benefits of the outdoor world. Most of modern life is so conditioned and shaped by the stresses and strains of a man-made environment that in many cases the healing influence of mountains, trees, streams, birds, fields and flowers is unknown and foreign to us. Perhaps this book can help reverse this tragic trend.

At the beginning of this introduction the assertion was made that our Father had certain specific reasons for bringing Ursula and me back to this mountain region. Unknown to us at that time was the responsibility of having our lives closely intertwined with families who faced terminal illness.

In just a little over a year we had, in a truly spiritual dimension, lived on the "sky edge" with fourteen families who faced death and all of its formidable consequences. Of these one was my own dearest friend, Harvie Murfitt, to whom this book has been dedicated. Up until six months ago he and I climbed, hiked and relished the high country together. Now he has gone on to even higher ground. He was a gracious, gentle, strong man. There are few like him around. How he is missed!

Besides him four others have crossed over the edge of the sky. And so it is that out of the deep sorrow, the intense suffering, the anguish of spirit that has been endured, some of the great principles explained here have been born. We have known in some small measure what Isaiah of old meant when he spoke of Christ as the One who bore our griefs and carried our sorrows.

This is not a shallow book designed just to entertain the reader. In parable form it deals with some of the most profound questions which confront us. The parables give sharp, clear glimpses into spiritual verities that transcend time and our few fleeting years upon the planet. They come to us bringing courage, consolation and serenity of soul.

My earnest hope is that through them our Father will give you bright light for the trail you tramp here. May He also give you sure and steadfast hope for life beyond the edge of the sky!

2
Four Bears and . . .

ONE MOUNTAIN RIDGE I had often dreamed of climbing with Harvie lay just a few miles west of our home. It was typical of our high, dry, semidesert terrain. Like a long, slim mountain lion, crouched low against higher ranges, it bore the tawny color of sun-scorched grass, co-mingled with gray sage and rock. Scattered here and there were tough, old, wind-twisted firs and sturdy Ponderosa Pines that found footing in the stony soil.

It was always a thrill to tramp the new and strange game trails that criss-crossed the high country. And as I climbed slowly but steadily toward the clouds my spirit ached fiercely for the comradeship of my friend. How he used to take these hills in full stride! How his big, tall, raw-boned frame seemed designed to lift him easily over the tough terrain.

But Harvie was not here.

I was very much on my own—yet not alone!

For in a strange yet sure way, I sensed and knew the presence of God's Spirit accompanying me on the trail. Whatever His intentions, I was open to His touch—receptive to any lesson He might wish me to learn in the dull overcast of that rainy day.

It was really a good day for a long, hard hike. The leaden sky and gentle drizzle cooled the late summer heat. The silver droplets of moisture clinging to every blade of grass and dry twig on the ground made for silent footfalls. So it was possible to pick up every sound that stirred in the soft silence of the lonesome hills.

As I topped the crest of the ridge I was startled to see it was cut off from the adjacent range by a deep, steep-walled canyon. On the far side sharp slopes of scree and broken rock rose sharply from the canyon floor.

Stopping to catch my breath, I stood in the shelter of a dense fir tree. Suddenly the sound of distant stones rolling down a slope caught my attention. Some sort of animal was on the move, loosening rocks that rumbled down into the canyon. All my senses were fully alert. What would it be?

Silently as the wraith of mist that swirled around me I moved along the rimrock of the canyon edge. I searched the opposite slopes for some sign of life, but could see nothing. Again there was the dull rumble of rolling rock. And once more I glided silently across the rain-softened ground. The whole world seemed so still, so serene, so at rest. Here was solitude of unusual intensity.

Through my binoculars I carefully scanned the rock slopes, shining with wetness. They seemed devoid of life until all at once my eyes caught the slight movement of the branches in a large serviceberry bush. Here we call them Olalla berries. In our upland world they often grow into massive shrubs up to fifteen feet tall and as many across.

A half-grown black bear, his coat glistening in the rain, was stripping the last of the summer fruit from the tall and slender branches. Within moments I found a second bear of similar size in another clump of brush, and then a third gathering the tender leaves from the tips of a hardy Vine Maple. Then as if to add a special delight to the day I discovered a fourth bear, a magnificent sow (female), obviously mother to the three younger ones, turning over rocks to find ants. It was she who had rolled the stones down the slopes.

Fortunately what feeble air currents were moving on the mountainside blew from the bears toward me. So it was possible to stalk them silently up my side of the deep defile until I was directly across the canyon from them. And now they were in full view.

What a rare and special treat this was! So often a man's encounter with wild bears is fleeting. Like dark shadows they slip away quietly into the trees and are lost to sight in a matter of moments.

How Harvie would have loved this interlude! How he revelled in watching wildlife! He would have grinned and chuckled with pure pleasure at such a show as this.

I spent the next four hours in constant company with those four beautiful bears. They were already heavy and rotund with the wild fruit that had flourished in such abundance during the summer.

Their coats, black as a polished old coal stove, shone with health, vitality and wellbeing, now doubly so because of the mountain mist that sparkled on their fur.

The obvious gentleness and cordiality with which the four bears treated one another made an enormous impression on me. I had noticed and observed the same sort of behavior among elephants when I studied their family life years ago in Kenya.

There simply was no pushing or shoving or angry rivalry among them. I was especially surprised at how quiet and silent every move was, every gesture, every interaction between them. There appeared to be an aura of courtesy and respect between the bears that warmed my own spirit in a strange yet wondrous way. If only human families were as cordial!

This was emphasized even further when I watched spellbound as one would actually bend over the branches of a bush and allow his companion to relish the fruit and leaves from it. Not once was there an outburst of anger or a hint of hostility.

Steadily but surely I stole closer and closer to the four until only about a hundred yards separated us. The old she-bear now decided it was time for an afternoon siesta. A giant, veteran fir had been blown down on the slope. It lay prostrate on the ground, a huge log now bare and stripped of bark. It would make a fine couch.

Here the four bears decided to stretch out and sleep away part of their afternoon. They curled up against each other, here a foreleg, there a hind leg, draped over one another's bodies. It was quite a scene and it surprised me none of them took umbrage at another for encroaching too close or shoving for the softest, smoothest spot.

I was being given a first-class object lesson in harmony of life. It appeared that utter peace and complete mutual understanding prevailed. There was no tension, no discord, no stress apparent.

After their siesta the four bears climbed down off the great gray log and began to forage for fruit and ants again. I began to call to them softly. The sound of my voice did not appear to disturb them. Rather, they seemed easily reconciled to my presence in their territory. It was a marvelous and touching finale to our time together.

I had been sitting quietly on a rugged, moss-covered outcropping of rock at the base of a gnarled tree that gave me shelter. As I stood up to leave I was startled by a huge mountain rattlesnake that had slipped up beside me unnoticed.

In swift, lightning-like action, he struck twice in rapid succession. Fortunately I had on heavy bush pants and high-laced hiking boots. Still his sudden attack made every hair on my arms, legs and chest stand erect. He was aroused, alert and angry—perhaps even alarmed to see me stand up suddenly so tall beside him.

His rattles whirring with agitation he slithered into a dark crack in the rock that had been fractured by the roots of the old fir. I walked around it carefully. On the other side lay his shed skin. It stretched out just about four feet long, lying there shining on the stones. It had been a close call indeed. But through it I learned an unforgettable lesson.

In great seriousness I mused over the events of the day as I tramped the long trail home. I had been given a clear and vivid glimpse into one of the most profound yet powerful spiritual principles in life.

Things are not always as they appear!

This had been such a tranquil day. The mountains all draped in soft veils of mist, rain and moisture seemed so serene and still. Even the gentle interlude with the four bears gave one the feeling of quiet contentment and special pleasure.

Yet in the very midst of it all there lurked death. The rattlesnake was certainly the handsomest of his species I had ever seen. His thick, powerful body was adorned in striking bronze and black markings of special design.

Had his long fangs found their mark in my flesh, it is most likely it would have been a mortal wound. So large a charge of venom in one as old as I am could have meant death before I could tramp the long miles home.

It was a microcosm of life itself. For in the midst of our days, death is never really far removed. At almost any hour, from some unexpected quarter, the last and final call may come swiftly and in a most surprising way. We never can tell when the fatal moment will appear.

So the serious, sobering questions must be asked:

"Do I live ready to die?
Is my life in order?
Do I know and love God as my Father?
Is Christ my closest friend?
Is all well between me and others?"

Just a few months before this incident Harvie and I had made a late winter climb together. It had been such a joyous adventure, filled with fun and good cheer.

I recall so clearly how we scaled the last ridge all shining with deep snow. There in a sheltered spot we shared our sandwiches and tea while the sparkling midday sun warmed our faces and hands. Never, never, never did either of us dream that terminal cancer would soon snatch him away. Death stalked the dear fellow that day and we did not know it.

So, things are not always as they may appear. And the only guarantee we can have not to be taken unaware is to have made our peace with God through the great generosity of the wondrous, amazing grace of Christ. Then the call home can come at any moment. And all is well!

The second startling insight which God's gracious Spirit imprinted upon my own spirit that day was this: *Even in the most harmonious settings, the enemy of our souls is at hand to disturb.*

As God's people we sometimes delude ourselves into believing that we can live lives of serenity here on earth without fear of attack from the evil one. It simply is not so. Satan appeared in paradise to disrupt the sublime arrangements made for Adam and Eve. He appeared in the desert to assail our Lord and Master Jesus Christ in His great enterprise for our salvation. So he is bound to bother us.

The serpent is not a figment of man's imagination. He is not some superstitious fabrication of ancient folklore. A deadly foe opposed to all that is fine and noble and upright in the earth, he is the implacable enemy of God and His people. He insists on insinuating himself into the most harmonious of our situations. He poses a perilous threat even in the most sanguine of our days. He is swift to move and ready to attack in the most unlikely moments.

It is for this reason that the Spirit of God alerts us again and again to be on our guard against the evil one. Even our Lord, with enormous understanding, taught us to pray daily: *"Our Father who art in heaven. . . . deliver us from evil"* (or the evil one).

Fortunately for me, long years of wilderness experience had taught me the basic behavior essential to survival in the high country. One went properly attired in heavy bush pants, high-laced hiking boots, warm clothing and, above all, with alert senses. Reflexes must be swift and smooth and silent.

So it is, too, in the Christian experience. Our walk with God through the tangled trails of this brief earthly sojourn is not without its perils. There are abroad in the wilderness of our days not only high adventures with Christ but also some severe risks. The Word of God alerts us to these.

In passages such as the sixth chapter of Ephesians we are given explicit instructions as to what antagonists we can and will encounter. We are supplied with specific information on how to equip and garb ourselves so that we can survive unexpected emergencies.

Sometimes we are startled by the sudden appearance of the enemy, no matter what guise he assumes. But this does not mean we need to fall prey to his devices. If we are properly equipped in soul and spirit against his attack it will come to nothing. When we are fully alert with the Word of God active in our lives, we survive unscathed.

There are precautions we must take as Christians. There need not be disaster even if there is great danger abroad. Provision is made for our overcoming the evil one if we will calmly obey our Master's instructions and quietly carry out His directions for our lives.

He will lead us in paths of righteousness and peace. But we must allow Him to be our constant companion on the trails of life.

3
The Beauty of Bunch Grass

IN OUR LOFTY landscapes, where the mountains push their ragged ridges against the edge of the sky, one of the most common scenes is a swath of golden grass, spread like a tufted blanket between the trees. For only a few weeks in early spring does this golden glory appear as a faint mantle of tender green.

The clear, clean, sun-drenched atmosphere of the high country quickly turns the bunch grass slopes to burnished bronze. Ours is essentially a rangeland of sun-bleached golden grass with dark and handsome trees scattered across it to give the impression of open parkland.

This is the region where fine herds of cattle graze the summer range. Deer abound and the mountain winds blow softly, whispering among the trees, bending the grass like waves of flowing gold. It is glorious country in which to hike or ride a horse. A realm of long views and wide expanses, its high horizons challenge the spirit and call to the wild, free emotions of a mountain man.

Some of my most memorable years have been spent in this rugged mountain world. At one time I owned nearly a thousand acres in one of the upland valleys. There was an ancient log cabin there, perched beside a tiny stream that tumbled over the cliffs into a lake nearby. I wrote seven books in the rough shelter of that thick-walled cabin—books filled with beautiful photos and passionate cries for the preservation of all things wild. They had such titles as *Under Wilderness Skies* and *Under Desert Skies*. Their basic uplift and inspiration were born in the thrilling atmosphere of the high bunch grass ranges.

Our native bunch grass has been called one of the most noble living plants upon the planet. Some ecologists consider it to be the supreme species of grass in North America. Other specialists call it "the great healer." This is because of the remarkable benefits it bestows on the land.

To those who generally think of grass as a smooth green lawn, closely clipped and meticulously manicured by man, our native mountain variety comes as a rough, tough surprise. It grows in sturdy clumps, really like a tussock of tough stems intertwined with slender leaves that can feel rough to the touch.

Each tussock is separated from its fellows by bare soil or open ground. This space between the bunches of grass is often shaded by the tall stems of the seed heads which in good grass country may be two or three feet tall. Seldom is the stand of grass so dense or thick as to form a solid mat. Rather, it appears like an old-fashioned tufted rug flung casually across the countryside. Each bundle of tough plant fibers glows gold against the dark underlayer of the land itself.

This covering of grass will and can grow on stony slopes so steep that they are almost vertical. It is so sturdy, so deep rooted, so tenacious it can thrive on thin soils where other plants succumb. Despite blazing summer days when heat in these hot hills pushes well above 100° F it still flourishes under the burning skies. Where wind and weather and trampling hooves and human abuse would wipe out any other grass, this hardy species still survives.

The secret lies in its tremendous root system.

A single clump of bunch grass may have miles of hairlike underground roots that reach out to tap the hidden nutrients in the soil. Each plant sends out an intricate network of rootlets that not only anchor it to the slopes but draw life, moisture and sustenance from the mountain terrain.

So deep, so far reaching, so extensive is the bunch grass root system that intensive scientific studies have shown a single plant to have up to seventeen miles of rugged roots! Little wonder this sturdy species can withstand so much grazing, so much trampling, so much abuse from reckless ranchers who often overgraze the range.

Year after year the bunch grass patiently puts out new growth. Season after season it sends up fresh shoots to shimmer in the sun. Generation after generation its golden glory cloaks the high country to gladden our spirits and nourish all those who rely on it for sustenance.

Cattle come down off the bountiful bunch grass ranges in fall, so fat, so well nourished that they appear to have been stall-fed on grain. The rich protein content of the grass is some of the finest forage in all the world. Even when it is bleached and glowing bronze it bears within its fibers a level of nutrition seldom matched by any other plant material.

When winter storms blanket the ranges in snow, deer and mountain sheep and range horses will seek out the open, southwest slopes to feed on the sturdy bunch grass clumps. The tough fibers, so rich in protein, like well-cured hay, will fuel their inner fires fighting off the chilling cold.

Yes, in spring, summer, fall and even in winter, bunch grass is beautiful. It is the gentle healer of the hills, the sustainer of life, the golden carpet flung so freely over the land by our Father's generous care.

Several days ago the dawn broke calm and clear and cloudless. It was a typical late summer morning in our mountain valley. The golden light of the sun's low rays stretched softly across the tawny bunch grass hills that partially fill the views from our wide front windows. The warm glow of the open range was like an eager invitation to go out and climb the ridges. So I responded at once.

Happily for me, the areas adjacent to our home are some of the choicest bunch grass country I have ever known. For one reason and another they have not been abused, burned, overgrazed or even trampled too much. These bunch grass hills are still in a pristine state of natural splendor seldom seen.

Droplets of moisture clung to the clumps of grass as I climbed the steep rock ridges above our house. The dense tufts, now heavy with their annual seed heads, carpeted the steep slopes in beautiful bronze shades. As I broke out over the summit I came across fresh deer tracks where a band of Mule Deer had been feeding in the dawn.

Then suddenly I stepped from the shaded side of the rock ridge into the full glory of the morning sun on the south side. The scene made me stand in awe, stunned by the exquisite beauty of the bunch grass. Never had I seen it in quite such an enchanting light.

The low slanting rays of the rising sun ran almost parallel with the slope. The soft light touched each individual tussock so that it glowed from within. It was as if ten million lamps strewn at random across the undulating range had suddenly been lit, each with a living flame of golden inner fire. It was one of those sublime, passing, precious moments in time, etched forever on the memory.

And in that instant of time my spirit was touched deeply!

As I stood in silence the questions came swiftly.

The gracious Spirit of the living God was dealing with my soul in profound intensity.

Did this little life of mine, lived out quietly on the edge of the sky, in any way remotely resemble bunch grass?

Was there anything beautiful about it, even if it seemed so very ordinary?

Could it be said of me that I was one who brought healing to these hills, help to those around me?

Did my presence in this place contribute to the well-being and nourishment of those who in quiet trust turned to me for sustenance?

Were the roots of my being so deeply driven into the very life of the living Christ that there I found the ground of my being?

Was it the very vitality of His vigorous life that sustained me amid all the vicissitudes of my experiences?

Could my Master say of me with calm approval that in season, out of season, my days had been a delight to Him, a benediction to His people, a benefit to my generation?

Despite the reverses of life; despite the heat of the day; despite the trampling of others; despite the carelessness of my contemporaries—did I still quietly put on new growth year after year?

Was I rich forage for famished people?

In times of stress and distress did someone here find sustenance to sustain them in their strain?

Were there those moments in time when my life glowed, touched and transformed by the warm light and gracious love of God, my Father?

I came down off that mountain deep in reflection, moved by those still moments of meditation. A rough mountain man had been touched by the Most High!

4
Mountain Climbing

AT THE AGE of fifteen I climbed my first major mountain. It was Mount Kilimanjaro on the border between Kenya and Tanzania in East Africa. The blood-tingling thrill of setting one's feet on high ground, against the edge of the sky, ignited a flame of enthusiasm for the high country then that has never left me.

Since that first mountain adventure, well over fifty years past, I have climbed ranges scattered throughout various regions of the world. Perhaps it is the wild, free spirit of my Swiss forebears that has produced such a passion within me for the high places. Still it is there. And though I am now well advanced in years, the lure of the peaks still grips me fiercely, constraining me again and again to respond to the challenge of the upward trail.

Above and beyond the adventure of getting onto higher ground, there lies deep within my being an intimate love for rugged hills, upthrust alp-lands and the splendor of shining snowfields that crown the summits. Unlike many climbers who see this realm as a mere fortress of rock, ice and snow to be beaten by brute strength, climbing skill and special rock techniques, I view it as a magnificent environment in which to move and live with awe and wonder.

I have written much about this in some of my previous books such as *Canada's Wild Glory* and *Mountain Splendor.* Both by word pictures and beautiful photographs an attempt has been made to share with the readers some of the majestic wonders of the high mountain realms I have explored.

But here I am concerned with the actual exercise of climbing followed by its immediate benefits to the climber. In short—what it means to climb!

Hiking in high-country places puts a certain strenuous demand upon one's strength and stamina. It is not a gentle stroll in the park. It calls for fortitude, for discipline of mind and muscle, for vigor of spirit to push toward the summit.

Often the climb begins with a rather tedious trail at the foot of the mountain. This leads through thick timber, windfalls and steep switchbacks where only here and there a distant glimpse of peaks encourages one to press on.

Bit by bit the trees begin to thin out. With increasing altitude the timber becomes more stunted, broken and beaten down by wind, snow and fierce ice storms. Here, too, the air becomes thinner, less charged with oxygen. Vistas widen, distant views quicken the pulse and the air is pungent with the perfume of pine, fir and spruce.

Then the trail breaks out above tree line. Sweeping alpine meadows of short grass, lowly heather, glowing wildflowers and broken rock beckon the climber to move higher. Here is the sky edge. This is where heaven seems to touch earth. It is a realm as yet unravaged or ruined by the hands of man.

Finally, for the hardiest of climbers there stands the summit. All sheathed in ice, snow and giant rock buttresses, its peaks comb the clouds, or, if the weather is clear, stand stark and beautiful against a brilliant blue sky.

It is a world of great stillness, punctuated only by the undulating sounds of a distant waterfall, a whistling marmot or the lone cry of an eagle. It is a realm of incredible grandeur and glory. Fields, aglow with millions of multihued wildflowers, stretch up to the ridges. Vast, wide valleys sweep away to the horizon. Mountain lakes sparkle in the sun. And all around lies commingled snow and sky and stone.

There is a stimulation, an uplift, an all-engulfing enthusiasm which energizes the soul in such a setting. The person who has spent time at the edge of the sky is never, ever, quite the same again. He or she has tasted the thrill of the lofty landscapes and learned to love them through intimate, personal contact.

This was especially true of my friend Harvie. His favorite mountain realm was "The Cathedrals," a rugged range lying about forty miles west of our homes. The first time I climbed there it impressed me so profoundly I immediately petitioned the Provincial Government to set the region aside as a park. In due time, by sheer patience and perseverance, this came about. So today it is one of the finest wilderness preserves in British Columbia.

Here was where Harvie loved to climb. This is where he went again and again for renewal of body and strong invigoration of spirit. And it is there where his ashes have been buried amid the splendors of the upland meadows he loved so dearly.

We often hiked in the foothills of that range together, even in mid-winter when snow blanketed the slopes and ice had locked the rushing rivers in its blue embrace. Still we would hike there to watch the deer, to see the wild sheep, to find the mountain goats on their cliffs—but most important just to be together in the high country.

From long experience we had learned to set a calm, steady, even pace. We did not try to rush the slopes in a sudden burst of energy. Often we paused, but only briefly to catch our breath, to rest our muscles, to renew our vigor. We took time to study the birds we met, to read the wildlife tracks along the trail, to relish the ever-widening views. We would stop to sit in the sun and enjoy a sandwich, a cup of tea or a jovial chat. There would be creeks to cross, rocks to climb and windfalls to get over. But it was all mountain climbing. So we took it in stride and loved it all.

Getting onto "higher ground" with God is much the same. There are too many Christians who seem sure they can attain the summit of spiritual experience with a single startling surge of energy. It is almost as if they thought the lofty life of communing with Christ could be achieved with one bold leap of faith, or some single session at a weekend retreat.

This simply is not so.

Our Father invites us to walk with Him steadily and surely, day by day, taking one step of faith after another in calm succession. There will be interludes in which the trail may seem very tedious. It may even appear to go up, then down, back and forth, in rather boring switchbacks. There will be times when nothing thrilling excites our view. Yet we can still be gaining ground.

As we go on with God we are bound to encounter some windfalls and downed timber as well as rushing creeks of misfortune. There are going to be obstacles to surmount, deep waters to ford, before we get out of the woods. Christ never guaranteed that the going would all be easy.

Even when we do break out into the open alpine meadows above timber line there will be miry stretches along the trail. The chill, upland atmosphere can cut to one's bones. The experience of wide horizons and awesome vistas can be tempered by biting winds and driving sleet. It is worth them all.

When we keep company with Christ in the lofty life of separation from the common crowd, we find there is a high cost. That cost is one of accepting the challenge daily to do His will and comply with His wishes. It might seem much easier just to settle down in a soft spot. It may entail the criticism of others around us.

But He calls us to push on with Him steadily. Our Lord wants us to take the upward view of the sky edge. He calls us to live dangerously with Him in the full and abundant joy of His hearty companionship in the high country.

Yesterday was a classic example of this principle. The day broke dull with a gray, leaden sky hanging low over the hills. A raw wind, with ice on its breath, blew down the slopes from the first heavy snowfall of the autumn season that decorated the ridge tops.

It would have been so easy, so comfortable, so pleasant just to lay a crackling fire in the hearth; to draw up my favorite reading chair by the laughing flames; to settle down and enjoy an engrossing book, then, with Puma (our cat) lying on my lap, while away the morning in luxurious ease.

But the call of the mountain trail was insistent.

The challenge to go out into the high country was clear.

The cost of climbing was considered and accepted.

Quietly I slipped into long winter underwear. The sturdy boots for mountain climbing were laced securely. A heavy wool shirt that has taken me through a hundred storms was buttoned over my chest. A well-worn windbreaker and snug wool cap completed my attire. Then I was off for the hills.

The chill wind made my lungs ache. The steep trail put a fierce strain on my legs and thighs. They cried for relief. But I pushed on steadily. I was determined to scale the ridge to reach the summit of a range I had never been on before.

That is really what the challenge of Christian life on high ground is like. It is a series of choices. Am I going to accept the challenge, count the cost and move out of my comfortable lifestyle to tramp the trail of testing and self-discipline with Him? Am I willing to be "wrung out," exposed to hardship and exercised to the limit to gain ground with God?

Do I truly love Him with all my mind, soul, strength and heart as I love the sky edge?

"To truly love God with all one's heart" is perhaps the most maligned and least understood phrase in the church today. Its counterpart, "and love your neighbor as yourself," is equally obscure and distorted by our soft society.

From God's perspective, "to love" is to entertain and express good will toward another. It is to set the will to seek the best for all concerned. It is abandoning every element of selfish self-indulgence to expend one's self fully for the well-being of all others.

This is the high calling to which Christ calls His followers. Not until we walk this noble way do we know anything of living the lofty life to which He summons us. There is a high cost to it. It is not the soft, sensual sentiments of people who are pursuing an "emotional high" assuming it to be the quintessence of spiritual experience.

As I climbed yesterday this truth came home to me with a clarity as sharp, cutting and acutely defined as the biting wind that cut across my cheeks and numbed my hands.

No, mountain climbing is not a stroll in the park. It is not always a saunter in the warm sunshine of a spring day. It can be a tough ordeal in which a man must face sleet and rain, cold or heat, snow-laden skies and sometimes blue skies. He has to be prepared and ready for any weather.

As I broke out above the clouds, a soft, subdued glow of Indian summer sunshine enveloped the open mountain meadows. Its warm light touched the flaming Vine Maples, igniting them with its glory. It lit up the burnished coat of a magnificent Mule Deer that bounded up the slope. It glistened from the wings of a skein of geese gliding across the sky edge.

It had been worth climbing the challenging heights.

I basked in the sun at the crest of the ridge. All was well!

For a few moments I snuggled down into the silver sage that grew on the summit of the range I had climbed. It had been touched by frost. Its pungent aroma permeated the clean, crisp mountain atmosphere. It was pure delight to inhale its fragrance, to sense the stimulation of its uplifting perfume.

This was the essence of the sweeping upland range. It was the exhilaration of the sky edge where the mountains met the sky. This wild, free, upland realm was where eagles rode the thermals and Meadowlarks sang in the sage.

Rare interludes like this are precious moments a man can store in the vault of his memory. They are beautiful bonuses given from my Father's generous hand. They are gifts of pure pleasure bestowed by His bounty.

But they would never have been mine had I chosen instead just to sit softly by my hearth. They would have been missed had I preferred just to stay at home, refusing to risk the storm or tackle the trail.

Contentedly I gazed out across the sweeping panorama of upland valleys and upthrust ranges that lay stretched out beneath me like a giant relief map. I could see more than fifty miles from my high vantage point. The whole world lay still, subdued, wrapped in the faint blue haze so typical of early autumn.

Only the distant cry of the wild geese at the very edge of the sky drifted down to the lone man high on the hill. But I was not alone, for God very God, by His Spirit was present in that splendid mountain sanctuary.

Sharing the interlude with me, He had quickened my spirit. He had stirred my soul to the depths.

With joyous stride I headed home down the slopes, plunging through the clumps of bunch grass and broken rocks. On the way I gathered a bundle of flaming maple leaves to decorate the hearth at home.

It was a triumphant farewell to a splendid mountain climb.

5
Eagles in the Wind

THE AFTERNOON WAS wrapped in September sunshine. Warm air filled the river valley below the cliff on which I sat. From my lookout I could scan the ranges that stretched away into blue smudges on the farthest horizon. This was immense country over which eagles could circle wide in the air against a backdrop of cumulus clouds.

Lost in the luxury of the day's deep contentment, I lay on my back watching the drifting clouds. The fragrance of the tender grass pressed beneath my body scented the air, mingling with the piney aroma of sap oozing from the branches of the craggy old snag beside me.

I knew this particular tree was a favorite perch for the eagles. Long ago its majestic crown had been broken beneath the blast of a brutal ice storm. The shattered limbs, twisted and torn from their sockets in the trunk, dangled in dejection from the proud old tree, growing gray and hard as bone with years of wind and weather. Near the base of the tree a fragment of daring greenery still survived. Here the sap still struggled in spring to push out a spray of new needles and fresh cones from its stubby, twisted branches.

Despite its broken crown, one sturdy old limb stood defiant in death, like an upthrust arm with knotted muscles against the stern sky. Here the eagles sat and scanned the valley below. Patiently they came to wait for the rising warm air currents that would lift them high above the rock ridges of their wild realm. Here they sat and screeched their high-pitched cries that slanted down across the rock cliffs below them.

So I lay there on this dreamy day, a grass stem between my teeth, my head propped on a gnarled root for a pillow. But as the afternoon passed into evening I found I was not alone. High above my head two tiny specks, scarcely visible to my naked eyes, cut long spirals against the clouds. It was a pair of eagles, and I watched them circle slowly toward their tree where they would wait out the night.

The beautiful scene from Isaiah 40:31 leaped into my mind: "They that wait upon the Lord shall renew their strength; they shall mount up with wings as eagles; they shall run, and not be weary; and they shall walk, and not faint."

Entranced with the eloquent language, so simple yet so descriptive, I watched the great birds soaring on the warm air currents. Slowly there penetrated my mind and heart an acute appreciation of the precise picture that the grand old prophet, Isaiah, was trying to portray to his discouraged people. Most of his audience were simple country folk who, if they had never seen eagles, at least were familiar with the kites and vultures that are so prominent a part of rural life in the Middle East.

But for me on this summer day these two birds soaring majestically over their wilderness domain were the pristine picture of the Christian as a conqueror.

"They that wait upon the Lord shall renew their strength. . . ." The words kept running through my mind time and time again. Waiting—wasn't this precisely what I had watched eagles doing so often—just sitting, resting, waiting?

All through the darkest nights, through the cold, gray gloom of morning the birds simply rested patiently, renewing their strength, waiting, perched on some dead snag or crag of rock.

The eagles know from experience that as the sunshine floods the valleys and warms the rocks and earth, gentle updrafts of air will start to rise above the surrounding ridges. It is on these thermal currents that they will soon soar with ease.

So they sit quietly, not fretting or worrying about whether they will be taken aloft. They know they will be. They renew their strength while they wait.

This is the picture of a Christian passing through the dark hours of danger and discouragement. All around him he can sense the chill downdrafts of frustration and reverses. It seems God's face is hidden from him and he cannot see ahead. Yet he need not be despondent. Rather, this is the time to wait for the Lord, to rest in the confidence that He is true to Himself in utter faithfulness.

Then it is that the first rays of morning sunshine reach the crest of the cliff and touch the eagle's feathers. He shakes himself, fluffs his plumage and with new interest watches the valley below him fill with golden light. Since he knew this would happen, his calm waiting has restored his strength and renewed his vigor.

At first, almost imperceptibly, but growing ever stronger, he feels the warm air currents rising around him, lifting gently from the valley floor past his perch.

Presently the regal bird spreads his wings and launches himself confidently into space. At once the thermal currents are bearing up beneath his wings and he rides them splendidly. By deliberate effort the eagle keeps himself in the center of the updrafts, rising higher and higher, borne aloft, mounting ever upward until he is lost to sight.

What a sublime etching this is of the Christian in his relationship to God. On the outstretched wings of prayer and praise he launches himself out upon the promises of God, depending on the great updrafts of His faithfulness to bear him up.

It takes courage to do this. A daring act of faith is required for us to let go of the limb to which we have clung for so long and launch ourselves fearlessly into the great open space before us.

As the bird by the discipline of keeping his wings outstretched to catch every eddy of air mounts up with ease, so the Christian, if he would overcome, must school himself continually to spread his heart before God in an attitude of never-ceasing prayer and praise, looking to Christ.

The updrafts of God's faithfulness are forever. It is up to us to rest upon that faithfulness. This we can do only by holding ourselves in the center of His purpose through a deliberate and continuous attitude of prayer and praise.

Probably the thing that impresses anyone who has watched eagles soaring the most is the apparent ease and utter serenity with which they fly. Of course this would be impossible without the skill that comes from long practice.

The demands made upon the Christian who would lead a triumphant and serene life are no less exacting. The young believer will often grow weary. He or she will be tempted to relax vigilance.

One will be impulsive and prone to a faltering up-and-down experience. Like a young eagle, one will do a good deal of flapping and flopping around before he or she has mastered the art of continuous soaring. In fact, one might become quite exhausted and downcast on occasion from trying so hard to fly on one's own strength instead of just resting on God's faithfulness.

All these thoughts poured through my heart on that warm day. Evening was settling over the ridges, and I watched the proud birds circling slowly down toward the tree where I sat.

For them darkness was approaching, and in the cool of the night they would rest and wait upon the gnarled branch of the old pine, renewing the strength that had been spent in keeping their wings outstretched all day.

With the rising of the sun tomorrow they would mount up on fresh wings.

The glorious flight of the regal birds is not always without adversity. Eagles, too, have times when they are tested and tormented by rowdy attacks from lesser birds.

One day, hiking in the hills west of my cottage, I was astonished to see a mob of crows pursuing an eagle at treetop level. The daring "black jacks" would dive down on the beleaguered bird in angry attacks. Crow after crow hurtled down on the eagle like black bombers bent on destruction.

Though the great bird twisted and turned in mid-flight, lashing out in self-defense with sharp talons and rapier beak, he was no match for the infuriated mob of black bandits. They were doing their best to drive the regal eagle into the timber.

Suddenly, to my unbounded surprise, the great bird swooped up to a giant old snag that stood etched against the sky on a granite cliff. In a split second he had settled securely on a gnarled limb. He shook out his ruffled feathers, adjusted his strong stance, then peered about him with piercing eyes.

Instantly the crows called off their attack. As if by a supersensitive signal every one of the daring black acrobats peeled off from the attack to fly away in disarray. The monarch of the air was supreme where he stood, waiting calmly for any crow foolish enough to come within reach of his flashing, swordlike bill.

Standing there on the ancient, twisted tree, the eagle was again at ease. Every movement of his magnificent head and glowing eyes spoke of strength, assurance, power and prestige. He was waiting, ready for the worst that never came. He was in control again.

The eagle had shown that he was more than a match for any mob of crows trying to gang up on him. He was able to meet their attack and master their daring devices. But to do so he had long ago discovered he could do it best by simply waiting quietly in strength.

There was a most profound lesson for me in that brief episode that afternoon. The best of believers have those moments in life when suddenly they feel mobbed and harried by either adverse circumstances that suddenly arise on the horizon, or the cruel attacks of their contemporaries.

One simply cannot get through life without excruciating experiences of this kind. It is absolutely inevitable that there will be days when it seems we are going to be driven into destruction. People or events just do gang up on us. The irony of life is that calamities, like the crows, come in bunches of unexpected, rapid sequence, one rushing in upon another.

Often our first impulse is to flee or take flight. Somehow we want to take to the trees. We lash out left and right hoping to keep the destruction at bay. But we seldom succeed.

The more prudent move is to settle down in stillness, waiting quietly for the crisis to pass. This is not an easy decision to make. It often seems much more heroic to try to fight our way out of the fray. Yet that is not the best way.

The longer I live, the more often I discover that to wait patiently is the secret to power and peace. Standing quietly, serene in the strength that comes from knowing Christ, one can overcome. Wait upon the Most High. Trust in His remarkable wisdom. Let the strength of His Spirit support us. All will be well!

6
Snow-fed Streams

CLEAR, COLD, PURE water pouring out of the high country in constant, abundant supply is one of the exhilarating joys of the sky edge. Singing streams, tumbling waterfalls, roaring rivers all rumbling down their valleys are as eternal as the snowfields that comprise their source.

As long as winter and summer, springtime and autumn move majestically across the mountains, so will the snow-fed streams refresh the hills and nourish the valleys below. In the flowing water there is life and power and renewal for the earth.

In our rugged northern ranges the snow and rain have their origin in the uncharted, windswept reaches of the vast north Pacific. From out of the immensity of the ocean depths great winds pick up their burden of moisture and carry it aloft across the coast to set it down upon our western slopes. There in giant drifts of snow, some eighty feet deep, the precious moisture seeps into the soil and percolates gently into bubbling springs and melting freshets.

Ultimately, after weeks and months of travel down the mighty mountain valleys, the water returns again to the sea whence it came. The cycle is completed. The water has run its course. And there it lies again, ready to be borne aloft and carried over the land.

This powerful process is as ancient as the earth itself. It is as eternal as the tides. It is as enduring as the rock over which the water runs. All of these are relative aspects of a planet which had a specific beginning in time and will come to a significant end in future. But for the brief duration of our earth days it appears to us to be everlasting.

This is why poets, philosophers and mystics have always turned to the eternal hills for uplift and inspiration. It is why they have sought the solace of the sea in their soliloquies. It is why they have written and sung of flowing streams and deep-running rivers.

Instinctively man's soul seeks that which endures. His spirit yearns for something no longer transient but eternal. His innermost being longs to be identified with the everlasting, for in truth his spirit is indestructible.

Often, without shame or embarrassment, I have turned to the sky edge with its tumbling streams and melodious sounds to find solace for my soul, healing for my heart. There comes gentle strength and quiet assurance in the acute awareness that these upper springs have flowed undiminished, unchanged for ten thousand years. There can be renewal here at the edge of a snow-fed stream that flows from the rock with pristine purity as clean as the wind-driven snow on the summit.

Again and again, in a long lifetime of wilderness trails and testing mountain climbs, I have stooped to bury my face in the swift running rivulets of an upland stream. Long and deeply have I drunk of its cold delicious fluid. I have been refreshed, renewed, ready to push on again with the heavy pack on my back.

Besides the physical refreshment of a snow-fed stream, there is a unique and special quality to the music it makes: the murmuring of its soft flow beneath the stones; the muted tones of its gentle laugh as it tumbles over ledges of rock; its low rumble when it rolls the boulders in its bed in full flood. Depending on the mountain breezes, these sounds rise and fall with constant variations as if played by a celestial orchestra.

Yes, there is music in the mountains. There is uplift for the weary soul. Rejuvenation awaits the spirit ready to listen and be refreshed. This is music of divine origin. Its melodies caressed the creation long before man set foot on the scene. Its harmony can heal in wondrous ways. There is deep and profound therapy in the flow of water, in the songs of a stream.

Modern man, far removed from the natural balm of such a serene source of inspiration, is only just beginning to rediscover the wonders of running water. Creeping shyly out of the grim ghettos of their own building, a few are seeking solace at the sky edge where streams still run clear.

But we mountaineers have always known that there was help and healing in the high country. We have turned our tired feet toward the upward trails. We have found peace and rest and splendid strength in the streams that were suckled by the shining snow.

This was true for me when Harvie passed over "the great divide." When the final tribute had been paid to this splendid man, I turned to the high mountains and sought solace beside a rushing stream that carved a mighty channel through the untamed wilderness.

I needed desperately to be reassured that life could still go on flowing in strength as did this fine river. I needed to hear the pulsing, profound music that had endured an eternity and could be composed just as surely in my own agonizing soul. I needed to sense the power, the purity, the life, the potency that flowed from above.

My Father did not disappoint me. In the serenity and strength of that stream He spoke to me emphatically. He touched me in unmistakable terms.

It was a warm summer afternoon when I made camp near the stream. The heavy pungency of hemlock and fir needles, stressed by the sun, hung in the air. Underfoot a deep carpet of needles and cones cushioned my footfalls. Chipmunks scurried through the underbrush. And in the distance there played the soft music of the stream, its melodies drifting through the trees. It invited me to draw near, to listen to its song and drink of its coolness.

Taking a thick terry towel and my well-worn Testament, I started down the trail to the stream bank. Deer, bears and coyotes had made a well-used trail down to the water's edge. It ran over ancient, gnarled roots of poplars, pines and dense cedar thickets. Gently I worked my way along the stream until I found a giant slab of stone that jutted out into the swiftly moving current.

Here I spread my towel on the sun-warmed rock and stretched myself beside the singing waters. I was opening my soul to any message the stream might bring to me from my Father's great heart of compassion. Crushed with the departure of one I held so dear, I needed healing and restoration.

The first powerful impression that swept into my soul was the incredible clarity and pristine purity of the water pouring over the rocks all around me. The fluid was utterly transparent, so free of any contamination that I could see every pebble, every stone, every grain of sand in the stream bed.

This was virgin snow water, as cold as ice, as clear as the finest crystal. It surged down the valley cleansing, refreshing, stimulating every life form it touched.

"Exactly like the life of God!" I mused to myself. "The life that comes flowing to me from the eternal Christ is utterly pure—free of any pollution. It carries no silt, no mud, no debris, no contamination into the complexity of our earth days!"

With sudden, startling insight I realized that just as I had drawn near to this stream to drink deeply of its freshness, to plunge my face into its cooling depths, so Christ had invited me to come to Him and drink deeply of His invigorating, ever-abundant life. The source was inexhaustible, the supply ever new, the flow unceasing.

In a private, deliberate act of profound faith I lifted my face toward the slanting rays of the late afternoon sun and spoke softly: "Oh my Master, my Friend, my Father, I take of Your very life and drink it to the depths!"

In that moment I sensed the surge of His gracious Spirit flowing into mine to renew and revitalize my ravaged soul. The dynamic of divine life was restoring me.

The second compelling awareness that swept over me was the persistent power and vitality inherent in the flowing waters. They poured over the rocks in gushing torrents that tumbled the small stones along the stream bed. The flowing action wore away rock, shaped stones and carved even deeper in the hills the channel to the sea.

So it is with the great good will of God. It is an irresistible force in the universe that flows steadily to shape the destinies of us all. His intentions toward us are grand and good and noble. It is His great, persistent power that shapes our history and directs our days.

"The events He allows to intrude upon our little lives are not intended for our undoing," I murmured to myself in quiet soliloquy. "Rather they are intended to conform us to the greatness of His own wondrous character."

The sorrow, the suffering, the shaping of our lives would in time see the contours of our characters likened to His own lofty ideals and purposes for us as His people. Through the deep-cut valleys of our days His own sublime life could flow in refreshment to others who suffered as we did, who tramped the trail of tears that we had trod.

Almost immediately I became acutely aware that out of my own deep grief God could bring balm to other broken lives. He could flow through the anguish and agony of my loss to touch others in their loss.

As the sun warmed my body, caressed my face and sparkled in the stream, I was struck with the remarkable potency of the river. Everything it touched it transformed. There was vigor and vitality in every tree, shrub, blade of grass or mountain flower that flourished on its banks.

It was as if in loud, clear tones it stated boldly, *"Life-life-life!"* Here was the source, the strength, the surge of life itself poured out, spilling over, quickening everything it touched. From this singing, spilling, shining stream came the vitality of all the vegetation of the valley. More than even that, beyond the forest, grass and flowers, were the birds that dropped down here to drink; the wildlife that came here to slake their thirst; the solitary person who came to find new life to face the future.

"O Lord, my God, how generous You are; how gracious to this weary one; how merciful to a man deep in distress!" The words were not spoken aloud. They were the profound inner expression of a spirit being renewed by the gracious inflowing presence of the Living Christ.

He had come to me in the solitude of that high mountain stream and renewed my spirit. Vigor, vitality of divine origin swept into my soul bringing life, life—life from above—from the edge of the sky, from Himself.

It is not surprising that the grand old apostle John in his sublime vision of the eternal city of our God should see a shining stream flowing as a river of life from beneath the very mercy seat and eternal throne of God. There could be no more pure or poetic language in all the earth to describe the glory of the life of God flowing forever to His people.

What he had seen, I, too, in living reality had experienced on this still summer afternoon high in the mountains. New life, dynamic energy and fresh vigor filled my soul from the eternal source of God Himself.

As the evening sun settled slowly over the last high ridges of the sky edge, the warm rays laid a golden glow of sheer glory over the stream. Never in all my years in the wilderness had I seen flowing water take on such wondrous beauty. Breath-taking shades of green and gold, of blue and silver, flashed in the current and gleamed from the running waters.

It seemed almost every color of the spectrum shone like light glinting from a thousand gems that sparkled in the stream. Even the intense whiteness of the tumbling rivulets turned the whole scene into a dazzling display of artistic loveliness.

And again the vivid, moving, majestic realization came to me with shining clarity: *"Life does go on. Life can be beautiful. Life is touched with wonder . . . because of my Father's perpetual presence!"*

My part was to look for the glory of the Lord as it was reflected to my watching gaze from day to day. Just as the sun touched the stream and turned it into a glowing scene of dazzling beauty, so the effulgence of the glory of God could transform my little life into a thing of shining beauty and gentle wonder.

In the evening shadows I strolled back quietly to my camp. The Eternal One had touched my spirit with His Own that afternoon. Healing and help and hope had come flowing to my soul that assured me, *"All was well!"*

7
The Olalla Bush

LONG, LONG BEFORE the white settlers pushed their way across the prairies and into the western mountain region, wild serviceberries comprised an important part of the Indian's diet. The prolific purple fruit, similar in size and shape to the better known blueberries, was gathered in great quantities by the various tribes. Some of the berries were eaten fresh, but the greater portion, mixed with animal fat, were made into pemmican. Pemmican was the staple food used on the trail and consumed in severe winter weather.

Out on the prairies serviceberries generally grow as rather stunted shrubs clinging tenaciously to deep draws or cut banks in the coulees. There the hardy bushes find shelter from the blinding blizzards and cutting winds of the long harsh winter.

In our high mountain region with long valleys and sun-splashed slopes facing south, the serviceberry grows into a large imposing clump of sturdy brush. Some of these, in choice locations, will reach a height of fifteen feet, with an elegant vase shape that is almost as wide as it is tall. The long slender limbs are tough, durable wood that can endure the relentless lashing of the wind without ever breaking under its force.

Only when the bush has become very aged and dies from natural causes do the branches become gray and brittle. Then they will snap under the weight of heavy snow or give way if battered by a bull or shredded by a buck in rut.

The Indian name for our mountain serviceberry is the *Olalla*. It is a lovely name. Its lilting sound is suited to a shrub so beloved by both outdoorsmen and the wildlife of the hills. All winter the picturesque lacelike limbs, shorn of their little round leaves, stand in sharp silhouette on the white slopes where the snow lies deep. They decorate steep rock slides, deep rugged draws and unlikely barren spots where bears, coyotes or wild birds may have dropped the seeds in their dung.

No man, at least to my knowledge, has ever planted an Olalla bush for decoration. Yet in the spring of the year, which comes early in our sheltered upland valleys, the Olallas burst into clouds of delicate beauty. Fragrant clusters of creamy white blossoms decorate the slender branches, hanging in splendid profusion from every twig, like piles of puffed rice.

Their sweet nectar attracts swarms of bees and lesser insects to hover over the blossoms. A gentle, intense hum of wings fills the spring air as each bush welcomes the host of winged visitors. And all across the countryside the billowing white clumps of Olallas embellish the stark slopes and gray rock slides.

Soon the white petals fall in sparkling showers. The breezes blow them in snowy drifts across the ground. In their place come the first fruit and tender green leaves which are browsed eagerly by both game and livestock.

Rapidly the fruit forms. With astonishing speed the berries swell on the stem. If spring showers are frequent the limber branches soon begin to bend in graceful arcs beneath their heavy load of rich purple berries. In favorable spots the fruit is large and luscious, a banquet for birds, bears, coyotes, chipmunks and passing people.

Indian summer weather finally turns the Olalla leaves to burnished bronze. The edges, trimmed with brown, give the shrub the strange glow of a bush on fire when touched by the sun . . . yet not consumed by the incandescent glory of its own inner light.

One warm day this past summer I went in search of a special bush that I had marked carefully on one of my hikes. It stood all alone on a steep, stony slope far removed from any other bushes of its kind. It was laden with beautiful berries of unusual size. So when they were fully ripe I was determined to return and harvest the wild bounty.

The impressive size of this particular bush was enough to attract my attention. Only because it grew on such a steep slope was it possible to reach the bent limbs that hung down close to the ground on the upper side. There, in the thin shade of its rather sparse foliage, I could readily strip the abundant fruit from the arched branches. In no time at all, my large bucket was filled, heaped up and overflowing with the luscious fruit. Every berry was fully ripe, turgid with juice, sweet to the taste.

Before I had come that morning the wild ones had been there before me. The lower limbs, easily reached by cunning coyotes, had been stripped. The upper clusters had been picked over by the birds. So I was fortunate to find an ample abundance still remained for me to harvest.

As I picked my share I marveled at such bounty coming from an uncultivated, untended tree in such an unlikely spot. Here the soil was thin, stony, riddled with rocks, and baked by the relentless sun. The seasonal winds whipped the bush back and forth without mercy, lashing its limbs with every savage blow. And the heavy loads of winter snows fell upon the branches, bending some to the ground, drifting over its base with ice and frost.

In spite of all the adversities of its environment, all the abuse of rough weather, all the stresses of its stern and tough location, the Olalla bush flowered and fruited in this spot with joyous abandon.

It was a vivid, living demonstration of that ancient adage—"*Just bloom where you are planted!*" It sounds so simple. Sometimes it has an almost romantic touch to it. Like so many spiritual concepts it is often spoken too swiftly and glibly by someone who has never faced the fierce, formidable challenges of living a truly productive life in a most desolate and desperate environment.

Often as I have been out on the mountains, hiking hard on a remote ridge at the edge of the sky, it has startled me to come across a lone Olalla bush, bursting with blossoms or laden with delicious fruit. By the superb miracle of my Father's loving arrangement, beauty of bloom and a banquet of fruit have been distilled from the tough raw materials of stony soil, burning sunlight and hidden underground seeps of moisture.

On the gaunt granite He has laid out some of the most beautiful bouquets in all the earth. And there too He has turned rain, sunshine and gravel into the most delectable fruit and juice for the gentle refreshment of all who pass by.

Our modern preachers and hyper-evangelists urge us to demand our "miracles" from God. They rant at us to claim our rights and receive some sort of dramatic demonstration from the divine. They insist that only by special signs and wonders will the world ever come to acknowledge Christ as God very God.

He Himself told us no such spectacular displays were necessary to demonstrate His deity!

Instead He urged us to look around and quietly notice the lily of the field, the fledgling sparrow fallen from its nest, the Olalla bush blowing in the breeze. There in the ordinary events of the natural world around us lay a thousand miracles of His making, the lovely touch of our Father's care.

It is not that He chooses to deprive us of staggering, mind-bending demonstrations of His splendor. Rather, the difficulty is that we are so slow of spiritual perception, so dull of divine insight that we are impervious to the remarkable display of His magnificent prowess all around us. Eyes we have that do not see and ears that do not hear.

An avalanche lily, pure as the finest gold, pushes its lovely bloom through the snow on some remote mountain meadow. We simply nod our heads in momentary surprise, then stroll on—never considering that no man's hand had any part in such a spectacle, such a complex creation. A skein of geese, hurtling across the loftiest ranges at a steady 60 MPH, hour after hour, dead on course, without the aid of computers or other electronic gadgetry, will find their winter haven 4,000 miles to the south. A gorgeous Olalla bush all aglow in glorious attire, no matter the season—graceful lacework in winter, perfumed blooms in spring, purple with fruit in summer, ablaze with gold in fall—to us dull mortals is all just "part of the scene."

O, to have the scales of human skepticism stripped from our eyes now dimmed by the madness of our man-made media! O, to have the sensitivity of our spirits reborn after being so long imprisoned by the crude and crass culture of our cities! O, to have the strings of our souls stirred once more by the splendor and the glory of our God and Father which in fact fill all the earth!

It takes time, much time, precious time alone, in company with Christ, for the dynamic reality of His life and light and love to break through the darkness of our delusion and set us free. We do not need to seek some special services or attend some sensational staged event to witness the miracles of His power.

The glory of His grace, the loveliness of His presence can be seen even in the lowly beauty of an Olalla bush. He surrounds me with new miracles every morning.

It is such an acute awareness of Christ's presence in the world of plants and trees, grass and flowers, sun and rain, clouds and earth, moon and stars, sunrise and sunset that can enable the most ordinary person "to blossom where you are planted."

One of my dear friends is an elderly widow who lives in an austere retirement center in the very heart of the city. Endless traffic and crowds of pedestrians press in around her residence in a constant cacophony of noise and confusion. The halls she walks are dim, dark, haunted by aged people who for the most part have given up hope. Her own tiny room is almost like a narrow cell with a limited outlook between the building's concrete walls.

Yet in such a stark setting this loving lady pours out the perfume of her gracious personality upon every life she touches. Every day she is fit enough to get out, she takes walks to pick any stray flowers, or leaves, or even decorative wayside weeds she can find. These she brings back to share with others who are shut-ins, or in the hospital.

Every book, every pamphlet, every magazine that comes into her possession she passes on to someone else to enjoy. Her tiny figure is filled with laughter, fun and the joyous optimism of one who loves her Father and revels in His company. The sunshine of the sky, the wonder of the stars, the fragrance of flowers, the healing touch of trees and grass are reflected in gentle love from the soul and spirit of this saint.

Wherever she goes, she leaves behind a legacy of hope, of cheer, of good will to those she meets. Through her little life there radiates to all around her the character of Christ, the gentle glory of God. She, too, is a living miracle, a divine demonstration of our Father's life touching and transforming her life at the edge of the sky.

For she, too, is like the Olalla bush that blossoms where God has planted her, even among the indigent and dying all around her.

8
Trees above Timber Line

ONE OF THE rare and special thrills of hiking in high country is to break out above timber line into the stillness and solitude of the alp-lands. These lofty alpine meadows lie at the sky edge, wedged between the trees at lower levels and the soaring ice slopes sharp against the sky.

As a younger man I spent weeks and months in these "gardens of God." It was here, where ramparts of rock, ice and snow stood in majesty above the wildflower fields that I stalked the monarch of the mountains, the Grizzly, and the Mountain Caribou, the Bighorn Sheep and hardy Mountain Goats. I was studying their life habits, recording their migration routes, filming the intimacy of their day-to-day behavior.

Amid such grandeur I was always stirred by the solitary trees that found footing and flourished in this harsh and rugged upland realm. Occasionally the trees grew utterly alone, clinging tenaciously to some crack in a cliff or standing sturdily on a rock outcrop where wind and weather lashed them mercilessly. More often they grew in little clusters, a few unyielding individuals giving mutual support to each other in the exposed and perilous paths of hail, sleet, snow and roaring winds.

Unlike animals, birds or men, trees simply cannot shift or move about to protect themselves from the adverse vagaries of weather. Rooted to one spot they must stand there and survive the onslaught of sun, wind, snow, storms, blizzards and all the ravages of time and tempest. The passing seasons and pressure of environmental forces so move upon the tree that often it barely survives the stresses and strains of its formidable setting.

Such solitary trees, wind-twisted and storm-tossed, are not always the perfectly shaped specimens of their kind.

To the onlooker they may appear contorted, misshapen, yes, sometimes even broken and blasted by ice and hail and winter gales. Yet they own a special glory born of adversity. They reflect a unique strength that has stood the stress of a thousand mountain storms. They possess a beauty that can emerge only out of great agony and solitary suffering.

It is this steadfast character of the tough trees above timber line that has elicited my own personal awe, respect and interest. It is this unique quality of grandeur that fascinates the photographer; that excites the artist; that arrests the passerby.

Standing alone at the sky edge, the sturdy trunks, dwarfed and shortened by so much snow and ice, often appear compressed by the constriction of such an arctic climate. The branches, beaten and battered by nonrelenting wind with sleet in its teeth and snow on its wings, seem stubby and foreshortened. Here, one may have been torn away in a roaring gust. There, another may have been bent and twisted like a knotted arm held up in bold defiance against the storms of life. Sometimes the crown has been broken in a winter avalanche of snow and a new leader has emerged to push its twisted trunk into the clouds and mist that swirl through the peaks.

Still the trees survive. Still their sparse foliage reflects the upland sun. Still they stand silhouetted in royal splendor against their gaunt backdrop of snow fields, rock ridges and shining skies at the edge of the horizon. Still they put on new wood from season to season.

In their quiet fortitude lies a stirring example of the benefits of adversity. In their unusual beauty, mortal man can discover something of our Father's grand design for shaping special people.

First of all, it is of more than passing interest that these trees of unusual inspiration are not a part of the full forest of the lower slopes. They are rugged individuals set apart from the common crowd that make up the usual stand of timber. Isolated from their fellows, they are often rooted in some remote spot where they must stand alone against the storms. They do not enjoy the shelter of ten thousand other trees that might offer respite from the wind or shade from the sun.

Their life is spent in the solitude of the sky edge.

Their seasons are passed in the rare upland realm of the alplands.

Their life must be lived in the maelstrom of stress at the extreme edge of survival.

And in the economy of God, the same is true of those who are willing to live separated lives, apart from the common crowd of our human society. There is such a thing as being too sheltered by our "comfortable culture"—too coddled by our contemporaries, too indulged by our affluent age.

If certain of us are going to be shaped into special specimens of rare quality, it calls for some suffering alone. Rugged strength is not developed in the soft security of our associates. There has to be that deep grounding of our lives in the very bedrock of Christ's character if we are to endure the blasts of adversity.

Christian leaders speak too easily, too glibly, too romantically of "getting onto higher ground with God." It is almost as if they are inviting their listeners to take a stroll into a summer rose garden.

To get onto a higher life with the Risen Christ demands great discipline from the disciple. It calls for separation from the world's soft and cozy associations. It means strong self-denial, standing alone in noble, lofty living. It entails suffering, sorrow, pain and the drastic endurance of adversity.

Christ came to us as "a man of sorrows and acquainted with grief." He was one cut off from the comfortable, easy companionship of His contemporaries. He stood alone in His suffering that He might prove to us the unfailing fortitude of the living God. Despite the worst the world could hurl at Him, He emerged triumphant—beaten, broken, bruised on our behalf, yet able to bring us to Himself in great glory.

If we of the late twentieth century are to claim His name, then it is incumbent on us to be prepared to be His separate people. The indulgent, soft, cozy church of our day does not challenge Christians to come out from the corrupt culture of our times. It does not demand that we stand boldly, bravely against the blasts of adversity which are bound to assail us. It prefers to keep us soft, sheltered, comfortable and complacent in our padded pews. There we can have our good fellowship, good fun and good food without ever facing the fury of the fierce elements in the world.

Those prepared to be apart, strained and stressed by the agonies of our age, are few and far between. Those who will endure hardship in solitude are rare indeed. Those who, despite the suffering, will stand strong are as thrilling to encounter as any wind-shaped tree at the sky edge.

One dear couple, longtime friends of mine, are of this caliber. Both in their late eighties, bent and beaten by the storms of life, they live in noble dignity. She is blind. He is crippled with arthritis, both hip joints replaced with artificial sockets. Yet every week at tremendous personal pain they visit the aged. She plays the piano while he sings lustily to lift the spirits of those downcast. Season after season, sun or snow, they visit in children's camps to bring inspiration to the young.

This is what it means to live on the high ground of God's choosing apart from the crowd.

This is what it means to see the beauty of the Most High expressed in the humble conduct of His followers.

This is to encounter something of the very character of Christ in a common woman and man of rare loveliness.

Thus amid all the lashing storms of life and winds of adverse suffering there is demonstrated the noble faithfulness of our Father who empowers them to prevail. We look on in awe and wonder, moved and inspired by their brave fortitude, their quiet faith in Christ, their flowing love that uplifts a hundred other hearts.

Turning back to the trees above timber line we see a second dimension to their growth not often recognized by the casual passerby.

It is the rare and elegant quality of the actual wood produced within the wind-tossed tree. Its grain is of exquisite texture interspersed with whorls and curving lines of unusual gracefulness. The stresses and strains of being tossed and twisted by the wind and sleet and deep snows of winter produce an extra flow of resins in the tree. Not only does this give the fibers a remarkable tight-grained texture but it gives off also an exquisite fragrance.

An expert violin maker, who is a master craftsman, tells me that he spends weeks each summer searching for special trees above timber line. From these he takes his choicest material to create musical instruments of the finest quality and tone.

Wood produced in the high and tough terrain above the usual timber stands bears within it a rare timbre and lovely resonance not found in ordinary lumber cut at lower elevations. The fury of storms, the shortness of the growing season, the wrenching of the winds, the strain of survival in such an austere setting—all these combine to produce some of the toughest, choicest, most wondrous wood in all the world.

Here is wood grown on a gaunt rock ridge on some remote mountain range that one day will grace a violin, cello or guitar in Lincoln Center. From those tree fibers will come the finest music ever made by man. Its melodies and notes will enrich a thousand listeners, and, by modern communication, encircle the globe to inspire a million more.

But it all began with a sturdy tree, set apart, growing slowly, unknown, all alone on a distant hill against the sky edge.

Precisely the same principle is true for us as God's chosen people. Choice characters, fragrant lives, rare quality of life are not produced without the strain of sorrow and the suffering of adversity. Some of us will have to endure privation in personal isolation and more than likely without any public acclaim. Most of our inner anguish of soul is borne alone in the solitude of our own lives. We are not public performers, playing to a rapt but fickle audience.

Our greatest griefs are more often than not those of the spirit. Our stresses come most painfully within the very fibers of our souls. The agonizing separation within that attends the onslaught of suffering, the agony of losing loved ones, the betrayal of friends can be healed only by the gracious ministrations of God's own Gracious Spirit. But He does bind us up. He does inject His own presence into our lives. He does enable us to grow more beautiful, more gracious, more resonant with His compassion.

The end result is that our own characters do become more desirable. We do mature into men and women of wondrous warmth. We do, little by little, develop into fit material for the Master's use.

And out of it all, one day, there will emerge celestial music and glorious melodies that can enrich and uplift others clear around the earth because we grew at the sky edge.

9
Fire on the Mountains

VIRTUALLY EVERY MOUNTAIN in our region has, at some time or other, been scorched by fire. Ridge after ridge bears the ancient scars, now healed over, of drastic lightning strikes. Here and there, because of intense mineralization in the rock formation, numerous old twisted trees are splintered and shattered on the sky edge where the high voltage electrical charges went to ground.

During the severe heat of our long summer weather it is common for gigantic cumulus clouds to build up over the ranges. Out of these huge "thunderheads," with their intense electrical energy, lightning flashes across the uplands and thunder rolls in the deep valleys. It is a moving and majestic display of formidable power in the high country.

Sometimes the electrical display will last for several hours. Blinding light of blue-white intensity illuminates every tree, shrub, rock and peak in vivid clarity. It is a celestial display a thousand times more majestic than any manmade carnival creation with its gaudy lights.

As the thunder rumbles across the high ridges it resembles the approach of the apocalypse. The tremendous sounds reverberate across the mountains, echo from the canyon walls and boom against the rocks like gunfire in giant battle. When thunder is close by, the earth trembles in the tumult and trees toss about in the tempest of the gusting winds that accompany the electrical storms.

Lightning bolts crash to earth. Fingers of fire like a cougar's long claws reach for the ridges and zigzag across the sky edge. Rocks are shattered. Trees are split and splintered. Dry brush, grass and forest duff explode in flames.

It is all an ancient part of the natural weather forces that have shaped our lofty upland world. Fire has always been a formidable factor in controlling forest growth, regulating the succession of plant communities in the region and removing excessive stands of undesirable timber growth.

Even the primitive Indian races seemed to understand and grasp the benefit of burning off part of the wilderness every year. This way the region was being given the chance to be cleared of undesirable undergrowth. The raging fires removed and consumed low-quality ground cover like cheat-grass and knap-weed that invaded the upland ranges. The searing heat destroyed ravening insect populations and gave the high country a chance for a whole new generation of pioneer plants to be reborn out of the cinders and ashes that remained.

The emergence of new forage and the growth of fresh grass fertilized by the abundant mineral content of the ashes, the stimulation of new and nutritious shoots and seedlings from the scorched earth, all combine to produce a bountiful wildlife habitat that attracts birds and animals in large numbers. This all made for good hunting and in more recent times for better grazing.

Modern forest and range management is beginning to use "controlled burning" as a means to improve and enhance the natural habitat. But before that concept came into use, forest and brush fires were somehow always considered to be a great evil—probably because they were regarded as a profligate waste of valuable timber or the destruction of worthwhile watersheds where dense forest cover is desirable for percolation purposes.

When I was a very young man, one of my early adventures in the western mountains was to work on a fire crew in the Cascade Mountains of Washington. It was a startling and exciting introduction into the high country. The elements of danger and daring that such work demanded nourished my eager spirit of adventure. I fully believe no person has truly lived who has not, at some time, risked his or her very life in a cause greater than himself or herself.

Everything within my make-up responds energetically to the tough demands of a great challenge. My mind is quickened; my emotions are stirred; my will is set like steel to take the test, to run the risk, to overcome the obstacle.

To be on the fire line in midsummer under a blazing sun with the normal outside temperature around 100 degrees is a testing ordeal. Thirst becomes a terrible torture. One's throat is dry and sore as if seared by a hot iron. Excessive perspiration soaks shirts and trousers, leaving the body limp with lassitude. Tears stream from smoke-filled eyes. Often they are irritated and inflamed from cinders, ash, dust and particles of partially burned debris that float in the hot air.

Feet swell in soot-smudged boots heated from tramping across the scorched earth and blackened, smoking soil. Hair and skin are singed. Face and hands are grimed with streaks of sweat and soot, leaving one looking like a derelict, his stained clothes all askew.

> This is a measure of a man's mettle.
> Here a man's spirit shows true.
> What a test of character and will!
> This is where a daring spirit glows bright.
> Here there is no place for quitters.

All of this is lived out against a raging inferno of crackling flames that rushes through the trees, sweeps up the slopes in a wall of fire, then explodes in the branches above. Showers of burning twigs, glowing bits of flaming bark and cones fall to the forest floor. Huge clouds of blue and black smoke billow up from the burning debris. The sky darkens. The sun is shaded and a great rushing wind develops from the up-draft of the fire's ferocious heat.

Deer, bears, bobcats and a dozen other residents of the ridges smell the smoke and flee for their lives. Birds take wing and fly toward distant ranges.

All seems to be ruin and desolation.

But things are not always as they appear.

For out of this fire on the mountain, new life will emerge. New growth will come. A fresh forest will be re-created.

Perhaps the most dramatic demonstration of this process in modern times is the renewal of life on the devastated slopes of Mount Saint Helens. Biologists and environmentalists have been startled and delighted to see the incredible resurgence of new life in areas utterly devastated and burned over by the volcanic eruption.

Our lofty western mountains have been born and shaped by fire. Their very character and contours are the end product of burning. Their grand silhouettes against the sky, their mantles of forest cover, grassy ranges and glorious alp-lands all have been shaped by fire. Even the shining "silver forests" of stark fire-scorched trees with their blazing carpets of native wildflowers came to beauty by their burning.

I have mused much over this phenomenon in the natural realm. There is much to meditate over as one sits quietly beside a little campfire in the evening. The gentle crackle of the flames; the inviting warmth of the burning wood; the sweet fragrance of the blue smoke; the pungency of pine sap and spruce gum filling the night air—all promote long thoughts and deep reflection.

There is something profoundly primitive about man and fire. His most ancient traditions and oldest roots are shaped by fire. All the struggles to survive, the preparation of food, the shelter against the bitter wind and biting cold are bound up with fire. Beyond all this the celebration of life, the joy of comradeship, the intimacy of family ties, the offering of sacrifices and incense were entwined with fire—and still are.

Is it any wonder our Lord God sometimes refers to Himself as fire? Are we startled to see so many references in His Own divine revelation to us, as His earth children, that He comes to us as fire? Is it not understandable that even of old He would choose to appear to His chosen ones in flames of fire?

It was a flame of fire that moved among the pieces of Abraham's ancient sacrifice. It was fire and smoke and a great burning that descended in power on Mount Sinai when God's presence came down upon the sacred mountain. It was a divine flame that fell upon Mount Carmel to consume Elijah's bullock as well as even the water and stones of the altar. It was prophesied by John the Baptist that when Christ came He would bring fire on the earth. And visible, tangible evidence of the truth was clearly seen when flames of fire appeared upon the disciples on the Day of Pentecost in the upper room.

In the divine economy of the Most High, fire is an inescapable part of the impact of His presence on us.

That is a comparatively simple statement to make on paper. The reader may pass over it rather lightly. But its true spiritual implications, for the person prepared to take God seriously, are enormously profound.

Most of us do not take the bold, somewhat blunt statements of Scripture very seriously when they speak of fire in the life of the Christian. Too often these comments are relegated to romantic imagery or regarded as rather primitive language for conveying the idea of light, warmth or comfort to man.

We really do not want to deal with the dire results that a genuine conflagration of celestial burning might have on our cozy culture. The modern church of the late twentieth century in North America knows virtually nothing about fire on the mountain. Our fire suppression equipment has become so sophisticated, so ready on standby, so swift to respond to the first spark that smolders, that the Glorious Spirit of the Living Christ can hardly get a good blaze started in any soul!

The fierce burning that comes with shattering conviction of sin is scarcely known today. The sweeping, searing flames of fear of divine judgment and inescapable justice from a righteous God are no longer in the land. The intense inner fires of purification and cleansing and change that once swept through the souls of men like Wesley, Whitfield and Wilberforce are well-nigh a bed of ashes in the comfortable company of the contemporary church.

Where are the men and women today who do actually offer up their lives as a living sacrifice to be consumed in the flames of expendable service to the Most High? Where do we find those willing to be purged and purified by the in-rushing, invading, burning presence of God's Holy Spirit? Where do we see people so cleansed by the incandescent life and light and love of Christ that the corrupt culture of our times does not taint their souls nor stain their spirits?

The incoming of Christ's presence in power and great glory is a burning, scorching, searing experience that utterly changes the contours of our characters. Once we have been exposed to the fire of God's own purifying presence the old debris and detritus are destroyed, wiped out, purged from our lives. We are never, ever, the same again.

Only the burning, explosive, raging fires of God the Holy Ghost are ever going to clear the cheat-grass, the knap-weed, the thistles and thorns out of our tangled lives. The time has come when the fierce up-drafts of the wind of His Spirit need to sweep through our comfortable churches and compel people to fall on their faces in humble contrition. The day is long overdue when the fire from above flashes across the skies of our times to come crashing with lightning bolts into the stony ground of our rock-hard hearts. The hour is here when as a rotten society of overindulgent people we again hear the roar and rumble of the majestic voice of our Father calling us to be a cleansed and, respectfully, separate church.

Often as I hike alone in these high hills I cry out to the Most High to descend upon us in great power. I beseech Him to "break out" upon us with a fierce burning. I implore Him to release His Sovereign Spirit to sweep freely and fiercely across the earth convincing men of sin, righteousness and judgment to come.

Unless this happens there can be no renewal.

Only the purifying presence of the Lord God Himself will ever deliver us from our decadence. He alone can bring us new life, new vitality, new beauty.

There has to be fire on the mountains again.

10
Stillness

FOR SOME OF us the great glory of the high ridges and alpine basins is the sense of utter stillness and quiet grandeur that pervades the sky edge. The mountains were a realm rather far removed from the encroaching noise and clamor of human commerce and industry.

To a degree this is still true. Yet the formidable truth is that even the mountain stillness is being shattered by the increasing invasion of humanity and its mobile equipment. The scream of chain saws, the roar of bulldozers, the thunder of helicopters, the chatter of all-terrain vehicles, the blast of snowmobiles all combine to devastate the pristine stillness of the high country.

One has to go farther and farther afield to find secluded valleys or virgin ranges not yet ravished by the ruthless, grasping hands of modern "civilization." Logging roads and fire trails, recreational developments, mining operations and high-power transmission lines have spun a web of human technology across the wilderness. So it becomes ever more difficult to find a spot where stillness, quietness and true wilderness tranquillity prevail.

But here and there such precious places do remain. The area immediately adjacent to my present home is one of them. Just down the country road that winds through our upland valley is one of the largest radio telescopes in the west. It was located in that lovely mountain basin because of its seclusion. No aircraft are allowed to fly over the area. No chain saws, snowmobiles, dirt bikes or all-terrain vehicles are permitted. No commercial development is to be countenanced.

Here unusual peace prevails. And most of the time a serene stillness enfolds the valley.

As more and more people crowd the planet, it is inevitable that they must adjust to the ever-increasing noise of their civilization. This is especially true of larger metropolitan areas and industrialized urban centers. In those places noise is a way of life. It is a major part of the pressure which makes existence for millions stressful and painful—even though they may not be aware of this tension in their man-made environment.

In such a setting, try as he or she may, it is most difficult for any individual to think long thoughts—to meditate quietly over eternal verities, or even consider carefully the ultimate destiny of day-to-day decisions.

This explains why all through human history, if men were to be set aside for special service to their people, it was demanded that they first find some solitude and stillness where they could commune with their Creator. The ancient patriarchs, the flaming prophets of former times, the seers with burning eyes and great visions, the chosen saints with their profound spiritual perception were invariably those who had found the stillness of the high places, there to listen quietly to the soft solicitations of God's Gracious Spirit.

It is noteworthy that even Christ Himself, when He was here among us, continually separated Himself from the clamor of the crowds. He simply had to detach Himself from the pressure of people and the crush of the cities to find solitude on the mountain slopes. Nor is it mere accident that we are told this again and again by those who were closest to Him.

Finding stillness was an essential part of His life.

He did not neglect this exercise.

It was something He did continually at personal cost and the risk of gross misunderstanding.

It was the sure guarantee that His character would not be compressed or deformed by His contemporaries.

It was in the stillness of the night that He gave Himself to prayer, to meditation and to quiet spiritual communion with His Father. These were interludes of inspiration, uplift and restoration for His spirit.

If such moments were precious to Him, how much more so it must be true for us! It is in these quiet times that we can be open and receptive to the still, small voice of the Most High.

Of course we must recognize that not everyone has the opportunity to slip away into some secluded spot. Some are literally imprisoned in the canyons of concrete and steel that comprise our great cities. Millions more are cramped like cliff-dwellers in their high-rise apartments of brick and glass. So they have little choice but to find a private little nook someplace wherein a particle of privacy may be experienced for a few fleeting moments.

They have my utmost compassion. And, were I restricted as they are, it is quite certain my free spirit would soon be fractured. Within a few weeks my life would waste away in anguish.

For some of us, stillness, solitude and the vast immensity of great open spaces are the very breath of life itself. It is there, and only there, that we seem to discover the wellsprings of our spiritual well-being; the source of our strength in God our Father; the consolation of Christ to heal our deepest wounds; the comradeship of His Spirit to accompany us through the dark valleys of life.

This was utterly true for me when Harvie went on ahead into the realm of repose prepared for him. I needed desperately to rediscover the deep roots of my being in God. I needed stillness in company with Christ to restore my soul. I needed the strong solace of God's Spirit in the place of quietness.

As Harvie's physical strength diminished and the awareness of his imminent departure became ever more acute, I was in need of special grace to face this tearing wound in the fabric of life. There had to be divine reassurance that "all was well" when really from a purely human perspective a great gash of grief was gouging its way through my soul.

He had been such a noble man, so kind in attitude, so full of fun, so delightful to be with. It was unlikely anyone would be soon found to take his place in my affections as a friend.

In agony of spirit I sought for solace at the sky edge. Again and again my feet were turned to the high-country trails that lead away from the scenes of so much sorrow. I simply had to be alone—alone with my inner thoughts, alone with the utter loneliness of my spirit. Alone, yet not alone—for in the stillness of a lofty valley I sensed and knew the presence of my God.

There in the bright, brittle heat of early afternoon I took shelter in the shade of some high altitude trees growing beside a tiny mountain stream. Not unlike Elijah of old I cast myself down in their cool shadows in anguish of soul. It was not out of self-pity but out of a sense of profound pain at the apparent pointlessness of life. It was all so fleeting, so transient, so fragmented. Nothing appeared to endure, to last, to stand the passage of time.

What were the excruciating events of life doing to the contours of my character? This was not the first time I had passed through the searing flames of grievous losses in the circle of my family and friends. Again and again grief, separation and deep personal pain had swept through my life. What was the profound purpose in it all?

As I lay inert in the shade of the wind-stunted trees a gentle breeze began to blow through their boughs. It was cool, fresh, clean, coming from the snow-sheathed peaks that glistened white and blue above me. At first the movement of air was so light, so delicate, so nebulous, it seemed only an illusion. Its very essence only seemed to intensify the stillness of the hour.

But that mountain breeze bore on its gentle breath a message more moving than any I ever heard in any man-made sanctuary of steel and concrete. It spoke to my spirit in tones as clear and concise as any borne to me by the thrilling notes of a great organ:

> *"All the earth is in constant change.*
> *Even these majestic mountains weather away.*
> *The granite rocks are worn down by water.*
> *The giant valleys grow ever deeper.*
> *No tree, no shrub, no flower endures.*
> *The clouds come and go. So, too, night and day.*
> *The birds take wing. The insects perish.*
> *Even the bear, the buck and the chattering chipmunk*
> *are here but a breath in time.*
> *All is change. All is passing. All is perishable.*
> *Be still and know that I am God.*
> *Only I endure. Only I remain. Only I change not!"*

In utter silence of spirit I lay prostrate. In total quietness of soul I remained silent. In complete surrender of body I did not move a muscle.

I, a mere man, was alone with my Maker.
It was from Him that I had come.
It was to Him that I would return.
He and He alone was from everlasting to everlasting.

Only in Him was there life eternal that could surmount all the exigencies of my little life. Like the breeze from the snowfields, His very life enfolded me on every side.

From the day of my creation He had breathed into my being the very breath of His own eternal Spirit. All my life He had sustained and supported me by that same still Spirit that surrounded me on every hand and pursued me along every trail I took. Now in the face of death He, the Gracious Spirit of the Eternal God, in wonder and awe opened my tear-dimmed eyes to behold again the glory and hope our Father gives His children as they cross over to the other side.

He and only He could prepare for us a place of peace.
Soon Harvie would be there to repose in quietness.
The struggle and strain to survive would be over.
All would be well.
All was well!

He was here. . . . Peace!

The cooling breeze picked up strength as the quiet hours passed. It moved through the trees as surely as the breath of a master musician drawing lovely notes from his woodwind instrument. There was music in the wind, celestial music of the Master's making. It brought solace, comfort and healing to my aching heart. There was divine therapy in the gentle movement of the air that cooled my fevered face and dried my tear-stained cheeks.

When I first came to this still spot, it seemed I was so much, so very much alone. In the agony of my anguish, like Mary on the resurrection morn, it seemed no one else was there. Through her tear-blinded eyes she saw only dimly the outline of the empty tomb, the grave shapes of the gaunt gray olive trees.

But in that grim garden there was also the Lord of Glory—her Master—Rabboni. He spoke her name and she knew Him. In ecstasy she fell at His feet. And so, too, did I on this sparse mountainside.

There broke through again into my awareness the acute revelation: "O Christ, You never do leave us; You never do abandon us to the vagaries of life's constant changes; You never do let us tramp the trail of tears alone. You are ever near, ever dear, ever here."

Slowly, but surely, the long hours of that long summer day slipped by. Steadily the sun sank lower and lower in the western skies until it almost touched the horizon at the sky edge. For the first time that day I felt strong enough to rise and freshen my face with the cool water that ran in the tiny stream at my feet.

I bared my legs to the sun and let the mountain breeze run its fingers through my tousled hair. New vigor, fresh vitality, supernatural life began to course through my being. In quietness and in peace my strength was being restored. I was in the hills alone yet not alone, for there my strength was coming from my Father.

Suddenly a beautiful butterfly fluttered down the stream bed. It settled on my sun-warmed leg. There it paused briefly to preen itself and fold its gorgeous wings in quiet contentment. What a flash of glory, a splash of light, a touch of wonder to a wounded spirit!

Then from the rock-ribbed slope above me came the clear call of a Vesper Sparrow singing in a stunted spruce. The sun settled behind the western ranges. Long shadows crept down the valley as darkness began to descend.

But the sparrow's liquid notes filled the darkening twilight. The melodious tones rippled down the hill to me. Truly this was a song in the night! The grief was gone. In the stillness God had touched my sorrow. In the dawn there would be a new song in its stead.

11
The Season's First Heavy Snow

AUTUMN COMES GENTLY into our segment of the western mountains. Very seldom does the warm weather season end abruptly with the advent of raging blizzards or crushing ice storms as happens in some high country.

The progressive pageantry of fall colors and wildlife movements is one of the most magnificent natural spectacles on the continent. It may not be quite as sensational as the sudden flaming of the famous eastern hardwoods. But it is much more majestic because of the magnificent mountain backdrop that surrounds us on every side.

Indian summer can be the most glorious season of the entire year. The golden days splashed across the sleepy upland valleys are in a mellow mood. A soft blue haze hangs in the warm atmosphere. Ridge after ridge rises against the sky edge in serried ranks, each a little more faint—and lighter blue—as it reaches the farthest horizon.

The stunningly clear desert skies are alight with stars at night, sharp with the first frost and alive with the haunting, lilting cries of the coyotes. The same wide skies by day ring with the ancient, thrilling call of Sandhill Cranes crossing the mountains, of Canada Geese in wavering V's moving southward from the icy arctic.

In the mountain draws Vine Maples and Western Sumac flame like fire against the golden bunch grass hills. Along the streams and lakes, groves of Trembling Aspens and beautiful Black Birch are pure gold or burnished bronze. On the rock ridges Western Larch, some two hundred feet tall, wave their brilliant banners against the blue skies.

Little lakes and upland ponds are so still, smooth and shiny at this special time their surfaces shine silver like polished mirrors. Only here and there a flock of ducks or a passing deer, pausing to drink, will disturb the scene.

It is all so serene, so peaceful, so calm one could wish this gentle season would endure much longer than it does. Then one morning there is a glistening mantle of immaculate white draped softly over the highest crest of the loftiest peaks. The sky edge is adorned with the first fresh snow to touch the earth this autumn.

Though so far away, it is a clear, shining signal that the mountains are beginning to cool down. The gradual drop in temperatures is a gentle warning that winter is approaching. And with the advent of the icy season, strong winds, darkening skies and heavy snowstorms will move in from the gray immensity of the Gulf of Alaska.

The advance breezes that blow down the slopes are brisk and chill. They rattle the aspen leaves, stripping them from the white-barked trees. The gusting winds whine in the pines sending down showers of brown needles, old cones, bits of bark and broken twigs. The maples, sumac, birches and larch are shorn of their glowing foliage. Now they stand stark and bare, their dark gray frameworks gaunt against the lowering skies.

Hard frost turns the last green grass a soiled and saddened brown. Ice begins to creep across the lakes and ponds locking them in a gray shell. Bit by bit the whole upland world is transformed into a realm of rock-hard soil frozen solid. An eerie silence steals across the valleys. The songs of birds are stilled. All the earth is waiting for winter.

Then one night it comes!

Snow begins to fall. Ten million times ten million drifting flakes, each perfect and distinct in pattern, float down out of the heavy overcast. They drift down through the trees, settle among the shrubs, adorn every twig, cone, blade of grass or stone upon the ground.

The storm is not noisy. It does not come in with roaring force or thundering tones. It is almost imperceptible, yet utterly irresistible. Flake by flake, moment by moment, hour upon hour, it impresses itself upon the entire landscape.

Nothing escapes its impact. The whole world is suddenly being transformed by the pervasive whiteness. Everywhere the contours of the countryside are softened and smoothed with the enfolding mantle that crowns every stone, stump or broken fence rail.

Inch by inch the snow deepens. Two, four, five, perhaps even seven or maybe ten inches will settle out of the first heavy storm. Glowing pristine pure, it lies unmarked by a solitary track, untouched by a single hand. For a few brief moments before break of dawn the land lies immaculate in its dazzling whiteness.

Nothing stirs.

It is a moment of magnificent splendor.

A total transformation has come over the earth.

Exquisite loveliness has erased every scar upon the land. The last trace of waste, the worst signs of damage and devastation are covered over by the gracious mantle of gleaming purity.

As the sun breaks through from behind the scattering storm clouds a trillion sequins sparkle on the surface of the snow. Uncounted jewels of ice crystals catch the early light and reflect it in brilliant hues like a million diamonds shining in the sun.

Yesterday I went out to walk alone in the silence that follows such a snowfall. I climbed a remote ridge that stood sentinel above a broad upland basin of rolling hills. The whole world was wrapped in white, pensive, pure and still unmarked by man or his machines.

It was a morning to think long thoughts—as far-reaching as the distant views that stretched fifty miles to the far horizons of the sky edge. These were precious moments to muse over the meaning of life. They provided a gentle interlude in which I could be open and receptive to the soft, still impulses of God's Gracious Spirit.

It came home to me with intense clarity, equal to the brightness all about me, that just as the earth needed this great snowfall to make it utterly lovely, so, too, my life needed the enfolding purity of Christ's life to cover all my deficiencies. The ancient prophet of old, Isaiah, spoke of this in eloquent and moving language when he declared on God's behalf:

> *"Come now, and let us reason together,*
> *saith the* LORD: *though your sins be as scarlet,*
> *they shall be as white as snow"* (Isaiah 1:18).

There just have to be times in a person's life when the past is past, when bygones are bygones, when the gaunt, gray, forlorn memories of a former glory are buried under the supernatural loveliness of a new life from above.

For all of us there have to be new beginnings. There have to be fresh moments when we stand on a new height of land and look with widening eyes upon fresh vistas of our Father's great intentions for us. He and He alone can come down upon our soiled souls, our grieving spirits, our wounded hearts to enfold them in His wondrous ways.

As an author it is natural that I should always see life like a book. It is an unfolding tale that is being told chapter by chapter. Though it may appear superficially as one continuous whole, in reality it is not, for each of our lives is fragmented into segments. Each section has a significant beginning and a very specific end. And when that chapter is closed, it is closed! Then comes the time to move on to new adventures, to tackle new challenges, to reach for new insights, to find wider service with the Most High.

Just as summer gives way to fall, then in turn autumn is superseded by winter, so in the life of God's person there are succeeding steps by which we are led to follow Christ and pass from scene to scene in the grand pageantry of His purposes for us.

Summer is not fall. Nor is the autumn winter. Each is a season to itself. Each has a special splendor of its own. But likewise each has the fall-out of wasted opportunities, squandered time, wrong choices and willful waywardness that mar the memories of our better moments.

From time to time these demand a drastic change. There has to be a clean-up of the clutter, a renewal of the soul, a cleansing of the conscience, a fresh effulgence of Christ's life from above and a new falling of God's Spirit upon us to bring beauty into our spirits.

Like the chill winds of November, the stern events of our little lives can quickly make our days seem gaunt with grief and grim with the struggle to sustain enthusiasm. Some seasons it seems sorrow is added to sorrow until only the gray framework remains of what had once been beautiful and bright adventures. In the past eighteen months my wife and I have shared in the deepening gloom of no fewer than fourteen families who faced the scourge of terminal illness.

At such times of stress and distress a man needs more than sentiment or sympathy. He needs more than pious platitudes or easy pleasantries. He needs God—in all His majesty and glory and might!

Only the transforming touch of the Risen Christ upon the life can change the dark contours of the circumstances. He alone can descend upon the darkness of the soul in sorrow, bringing exuberant brightness and whiteness to dispel the doubts and gloom. He alone can transform the very outlook from one of despair to that of eager anticipation.

If this is to happen then we must be open and receptive to the presence and power of the Living Lord who gladly comes to engulf us with the wonder of His own person.

As I stood alone upon that snow-mantled mountain there came to me clearly the awareness that my Father, in His mercy and generosity, could again make all things bright and beautiful in my life. It was He who could erase the resentments at the grievous loss of my friends. It was He who could heal the deep hurt of seeing so much suffering. It was He who could cleanse away the criticism of so much pain and pathos.

Yes, there had been scarlet stains upon my soul. It was not a question of hiding them from Him. Rather it was a time to admit them openly, to lay them honestly before Him, to see that only the profound out-pouring of His Own wondrous life could ever cover them completely with the purity of His presence.

I came down off that snowy ridge a man renewed with a right spirit within me. I had met my Master at the edge of the sky. And in His own winsome way a tremendous fall of fresh snow, His righteousness, was enfolding all my life and outlook.

All would be well! Hope came afresh.

Not only was there hope for today, but even more exciting, hope for the years ahead.

Just as the first great fall of snow spoke of much more than the white splendor of the moment, so the presence of God's Spirit was a promise of new and exciting days to come. Winter was not the end of the seasons, it was but the preparation for spring. So sorrow was not the termination of time but the prelude to a new era of delight ordained for me by a loving, caring Father.

The deep blanket of snow draped across this high country would suckle the springs and replenish the streams that flowed from these slopes next April. The snow pack was the sure guarantee that next summer sparkling lakes would stand filled with cool, clear water to nourish a dry and thirsty land. Because these mountain slopes were buried under snow, ten thousand acres would flourish with emerald-green pastures next year—a carpet of wildflowers would be flung over the slopes. Herds of wild game would flourish on the bunch-grass ranges.

And so it was I saw clearly again the profound lessons that my Lord was imprinting indelibly upon my crushed and suffering spirit. Out of this pressure of pain, this stress of sorrow, would eventually flow streams of refreshment to others in the days to come.

Only out of the crucible of our calamities can there come the poured-out life that, though crushed, releases the fine wine of selflessness to enliven others amid their anguish. Yes, out of death comes life. Out of despair comes love. Out of darkness comes light.

It is always so with God. He is the source of all hope.

And it is He who imparts Himself to me.

12
Puma

"PUMA" IS THE very ancient native name for a Mountain Lion. In more recent times it has been replaced by such titles as Cougar or Panther. Of them all, "Puma" is by far the most appropriate and descriptive. For in its soft sound there is bound up all the stealth, strength and smooth conformation of the great cats of the western mountains.

That is the name I bestowed on a small, stray waif of a kitten that wandered out of the woods near our home one autumn day. The poor, wee creature was only a few weeks old, a mere bundle of thin bones and somewhat ragged skin. Yet even then, she bore the tawny, tabby markings of a wild cougar and moved with the quiet stealth of a mature mountain lion.

Of course she was not a true cougar kitten, but a tiny stray that someone lost by accident while traveling through our area. Or perhaps she was another kitten dropped off deliberately by some cruel and uncaring person who assumed she could survive on her own in the bush.

Anyway, it was a special mercy that she allowed my wife to pick her up and bring her to our little chalet among the pines. There she found a home where Ursula's tender care, and my own deep affection for all things wild, would assure her of a contented sanctuary.

She immediately surprised us with the unusual warmth of her affection. So many cats are rather aloof and distant in their demeanor. But from the moment we first met, this tiny bundle of life displayed the most moving gratitude for the love and kindness shown her. She immediately crawled up into my lap and began to purr up a storm.

That habit has never changed. If anything, it has intensified. She just loves to be with us, near us, a part of us. When I go to greet her in the morning she immediately responds with a soft mew as if to say, "So nice to see you, boss!" Then she stretches her sturdy body to its limit and reaches up to "touch noses" with me for a morning kiss. All the while she is purring like a well-oiled engine.

Puma came to us at a time of the great sorrow in our life of which I have written earlier in this book. It is inevitable that when friends and beloved associates pass on, there are genuine gaps of great grief left in our lives. This is bound to be true if our friendships are pure and profound. Separation of this sort tears a strip out of the fabric of our affections. And those wounds need more than mere words to heal the hurt and bind up the bruises.

My own conviction is that as humans we need something as strong as the consoling Spirit of God Himself to occupy the void. For those of us who truly know God as our Father, and Christ as our closest Friend, the presence of the Gracious Spirit of the Most High brings new life to our heavy hearts. He gives comfort to our sorrowing spirits. He supplies His Own vital energy to our emotions under deep distress.

In addition to all of which, from time to time, He sees fit to fill the empty place with a new life form as tangible as a bird, a kitten or even perhaps a colt. It is no accident that ravens were sent to feed Elijah in the terrible wastes of the Trans-Jordan region. It was no mere curiosity that a dove descended to settle upon Jesus at His baptism in the Jordan when He had returned from His awesome temptation in the desert. It was no happenstance that an unbroken colt quietly carried Christ into Jerusalem amid all the mayhem of the fickle crowds who shouted "Hosanna."

Certainly from my own personal perspective, God, my Father, could not have provided us with a more appropriate token of His profound concern than Puma. For into the drabness of our despair she suddenly brought unbounded delight. Amid the grief she brought endless good cheer and incredible gaiety.

Under Ursula's constant generosity and loving care, the kitten began to fill out in a remarkable manner. In just a few days her coat began to shine like satin. Quite obviously she had some Russian Blue blood in her make-up. For her fur, though unusually short, was thick and dense as the finest plush. It could readily resist the most intense cold of our mountain climate. To the touch it was as soft and smooth as the purest silk.

We have had her now for nearly four months. She has matured into a magnificent creature. She weighs well over ten pounds, a splendid specimen of grace and strength. She had survived in the bush by catching crickets, beetles and butterflies. In those weeks when she struggled to survive on such spartan fare she quickly learned to be swift and sure in her pursuit of any winged prey.

She has not forgotten her early skills. She is death to any fly, spider, wasp or insect that ever dares to enter through our great sliding doors. She can leap three feet in the air and catch an insect on the wing, so swift are her muscles.

Curled up on our laps, she literally revels in being stroked. She lays back her head, closes her eyes in quiet ecstasy, inviting us to tickle her chin or caress her cheeks and ears. She responds with pronounced, powerful purrs that rumble across the room in sheer animal pleasure. In all of this there is enormous contentment, gentle gratitude and profound affection.

We can only guess how old Puma is. At most she is not more than seven months of age. Though big, strong and swift she carries all the traits of a young and playful juvenile. At dusk she races around the house, which is very open in design, with wild abandon. She literally flies over the furniture, fights furiously with phantom foes in the form of tumbling golf balls or soft pom-poms on a string.

Her wild and unpredictable antics at times resemble those of an acrobatic monkey more than a cat. She has a favorite high-backed chair that she climbs over. On it she does acrobatics with incredible dexterity. All of which sends us into paroxysms of laughter. At times her antics are so absurd, so hilarious, so downright delightful I literally roll on the floor in glee.

All such good cheer, good will and glorious therapy could not be purchased at any price. I consider them a beautiful bonus bestowed upon us by the loving provision of our Heavenly Father. He, more than any of our human friends, knew how deeply we needed this element of gaiety, spontaneity and outright physical release in our lives.

Fortunately our furniture, of very simple design, but constructed from the toughest fabrics, has withstood all the onslaughts of Puma's claws with remarkable endurance. Hardly a piece shows the wear and tear of her energetic games. Here and there a claw mark scars the window frames where she climbs to view the wide world that stretches to the sky edge. But that is a small price to pay for so much joy commingled with the glorious memories of her happy coming.

Puma is a most astute animal. She seems well able to hold her own amid any company that comes to our home. She never runs or hides or cowers in a corner. Instead, she conducts herself with gentle dignity. She greets each guest with gracious good will.

She will accept discipline without sulking or holding any sort of grudge against the one who administers it. This is a most admirable trait! She is always quick to come back and make up. There are no old hostilities, no unsettled scores, no signs of attempts at revenge. She takes things in stride, is full of forgiveness and eager for good will.

All of this has been a tremendous tonic for me. If only human beings were more like my Puma—less prone to look for hidden motives, less given to holding grudges, less likely to think the worst. What a wonderful place the world might be!

With all of my rough and ready ways she has accepted me fully just as I am, as her loving friend. Despite my lack of consistency in every detail of life, she finds it fun and adventurous to share my days and enjoy our escapades. For Puma life is a game filled with new challenges. She does not live by the tired old theme of "safety first." And in large measure she has helped to reinject this dynamic dimension of excitement into my own outlook again.

She will pursue any bluejay that taunts her, to the topmost branch of our tallest pines. Tumbling and clawing, she will come scratching her way down without a particle of fear. She will chase her own shadow across the thick cedar shakes of our roof as if it was a game for the gods.

Yes, Puma has come into our lives blown here as it were by the inscrutable wind and wonder of the Great Spirit of our God. She is without a doubt a precious provision for two people in their pain. She has come to us as an angel in disguise. And because she came we are facing the future with great good will tinged by bright new hope.

13
Healing of the Hills

LOOKING SOUTH AND west from the great open windows of our home in the hills there stands on the horizon, at the extreme edge of the sky, a dark forested ridge. On clear spring days or under summer skies it is a rich green color with its cloak of pine and fir forests. In the fall it is often a misty blue almost lost to view against the hazy autumn skies. In winter it is the first of our adjacent heights to be rimmed in hoarfrost or mantled in a thick blanket of new snow.

Harvie and I often hiked this range. Somehow, because it was somewhat off the beaten tracks, few people were familiar with this lofty realm. In pioneer days it had been well-known to the hardy prospectors, rugged gold miners and tough old loggers who took all they could from its slopes. Even the earliest skiers, who had used its open slopes facing south and west for their sport, had long since moved to higher mountains with deeper snow. In more recent times it became a summer range for cattle ranchers.

Wherever our tramps across this high terrain took us, there remain grim reminders of days gone by when the tough teams of sturdy horses, and rugged boots of gold seekers, or bush loggers, tore the heart out of these hills.

Such spots had a special fascination for Harvie. He had a passionate love for the mountains, but particularly for those places plundered by man. In part this was because much of his life he had made his own livelihood by hauling tons of ore or logs out of the hills on treacherous winding roads. He seldom spoke of the great nostalgia which seemed to pervade his spirit about these intervals in his life.

On the other hand he expressed great concern over the carnage and waste of resources one saw wherever the ruthless hand of man had been at work. He often spoke vehemently of governmental policies that encouraged exploitation of the environment. His usual calm and cheerful demeanor would become aroused, angry and incensed by the sight of great gashes of cut-over country. His eyes would flash with fire when we passed beautiful mountain meadows or ice-fed streams marred by unbridled and selfish slashing of trees and soil.

Though he had worked hard all his life to wrest a living from the high country, still he held the hills in quiet reverence and loving respect. He knew and sensed with that profound intuition of spirit so seldom found in the sons of frontiersmen, that our very life reposed in a proper care of the earth. He knew that the earth did not belong to us to plunder, rape and abuse. Rather, he understood that we belonged to the earth, whose grandeur could only be preserved and perpetuated by the wise and prudent use of its bountiful resources.

Harvie and I often spoke of these things as we hiked the lofty ranges together. Often we sat beside a stream or high on a windswept ridge and mused over the future of this high, wild realm of rock, ice, open range and vanishing forests. What would it hold for our children and grandchildren? Would the snow-fed streams still run clear in these mountain valleys? Would there be feed left on these winter ranges to support a flourishing population of deer, grouse, mountain sheep and other native wildlife? Would these hills be healed so that in years to come another cutting of timber could be taken from the forest?

In a sentence it might be asked, "Could the destruction and devastation of a generation be renewed and restored in our time?"

I can recall with utter clarity the last time we climbed the faint, high, snow-covered ridge visible from my windows. It was mid-January. Winter had clamped its hard icy grip upon the country. Deep snow had fallen. The whole upland world was a spotless white. We climbed steadily toward the summit. Harvie was keen to show me the old mine shafts that had been sunk into the slopes above timber line.

Step by step, as if in slow motion, we took turns breaking trail through the deep snow. It hung heavy in the dark brooding trees. It clung to our boots, dragged heavy on our pantlegs, slowed our upward progress. Wisps of white vapor drifted about our faces from the heaving of our lungs and exhalation of our breath.

At last we broke out above timber line. And just as we did, the winter sun, too, broke out from behind the low-hanging winter clouds. Suddenly the whole upland realm was wrapped in blinding light and ultra whiteness. One could only see by squinting the eyes to mere slits. The world was wrapped in beautiful brilliance. Then as we reached the sun-swept meadows, pristine whiteness swept away beneath our gaze to the very edge of the sky in every direction. It was as if we were suspended in space where time stood still and not a single sound stirred in the great eternal silence.

It was as if momentarily we stood reverently, almost breathlessly, in the sublime sanctuary of the Most High. Neither of us spoke. It would have been a desecration. An interlude in time, it was a moment in our lives when eternity could be sensed in the soul, known by the spirit. For with intense awareness we were aware: "O God, our Father, You are here! The majesty of Your might and the glory of Your presence fill the earth and sky!"

A few drifting clouds crossed the face of the sun. Quickly we found shelter from the cold against the trunk of a gnarled, old, weather-beaten fir. There we broke out our sandwiches and washed them down with steaming cups of hot tea from the thermos in our packs. The burning liquid flowed through us like molten lava, driving out the frost and chill that penetrated our heavy winter clothes.

Suddenly a dense cloud of heavy fog moved up out of the distant valley below us. In a matter of moments it engulfed us in thick, dense folds of gray vapor. The sun was gone. And a darkness, almost like dusk, enshrouded the hills.

We started down the slope, glad to follow our own deep footprints in the snow. At least we would not need to search for a trail. Tired but deeply contented we tramped homeward, well rewarded for the efforts of the day, weary in muscle and tendon, but exhilarated in mind and emotions.

Harvie had often lamented to me the dreadful devastation of this particular range. Yet on this glorious day it had lain before us cloaked in pristine splendor. So I promised myself I would come there again to see it the following summer. And I did. But Harvie was not with me. He lay at death's door in a hospital over two hundred miles away.

What I saw would have cheered his spirits and lifted his morale. For a great healing had come to the hills. As I climbed the summit a pair of coyotes called across the open grasslands. A Mule Deer doe and her fawn bounded down the slope. A profusion of wildflowers flung themselves beneath the trees and over the ridges. A new forest of young and vigorous saplings covered the old mine scars and rotting stumps. Healing was everywhere!

That morning sparkling droplets of dew hung like suspended sequins of silver from every blade of grass, twig of tree and flower petal. A score of bird songs rose and fell with the symphony of soft mountain breezes that played through the timber. A pair of grouse burst up out of the dense grass before my boots; a big black bear had left his claw marks high on the snow-white bark of a poplar near a spring.

Life, new and fresh and vigorous, was all around me. The very pulse and power of renewal were at work in the upland world. None of it was planned by man nor programmed by science. Rather, it was the regeneration and restoration of a ravaged land by the inherent life and vitality of the biota itself. Once again these hills were becoming beautiful, beautiful! Once again fresh new forests would replace the carnage of cut-over country. Once again wildlife and wildflowers would flourish over a wasteland of old mine heaps and torn-up terrain.

This has always been our Father's way with the earth, so scarred, abused and ravaged by man.

And likewise it is always our Father's way with the soul of man so wounded, torn and scarred by sin, sorrow and the sickness of our society.

Only in Him can there be found the help, the healing, the health that restores us from utter ruin. Few people see this. Even fewer ever understand it. Most men and women do not have eyes to see nor ears to hear what is going on upon the earth. The understanding of their souls is too sotted with sorrow; their spirits are too stained by stress; their hearts are too tough, tempered by hard knocks, to grasp what God in Christ is doing in the world.

Most of us behave as though He did not exist. We act as if He were not here. In fact, in our puny pride we demand He prove Himself by some strange sign or wonder.

But our Father does not function in that way. He does not indulge us with dazzling fanfare. He does not turn to stunning theatrics to impress us with His power.

Instead, He proceeds quietly to restore our souls just as He restores the ravaged hills. He brings His own wondrous healing to our wounded hearts in the same way He heals the flattened forests and binds up the broken ranges. He renews our spirits exactly as He quickens again the streams and springs of the hill country—*by the gentle incoming of new life amid the desolation . . . yes, the miracle of His own life at work in the world.*

Everywhere one turns in the high hills of which I speak there is evidence of profound forces at work not arranged by the mind of man. On the gusting winds new seeds are blown in from afar that will revegetate the mountainsides. Birds and small mammals and even bears will distribute the new life germs in their droppings for miles across the country.

New growth will spring up wherever the soil has been disturbed, torn and trampled by the ruthless machinery of modern technology. When the whine of the chain saws, the roar of bulldozers and the thunder of trucks have departed, grass and herbs and brave pioneer plants will steal back softly to cover the scars and bind up the soil again.

I knew and sensed all of this as I stood on the summit of that range later in the summer. All about me on every side there was precious life pulsing strongly in the trees, in the undergrowth, in the riot of wildflowers, in the songs of the birds, in the abundance of big game. What had been a waste was becoming a wonderland.

So it is, too, of any person who will give God a chance to carry out His Own wondrous miracles of grace, mercy, compassion and restoration in the stony soil of their souls. Our greatest difficulty is that far too often we resist His coming into our experience; we close ourselves off from the healing of His presence; we harden our wills against the gracious work of His Gentle Spirit.

In addition to all of that, most of us want an instant fix. We want immediate renewal. We demand an overnight remedy for all our hurts.

We will not give God in Christ either the time or opportunities to bring us back from the bleak disasters that overwhelm us. Instead we turn to every sort of human device or man-made technology in an attempt to find consolation and comfort amid the chaos of our calamities.

The one great lesson I have learned above and beyond all others amid the great distress of recent months is this: *Be still, be quiet, be calm, and know that I am God!* It takes time to do this. It means one must, by a deliberate act of the will, learn to repose confidently in Christ . . . to rest assuredly in the faithfulness of our Father.

He is our hope.
He is our healing.
He is our helper.

The wondrous work which He accomplishes in our souls is done in silence. It is nothing less than the persistent incoming of His Own Presence to generate within us new life, new vitality, new confidence to carry on. He actually transmits to us His hope, His love, His energy, His ability to begin anew.

As the inspired poet wrote so long ago: "I will lift up mine eyes unto the hills, from whence cometh my help. My help cometh from the Lord, which made heaven and earth" (Psalm 121:1, 2).

As is the healing of the hills, so, also, is the healing of my spirit. Blessed be His name!

14
Wonder Springs Anew

WONDER, AWE AND enthusiasm comprise a tightly woven, three-strand initiative, which can be one of the most powerful influences to propel us through life. Often this is the element so quickly extinguished when the spirit is submerged, sunk down in sorrow.

> Wonder seems to evaporate.
> Awe slips away silently.
> Enthusiasm wanes like light fading at dusk.

Each of them is uniquely a gift from God. They come to us wrapped up in the irrepressible buoyancy of childhood. And, often, they are most readily restored through contact with a child. The contagion of seeing again through the eyes of a youngster, the wonder of sensing anew the glory of the earth through the senses of a child—these are delightful moments of restoration for one in the twilight of life.

This was the case for me when one of our eight grandchildren came to spend several days with us. He is an unusual lad of gentle disposition and quiet demeanor. His tousled head of hair gleams gold like a ripe field of wheat. His bright, bright blue eyes are clear, limpid and shining like a lake under summer skies. His tanned cheeks, sun-browned arms and lanky legs are smooth like the brown bark on a young birch tree.

We decided to spend a day hiking in the hills together. More than half a century separated us in age, but a steel-like bond of love for all things wild and free bridged the great span of time. We were content in each other's company. With my well-worn binoculars slung over his shoulders, and each of us with a brown bag of sandwiches in hand, we set off for some secret little marshy lakes I knew well.

We had scarcely started up the dusty summer trail when we

came to some Olalla bushes hanging heavy with rich dark berries. Though we had eaten a hearty breakfast, the delicious, winelike fruit lured us to stop briefly and relish the richness of its flavor.

Den (his full name is Dennis) had never set his teeth into wild fruit of this sort before. As the sweet juice of the berries burst in his mouth and trickled over his lips and tongue he could scarcely restrain his pleasure. The low, contented grunts of a boy in utter joy rumbled in his throat. His young face split into broad smiles now stained wine purple with the pungency of the fruit. He could eat all he wished. The wild bounty was his. It was free for the taking. He reveled in its abundance.

Somehow Olalla berries had never tasted so sweet to me before. As the blue stains marked our lips and moistened our fingers we sensed we were feasting the way wild bears and birds eat. For they too had banqueted on these bushes.

There were the distinct paw marks of a young bear in the dust on the path. We could see where the bushes were broken and battered by his harvesting. Along the trail the fresh dung of his passing was still soft under the morning dew.

Excitement, wonder and enthusiasm began to build between us. If we walked silently and softly, perhaps we would encounter him over the next knoll. Maybe it would be our pleasure to find the furry fellow feeding in another clump of berries.

As we started to climb the sage-covered slope a whole flock of young magpies burst up out of the tall brown grass. They were catching beetles, grasshoppers and ants. The current year's fledglings, such noisy but handsome birds, flew into some nearby trees and upbraided us for disturbing them.

I had seldom seen so many magpies in a single flock. Their raucous cries, their flashing black and white wings, their erratic flight from branch to branch of the Ponderosa Pines suddenly filled the hills with color, action and life. Both of us stood still, enthralled by all the flashing movement. We grinned from ear to ear.

Gently I led Den to a nearby clump of sturdy, thorny hawthorns. There the rough, ungainly, tangled masses of twigs wedged between the branches were a dead giveaway as to where most of the young magpies had been hatched and reared. The huge unsightly nests were vacant now. But in the future he would know where to look for the cunning birds that are such a menace to their lesser neighbors.

We came over the crest of the hill we were climbing. There below us, nestled like two silver plates shining in the sun, held in the hollow of the hills, were a couple of spring-fed ponds. Not too many people know about them. Only the local ranchers who graze their cattle on this high summer range are familiar with these waters.

Den gasped in startled wonder at the sight. The ponds were lovely in the simple purity of their unspoiled setting. He gulped in astonishment at the scores of ducks that dabbled in the shining waters. It was like looking at a painting.

Through the lad's eyes I too was seeing this gentle scene with fresh awe, joy and enthusiasm. We crouched low in the sagebrush and studied the birds through the binoculars. There were mallards, pintails, widgeon and teal moving across the ponds.

We stood up slowly, hoping to get a closer look.

"They may burst into flight any second!" I murmured softly. "Be ready for a great show!"

Suddenly there was an explosion of wings as scores of birds burst from the surface of the water. The droplets fell from their feet and feathers in a shower of silver rain. The sharp staccato of their wing beats literally filled the sky. Then wave after wave of hurtling bodies swept through the valley just over our heads. They were streaming away in a great circular flight to some other remote waters.

It was all over in moments.
But those brief seconds were charged with energy.
Enthusiasm, eager and ecstatic, welled up within us.
We were touched with the wonder of it all!
Indelible memories had been etched on our minds.

Den turned to me in that special, gentle, happy way of his. "Gee, Grandpa, wasn't that great?!" A look of enormous satisfaction stole over his features. Both of us were richer, much richer, than when we came.

We pushed on past the first pond, and came softly to the edge of the second. There in the soft mud the young bear's tracks were clearly visible in the moist earth. He had prowled all around its perimeter during the night, exploring all the scents and odors of other visitors to this little mountain glen.

I knew where a grand grove of aged firs grew in a cluster. The ground beneath the trees was like a wild park, shaded by the mountain monarchs, cool from the heat of the summer sun. We would go there just "to sit a spell"; to listen to the wind in the tall trees; to wait for some wildlife to wander into this quiet grove.

Den was very still, sensitive to the moods of the hills. He was open in spirit to the impulses of the natural world around us. I assured him in a whisper that we would not have long to wait. So we settled ourselves on a rock outcrop to see what would come.

We had not been there five minutes when there was a sudden stirring in the lower branches of a dense young pine about forty yards away. We fastened our attention on it. Suddenly an energetic little animal bounded into the tall grass beneath the tree. The tall fronds waved back and forth as it scurried back and forth, coming toward us.

"Don't even blink your eyes, Den," I muttered to my young companion. "Sit as still as a stone!"

We both sat as motionless as petrified rock.
Not a muscle moved.
Not a tendon twitched.
Not a sound escaped us in the mounting tension.

Suddenly a handsome Douglas Squirrel burst out of the grass. With great bounds he began to cross the clearing. Several times he changed direction, leaping over the ground in three-foot jumps that were startling to see.

Closer and closer he came, oblivious that we were even there, sitting still as two stones. The blood raced in my veins. He was so near now I was sure he might even leap right into Den's lap. Instead, he suddenly landed about eighteen inches in front of us. Momentarily he paused there. Somehow we seemed to be neither stones nor stumps.

He riveted us with his sharp eyes. Then he let out a burst of indignation at our intrusion into his terrain. After that he sped away chittering in alarm.

Both of us burst into laughter. What a happy moment. So close, yet so far! But in the brightness of that encounter a sense of beauty, awe and the sheer joy of living shot between us like a charge of electrical energy.

The boy was beyond himself with pure pleasure!

And I, the older one, was being renewed within by the splendor of this day, this golden day.

We stood up, shaking the moss, grass and twigs from our trousers. We were also shaking with gladness and good cheer. This had been an ecstasy shared and in the exuberance I had been brought back to my own boyhood.

Slowly we circled the pond again. Willows and birch and wild rose bushes overhung the far edge of the water. Stealthily we pushed our way through this tangle of dense undergrowth. I half expected to see a skunk or mink or perhaps even a pair of ruffed grouse. Instead I almost stepped on a Blue Racer. This is one of the rarest snakes in our high country. It is a very shy, slender reptile with exquisite blue markings on its slim body.

Den was absolutely captivated by the creature. He had never seen one in his whole life. It rivaled the most beautiful tropical fish in his aquarium at home. Surely we were surrounded with beauty in many forms in these rough mountains.

It was getting late when we finally reached the lake where I had planned for us to have lunch. We found a smooth, moss-covered outcrop of rock on a knoll at the water's edge. There we stretched ourselves in the sun and opened our brown bags. Delicious sandwiches, redolent with ham and cheese and sharp pickle slices, were a meal fit for a monarch.

As we sat munching our food, casting our glances across the sparkling waters of the lake, three black bears suddenly burst out of the trees and rushed up the bank across the little bay from us. At last we had caught up with the little characters whose tracks we had followed all morning.

It was as if a ghost of the imagination had suddenly taken

concrete shape in bone, muscle and shining black fur before our eyes. Like three phantoms come to life they hurried across a clearing and vanished into the timber.

For both of us it had been a day of joyous high adventure. The hours had been touched with awe at the unexpected. We had been inspired, stimulated with the wonder of the world. Fresh enthusiasm had mingled with vivid memories to lend a special splendor to our tramp.

Again I had looked, with warm excitement, through the eyes of a small boy. With the sense of fresh discovery I had tasted the sweet wine of wild berries. In that special sense of well-being, contentment and spontaneous delight of a lad, I again reveled in the flight of birds, the antics of an untamed squirrel, the smooth motion of a jewel-like snake.

Awe, wonder, enthusiasm were being reborn, rekindled, regenerated in an elderly gentleman who hiked in company with a small lad across the high hills against the sky edge.

I am fully confident the same identical sensation swept through the spirit of my Master during those difficult days He tramped the trails of Palestine so long ago. It does not surprise me one bit that He said: "Suffer [let] the little children to come unto me, and forbid them not: for of such is the kingdom of God" (Mark 10:14). He, too, in His time of stress and strain needed the re-quickening which can come from the companionship of a child.

In our age, with a society so jaded with cynicism, so bored with skepticism, what a bright fountain of youth can be found in the heart of a boy or the soul of a girl.

With eyes of wonder they still look out upon a lovely world created with such care by our Father. With souls stirred by awe they find joy in simple, natural life. With spirits of enthusiasm they energize our own. And in it all we can be renewed, if we will!

15
The Shaping of Stone

SMOOTH STONE, SHAPED and sculptured by natural forces in the high, wild mountain ranges, has always fascinated me. Few are the trips taken along a glacier-fed stream that I do not come home bearing some polished piece of granite, quartz or other rock in my well-worn pockets.

On the rugged stone mantlepiece of our fireplace two very special pieces of worn rock adorn the bright and spacious room. One is a smooth chunk shaped exactly like an ancient Indian tomahawk. Even its cutting edge is sharp as a well-honed knife. Given a wooden handle of tough birch, fastened with deerskin thongs, it could easily serve as a formidable battle-axe to slay an opponent.

The other polished stone is a lovely bit of blue-gray sedimentary rock shaped exactly like a wild mallard's head. It has the same salient facial features complete with a special hole for the eye at precisely the correct spot. Many visitors have been delighted by these stones.

Besides these, for many years we had a large glass jar filled with water, containing a lovely collection of small smooth stones, standing in the kitchen window. Children used to love to look at the smoothly polished pebbles that came in so many delicate colors from rich red to snow white. Each was a little treasure taken from the bed of a swift-flowing mountain stream or gathered from the edge of a sky-blue mountain lake.

There is a rare and unique quality to smooth stones shaped under the impulse of flowing water. The stones speak of long years of wear. Each is a silent tribute to great spans of time during which water was at work on the rock. It tells of patient, quiet subjection to the abrasive forces of the natural world.

Even more stunning and arresting than the small fragments a mountain man can carry home are the exquisite stream beds carved out of solid rock. Only in the highest streams that have their source at the sky edge may the ultimate beauty of this kind be seen. I say this with all due respect for the magnificent formations found in deep canyons at lower elevations. There, too, the bedrock is often shaped into the most wondrous planes and whorls. But the setting lacks the stupendous magnificence of a mountain backdrop with high snow-spangled peaks pushing into the clouds. There is missing the lure of glaciers thawing in the sun, the melt water from their blue ice charged with "glacial flour" so fine that it forms the most perfect abrasive.

This water, at the eternal verge of freezing, carries in suspension stone worn so fine it hangs suspended in the stream like thin milk. Millennia after millennia the ice-fed freshets flow relentlessly from their mountain source of snow and ice to carve an ever-deepening channel through the upthrust rock formations.

A favorite pastime of mine is to follow one of these highland streams ever upward to its source. The unexpected beauty of the stream bed itself often rivals all the other breathtaking scenery of the country through which the freshet flows. Depending on the type of rock formation, the colors revealed by the running water are of delicate hues. One that is a special favorite cuts through strata of rich red rock interlaced with streaks of brilliant white quartz.

Here the racing water whirls and curls its way over the surface of the stone with sparkling spray and shades of blue and white, reflecting the clear colors of the sky edge. The scene is enchanting.

I love to spend time sitting quietly in meditation beside these mountain streams. Here water has been at work for a very long time indeed. The change from season to season may seem imperceptible. Still the shaping, the smoothing, the sculpting goes on steadily.

Often these little high mountain streams are adorned with the most remarkable trees, shrubs and flowers. At the high altitudes the only trees which can survive are often small and stunted by the stern and rugged weather at the edge of the sky. Beaten down by winter winds, blasted by blizzards bearing tons of snow in their teeth, the little trees take root in some crack of the stone and draw their sustenance from the stream. They resemble bonsai trees, shaped with supreme care to match the elegance of the water-worn streambed.

Here and there a clump of wildflowers will find a sheltered foothold beside the running water. Plants of pioneer species, especially hardy and tough enough to endure the stormy climate of the remote ridges, bloom here in quiet glory. Again and again I have paused in astonishment at the loveliness of Water Willow Herbs, Northern Fireweed and clumps of Mountain Anemone that decorate the verges of these ancient rocks.

In simple truth such spots are the natural "Gardens of God." No man designed them. They were not arranged by human imagination nor brought into being by our horticultural ingenuity. They are the end product of eons of time during which year upon year ever-increasing loveliness has been brought out of the most unpromising material.

The seeds and spores of ferns and flowers, grass and shrubs, trees and herbs have blown across these ridges on the wind to take root in the rock and gravel. And so out of the most austere setting of ice, snow, gravel and stone there has emerged beauty, elegance and grandeur of divine design.

In the whole realm of outdoor art, there is a profound return to the reality of natural beauty. As a people we are rediscovering the inherent glory of God's creation. We are turning away from the confusion and meaningless expression of abstract art, all of which is a most wholesome trend.

But beyond all this there lies at even greater depths the profound spiritual perceptions which we need to discover as a modern society if we are to survive. Those principles are absolutely basic to any human understanding of what our Father's ultimate objectives are in shaping our lives to His ends.

I for one have become tired of listening to little men with giant self-importance pontificate on the plight of modern man. I am fed up with the flood of books published dealing with the dilemma of our self-centered society. Endless messages are given on the theme of "how people hurt." Amid all this outpouring of self-pity modern man would love to blame God for all that has gone wrong with the world. It is as if He really did not know what He was doing in allowing sorrow and suffering to be so much a part of life.

In my own search for spiritual reality in the midst of so much sadness, my footsteps have been led back again and again to the wonders of the natural world. As with our Master, I find true understanding in such simple things as water, rocks, trees and skies.

This must inevitably be the case. As the supreme Creator is was He who brought the earth into being. It was He who first conceived of things as lovely as sunsets, birds on wing, clouds against the sky or water shaping stone. And it was also He who brought man into being with all his convoluted character.

The principles of creation, re-creation and eternal duration apply equally whether they be in the natural realm of grass and sea and rock or in the supernatural realm of mind and will and stony spirits. This is a salient point which Jesus, the Living Christ, made again and again in His use of simple earthly parables to explain profound spiritual principles. The two realities of natural life and spiritual life are contiguous. They cannot be separated, even though our scholars and theologians would try to deceive us into believing otherwise. Too much, far too much of modern preaching and teaching is based upon purely human philosophy spawned by so-called "thinkers" whose mindset has emerged from the chaos of our man-made urban environment.

And so as I have sought solace and strength and reassurance for my own soul and spirit in recent months amid the agony of death on every side, I have turned away from the pious platitudes of preachers and teachers and scholars. There was no adequate explanation there for the unending stream of sorrow, the ever-flowing anguish of pain and separation which pours over the planet.

> It is not enough to cry out against the agony.
> It is not enough to submit sullenly to the sorrow.
> It is not enough to accept the separation stoically.

If we are truly Christians, if we are in reality children of the Most High, if we are at all sensitive to God's Gracious Spirit at work in this weary old world, we must be able to perceive our Father's purposes in all our pain.

Is it possible that amid all the mayhem He is actually bringing beauty out of the barrenness of our lives? Is He creating something of consummate loveliness out of our chaos? Is He in fact actually fashioning us to His Own character?

The unequivocal answer is, "*Yes,* He is!"

Somehow we simply must see this!

Again and again as I have sat alone by a singing mountain stream that flowed strongly over the hard bedrock, the acute awareness has come home to my soul. "That, God, is exactly how Your Own eternal, perpetual life flows over me!"

There is a river of divine energy that emerges ever from the very person of the Eternal One. It flows over the entire universe. But more particularly it moves relentlessly over me, around me, as a man. It exerts its influence and power in wondrous ways, some of which may not be even understood or known.

The eternal grace of God manifest in the outpouring of His kindness, compassion, patience and care, whether I deserve it or not, flows fresh and unfailing to me every day. The abundance of His life, His love, His light surround me on every side in joyous effulgence, whether I respond to their stimulation or not. The stirrings of His sweet Spirit surge over my spirit in a dozen ways, carried to me continuously by the constant coming of His presence to bring comfort, consolation and encouragement, whether I am even aware of Him or not.

> Across the years and across the tears, He is here!
> Ever, always, His quiet assurance is "*I come to you!*"
> Our difficulty lies in discerning His presence with us.

It is the constant coming, coming, coming of His life which enables us to understand that thus He truly transcends death. And this life comes to us in many forms and diverse ways that are much more than mere words or vague ideas.

That life comes to us in the integrity of His commitments to us as His people. He carries out His promises. His Spirit does actually bring us comfort. He does console us in the chaos. He does compensate us for our loss.

In the stream of His life that flows to us there may well be the sand and gravel of grievous events that grind us down. But they are the abrasive agents used in His purposes to shape us to His divine design. Just because we are Christians, there are no guarantees given to us by our Father that we shall be exempted or spared from the cutting circumstances of life.

It is often the individuals who have borne the greatest grief and endured the longest abuse who emerge beautiful in character, strong in spirit, unflinching in faith. It is they to whom we turn in our moments of despair. For it is they who have withstood the deep waters of suffering to become lovely in life.

At times, too, the very life of the Living Christ which comes to us may appear to us clouded, maybe even murky. We cannot fully comprehend why the stream of daily events flowing over our little lives resembles the cold, chill glacial streams that bear their burden of "glacial flour." Yet this is the polishing compound that puts the fine polish and smooth satin patina over every stone it touches.

It is the minute pangs of human misunderstandings, the crude, persistent rub of rudeness from others, the little lapses of ingratitude that press in upon us, the subconscious grief of insensitivity that move over us. These are all our Father's "glacial flour" for polishing people in their pangs of pain.

Out of all this there has come to me an acute awareness that nothing is permitted to touch my life except in the gracious good will of my Father for me. In His infinite concern He is shaping a character that not only in time here, but in eternity to come, will reflect something of the wondrous work He did in me.

Out of my stony spirit He has brought something of beauty and worth. It has taken sorrow and suffering. But anything of great value costs a great deal to create and shape.

16
The Splendor in the Clouds

MOUNTAIN SKIES HAVE a grandeur and glory about them rather different from the scenery elsewhere. Because of the higher altitude there is an intimacy and interaction with clouds and mist and storms not often experienced at lower levels.

Instead of observing the various weather systems that pass overhead from far below, in the mountains one is often very much "in the clouds." The high swirling veils of moisture pour through the passes, envelop the high ridges and drape themselves in delicate adornment over the trees and meadows of the high ranges.

We really do live at the sky edge. In the lower valleys the ground, especially in winter, is often bare and brown. But up at our elevation the whole world is wrapped in a wondrous white mantle of shining hoarfrost that sparkles with brilliance under the wide skies of the high mountain ridges.

Some days the moving clouds have deposited such a dense layer of hoarfrost on the trees and shrubs and rocks they appear to be blanketed by snow. But in a couple of hours of intense sunlight, most of the exquisite ice crystals are melted, sheathing every twig, needle and bit of bark in shining dampness.

Up where I live, at the edge of the sky, clouds come and go in a constant forming and dissolution. One hour they may appear to fill the whole inverted bowl of the sky. Then, just as suddenly, the wind may shift direction and the dense cover is torn to fragments that spill out of the sky and vanish into nothing but clear air.

It is much the same with the approach of snow and rain. It is not so much a sensation of feeling these elements are falling on one, as being in the midst of the downfall and watching the flakes or droplets of moisture descend on all sides around one. For anyone who has never lived in high country this may sound absurd but it really is the case.

I shall never forget the first summer showers that came. To the southwest the sky was clear and intensely blue. A strong sun filled the whole valley with brilliant light. Yet immediately around us there were heavy cumulus clouds through which rain was falling in gorgeous silver streams brilliant in the sunlight. It was as if we were at the center of the rain-making action.

This whole sensation becomes ever more spectacular during an electrical storm. All around us there are highly mineralized rock ridges to which the powerful high voltage charges are attracted. The roar of the thunder, the echo of its crashing along the crags, the flash of lightning, the splintering of trees all make for a majestic display of power and glory. Again it is not something happening at a great distance. It is a literal firestorm close at hand.

Some years, if the weather is dry, the lightning strikes ignite the forests. Great blue-gray clouds of smoke climb into the skies riding the heated updrafts of air. Then the sunrises and sunsets are accentuated with the most vivid colors of orange, red and mauve spread out across the smoky skies.

In winter the snowstorms which envelop us are just as intimate, intense and all-pervasive as the summer showers. There lingers always the peculiar impression: "This is very much a part of my personal life. It is not something remote and apart which is happening. It is here. I am a part of the weather pattern. It is a part of me!"

Often, often, when I go out to hike in the hills, as I attempt to do every day, those moving sentences uttered by the prophet Nahum so long ago come to me with tremendous force. "The Lord hath his way in the whirlwind and in the storm, and the clouds are the dust of his feet" (1:3).

Yes, He is everywhere present. He is everywhere active and at work in the world. Very much alive, He is aware of all that transpires upon the planet and in the lives of its people. Most of us sort of subscribe to this vague idea with mental assent. Precious few people consider the concept important enough to invest their confidence in the omnipresence of Christ. They refuse to have faith in our Father who is actually at work in every event that touches our lives. They do not seriously believe God's Spirit is everywhere active.

This becomes very obvious in times of great stress or emotional turmoil. It is one of the tragic truths that strikes with great impact when we see men and women surrounded with excruciating sorrow or enveloped in overwhelming grief. It is as if suddenly they feel abandoned by God. In the surging storms of sadness or darkness that sweep over the soul, hope vanishes, faith flees and good will evaporates away.

Again and again in recent months, since I began to write this book, we have literally been engulfed in storms of sorrow. I wrote in the opening pages that we had shared in the sadness of some fourteen families that faced terminal illness or other tragedies. Since those words were put on the page the number has doubled. One stands in awe at the winds and whirlwinds of grief and agony sweeping over our family and friends.

Just yesterday morning the phone rang. It was the wife of my next dearest friend in this area. Her strong man had suddenly been stricken with a massive stroke. Unable to speak, unable to articulate his thoughts, unable to move one side of his big sturdy frame, he now lay like a fallen tree.

This was the twenty-ninth person in our circle of friends to have the terrible threat of death descend like a dark cloud across the horizon of life. In eighteen months the tragic sort of story had swept over us in agonizing intensity almost thirty times. O the tears, the fears, the inner anguish!

Again and again, the stabbing, searing, searching questions come through trembling lips and tear-burned eyes: "Can God be in all of this? Is He really here? Does He truly care?"

In such moments pious platitudes will not do!
We cannot mumble sweet nothings!
There can be no vague ideas!

The excruciating crisis demands formidable faith in the Living Christ. It calls for unshakable confidence in the love of our Father. It must have the consolation and assurance of God's gracious Spirit.

"Yes!" Again and again I affirm the truth. "He has His way in the whirlwind and in the storm. The clouds are the dust of His feet." He, the Risen One, the Living God, is here present in our pain. He is at work in the whirlwind of our despair, moving behind the scenes in the dark clouds of our chaos and confusion.

Only He will or can bring beauty out of it all. Only He can bring help to our helplessness. Only He can restore joy for our sorrow. There is no other word of consolation or cheer that I can bring to those in dark places.

It may well be asked, how can you be so sure? My simple reply as a humble lay person is based upon three indisputable aspects of life. The first is the inviolate truth of our Father's Own Word to us as His people. Untold millions of individuals in their hour of sorrow have found faith and courage and calm strength coming to them from God in the midst of the storm.

Secondly, there has been my own private, moving discovery across the long years of my life that I am never alone in the times of trial. Christ has always been there in the turmoil of excruciating events which appear to be so threatening. Mary, who on the resurrection morning could not clearly recognize her Master through tear-stained eyes and could not comprehend His living Presence in the midst of death, exclaimed, "*Rabboni.*" Then He softly spoke her name. So I have seen Him dimly, but alive!

Thirdly, there is the subsequent result of all the storms and clouds and wild winds that sweep about us. At the hour they seem so tempestuous. But at a later date their benefits are clearly seen.

For out of the rain, out of the sleet, out of the snow, out of the storms there comes to the high country the cleansing, the refreshment, the moisture, the sustenance that eventually renews the mountains. Here in truth new beauty is born that adorns the high ridges with a mantle of shining white. Out of the stormy weather spills moisture that refreshes the alpine meadows, the lofty forests and sky edge rangelands.

Only because of clouds and mists and surging storms does moisture percolate through the soil to feed the mountain springs, to enliven the upland streams, to replenish the roaring rivers and fill the lakes anew.

Out of what appears to be death, new life emerges.

When today there is turmoil, stress and darkness, tomorrow new fields of flowers will flourish on the slopes.

In the skies so laden with heavy overcast, so charged with clouds and wind-driven snow this week, birds will soar on wing against the sun next spring. For this, too, will pass. The skies will be blue again.

All is change. Life is ever in flux. Nothing on earth remains constant. But in splendor and wonder those of us who know Christ shout with glad affirmation, *"O God, Thou changest not!"* Amid the mayhem in calm confidence we assert boldly, *"Forever, O Lord, Thou art faithful."*

A small parable illustrating this truth so forcibly was given to me as a gift by my wife on a handsome bookmark. It came home to my heart with remarkable clarity the morning I first read it. Since the author is unknown I share it here with the reader, written as concisely as possible in my own words.

The parable is entitled, "Footprints."

A man, near the end of his life, looked back to see all the events of his years played out before him again in rapid succession. He seemed to be strolling along the sand with the drama of his days being enacted on a giant screen against the sky edge.

He noticed that wherever he walked there were two sets of parallel footprints left upon the sand—his own and those of his Master, the Lord Christ.

As the drama of his days unfolded something else struck him forcibly. Whenever he passed through some very dark experience or there was a time of unusual sorrow or hardship, there was only one set of footprints.

Turning to the Lord he asked, "O Lord, You promised never to leave me! How is it there is only one set of footprints when the going was so rough?"

In tenderness and love the Master looked at him and replied: *"You did not know it. But it was then I carried you!"*

In essence that is the splendor, the glory, the majesty of the very love of God present in the storms of life. He is ever present with His people even in the darkest hour. It is He who carries us through. And on the other side we look back in retrospect to see His faithfulness every day, all the way, whatever men may say.

Clouds come and go. He remains constant.

Winds blow, storms subside. He is ever by our side.

Out of it all, He alone brings comfort, consolation and the great renewal which is such abundant compensation for all the crushing sorrow of our years—and the burning agony of our tears.

He, and He alone, makes all things new—both in this life and in the wider life yet to come beyond the skies. Bless His wondrous name forever and forever!

17
Hidden Springs

EARLIER IN THIS book it was mentioned that unlike many mountain regions, ours is dry terrain, almost arid in nature. On average, in any given year, less than twelve inches of moisture fall on this high country. This includes the winter snowpack. So in truth it almost approaches desert country.

For this reason springs, streams and mountain lakes are here considered jewels of great worth to be treasured. Without them these beautiful ranges that reach ever upward to the sky edge would be almost barren of life and destitute of vegetation.

Because I am an ardent outdoorsman with a fond affection for all things wild and natural, springs of water have always fascinated me. They are a vital source of life for trees, shrubs, grass, flowers, mammals, birds, livestock and even man. This was especially true in pioneer days when frontiersmen did not have use of modern power equipment with which to sink deep wells that could tap the subterranean water supplies. Then the hidden natural springs were rare treasures of great worth. To a certain degree they still are in our rugged mountains where it is not always possible to get in with power equipment.

In the long years of my mountain adventures I have drunk from scores of upland springs. The clear, cool water, free of any impurities, uncontaminated by man or his chemicals, is the sweetest drink available on the planet. Here the bears, the deer, the squirrels, the birds, the butterflies and other uncounted life forms come to slake their thirst. For they, too, know the hidden springs. From the free-flowing liquid they draw life and sustenance in the desert heat of summer and chilling frost of winter.

Yes, even in winter the springs still flow freely. The water emerging from beneath the mountain slopes remains at an almost constant temperature, melting away the accumulating snow and ice that forms a small basin around them.

Because I have always found special pleasure in discovering

where the hidden springs are in the hills, there has been a double delight in clearing them of dirt and debris which is bound to accumulate across the years. Deer, elk, wild sheep or domestic range cattle often trample the source of the spring. Rock and fallen earth may fall into the flow and almost shut it off. Broken branches or fallen leaves from the surrounding trees and shrubs that always encircle these lovely spots will often fill them with debris.

So I take the time to clear away the accumulation of decaying material. Sometimes it takes a sturdy effort to lift the rocks, stones and mud that block the flow. But the pure pleasure of seeing the mountain-fed water surge out strongly is a sensation of sweet satisfaction. I often enclose a small space with rocks that form a natural basin where all forms of wildlife can drink with ease and pleasure.

Here all my friends of hoof, wing and paw can come to refresh themselves. Here the game trails converge. Here the birds come swiftly and silently to assuage their thirst and freshen their plumage.

The water springs are also a special place where certain unique types of vegetation flourish. Because of crystal clear water that remains at an even temperature, watercress thrives in these spots. Not only do the deer and bears relish this delicacy, but so do I. Bunches of the herb are borne home for delectable sandwiches.

It is around the hidden springs in the hills that Red Osier Dogwood thrives. It is a magnificent water-loving shrub whose lacework branches form dense thickets around the springs. In spring they are brilliant green. In summer they are adorned with dense clusters of white berries that bears relish and on which birds gorge with pleasure. In fall the foliage turns crimson, filling the deep rock draws with red and purple hues.

Here, too, the native Hawthorne takes root. The sturdy little trees with their scarlet berries, shiny leaves and labyrinth of thorny branches are beloved of birds. Almost every mature "haw, haw" tree shelters at least one bird's nest. Nor is it possible to find their secret shelter until winter winds have stripped away the last gold and scarlet leaves.

The hidden springs are special spots of unusual beauty. In more open locations they are often encircled with a green sward of grass. I love to lie here in the sun and listen to the soft sounds of the clear water running between the rocks. Often the surrounding stones are sheathed in deep soft moss. Ferns and flowers grow among the rocks and nature shapes a bit of pristine paradise in this spot.

What is the secret of the hidden springs? How is it possible for so much life and vigor and beauty to be sustained in these austere surroundings? Whence the clear, pure-flowing streamlet that turns a waste of rock and sand and blasted mountain slope into a vale of refreshment?

The source lies in the great skies that arch over the lofty, shining peaks. It is the weather systems of cloud and mist and snow and rain that swathe these heights in veils of moisture. It is the shining snowfields on the summit of the ranges and crest of the high ridges. It is the gentle, persistent percolation of moisture through rock and soil and forest duff to emerge in this spot.

The mountain spring is not its own source of origin. Its story does not begin where it is born and come to light in the shining sun. The energy of its flow, the quickening of its waters are not inherent in the spring itself. Rather, the spring, amid so much desolation and desert dryness, gives life from a source outside itself, of eternal duration far beyond its own tiny boundaries.

The hidden springs high in the hills at the edge of the sky are an intimate, quiet, gentle expression of the eternal elements of the universe. Here compressed into a tiny stream of life-giving liquid lies a tiny fragment of the titanic forces of wind and weather that encircle the planet to determine its climate. These are the elemental sources of energy derived from sun, moon, stars and all the awesome arrangements ordained of God our Father in creation of the cosmos.

Often, in quiet solitude, I have reflected on such truths as I drank from a spring, then sat down gently to listen to its eternal music.

In utter sincerity, with soul-searching humility of spirit, I have asked myself, "Could my little life possibly be one of God's hidden springs in the wasteland of our world?" It is a perfectly legitimate and appropriate question. "Does there really flow out of my innermost being and through my person the pure, living water of the very life of the Living Christ?" These are sobering reflections. They call for honest answers in a culture that is as crude as a barren desert, a society as barren of belief as a rock slope. "Can men and women around me, jaded with sorrow, wrung out with pain, dry and bitter with remorse, find refreshment and new quickening in my company?"

When our Master walked among us He stated emphatically that it could be so. Just as He renewed and refreshed those who came to Him to drink of His life, so He declared the same could be true of us. But unlike Him, our source is not in ourselves. The vitality, the energy, the dynamic, the beauty, the renewal which emanates from me has its source in Him. Otherwise, it can never, ever, satisfy the thirsting soul.

The flow of life surging and pulsing through me to refresh this weary old world must be from God Himself. It must be the continuous out-pouring of His Presence by His Spirit which touches and transforms all around me. Any person naïve enough, arrogant enough, stupid enough to believe that it is his or her own charm, charisma or capabilities that change and enliven others lives in utter self-delusion.

One of the terrible tragedies of human behavior is for people to turn to other human beings in an effort to find sustenance for their spirits. They are always deluded, ever disappointed. Our spirits can only find life in the Living Spirit of the Living Lord. Our eternal quest for life-giving water can only be quenched by the eternal life of God Himself coming to us through the hidden springs of His own person who indwells those who are open channels for His life.

The best of us have lives that, like the mountain springs, are often plugged with debris and muddied with fallen earth and rock. The supply of live water is almost cut off because of the trampling of hooves, the accumulation of dead wood and leaves.

Most of us as God's people are really not vibrant springs through which there surges the very life of the eternal God. The hard knocks of life, the rocks of rank unbelief, the mud of trampled hopes and broken dreams, the silt of sorrow and sadness, the dead wood of death and despair, the fallen leaves of frustration often choke off Christ's life in us.

People come to us searching for strength, uplift, solace and refreshment. Instead, they find despair, defeat and dark bitterness. Too often our characters are choked up with the cares of life, the calamities of our corrupt society, the ennui of a cynical culture. We claim to be Christians, the children of the Most High, when in reality we are a reproach to our Father, a despair to His Spirit.

What we need, and need desperately, is to be renewed ourselves. We need a sudden cleansing, pulsing surge of God's Own Life to flush away the debris. We need His grace to scout away the silt and mud of a wrong mindset, to flow freely through us without hindrance.

As men and women search us out in the dry and barren hills of our times they will discover a quiet, gentle, hidden spring through which there pulses the very life of Christ. It is of Him they must drink, not of us! It is of His life and energy they must imbibe, not of our human personality. It is by His vitality they will be quickened, made alive, fully refreshed, not by our fallible human nature.

Jesus was very explicit when He stated categorically, "He that believeth on me, as the scripture hath said, out of his innermost being shall flow rivers of living water!" (John 7:38). To believe in Christ is to open one's life to Him completely. It is actually to allow Him unobstructed access into our souls and spirits. It is literally to permit Him to fill us with His presence. It is to take of His very life and imbibe of it fully. It is utterly to assimilate Him until our whole being is saturated, revitalized and overflowing with His life.

When this takes place we become the hidden springs through which the renewal and refreshment of God's very life flows to others. He it is, then, who touches and transforms all around us. It is He who brings life out of death, love out of despair and His joy out of our mourning.

18
Quiet Waters

ALL OF US need to find some quiet waters in life. Like the oasis for the caravan crossing the sun-scorched desert, so still waters are for the soul seared by the anguish of sorrow. There need to be moments of respite when in utter tranquillity of spirit our Father can be given opportunity to speak to us softly to renew our spirits.

Such times often come to me in the gentle company of high mountain lakes. These small sheets of shining water are cupped in the hills, sometimes surrounded by delicate stands of birch, poplar and willow. Others, above timber line, stand stark against the sky edge rimmed by rock and a few hardy reeds, tough enough to endure the environment of the high altitude.

The beauty and serenity of these still waters is duplicated by the incredible reflections mirrored in their shining surface. Every tree, snag, rock, distant ridge, soaring mountain peak and fluffy cloud suspended in the sky are reproduced as by a miracle in the gleaming water.

Here not a breath of air stirs the surface or wrinkles the water. It is as smooth as polished pewter. Sometimes on very chilly mornings after a clear night of extreme cold the lake will be locked in a sheet of glare ice which serves equally as a perfect mirror.

When autumn colors flame in the trees, and early frost has burnished the lake or marsh edge with tints of bronze and copper, the total effect is one of majestic splendor. It is as if a painting of huge proportions has been executed on the landscape by *a master artist.*

That, in fact, is exactly what has been done. For it was our Father who initially designed such loveliness to adorn the earth. And all subsequent art forms have found their inspiration at this source.

For the soul sensitive to the uplift of quiet waters there come moments, breathless moments, when in truth the whole earth speaks in hushed tones: *"O God, You are here! Your presence fills this place! Your peace enfolds these skies."*

And because He is there, my spirit, too, attuned to His, can find refreshment, renewal and restoration in such a spot. This is not to indulge in some spurious imagination of the mind. Rather, it is to discover the wholesome healing of the entire person in the presence of the Most High.

This element of utter serenity, of complete stillness, of lovely tranquillity in company with Christ, is a dimension of life that increasingly eludes us Americans. It is not that millions of us do not crave it. But it is unfortunately ever more difficult to find. The simple reason is that more and more multitudes are imprisoning themselves in large metropolitan centers where the roar and rumble of industry, traffic and commerce never cease.

Added to this is the insistence of modern man that wherever he goes, even into the countryside and remaining wilderness areas, he must take his twentieth-century gadgetry with him. The thunder of all-terrain vehicles, the drone of aircraft, the scream of snowmobiles or power boats, the staccato rattle of dirt bikes all shatter the stillness and desecrate the solitude of those who seek it.

Nevertheless all is not lost. Here and there stretches of unspoiled terrain remain. For those who will take the time and make the effort, quiet spots can still be found where serene waters bask in the sun and reflect the gentle glory of the sky edge.

There is one such spot just a few miles from my hearth. Tucked away between brown rock bluffs of very ancient lava these waters have somehow, as by a miracle, escaped the intrusion of modern man. Not once have I ever found an empty can or paper wrapping around their edge.

Whenever I come, I find a special tranquillity that defies description in common language. There is an element of profound peace that immediately permeates the awareness of anyone who enters the area with hushed steps. Loud language and coarse conversation are simply not acceptable. Human sounds are an intrusion. Crude use of any mechanical device would be a desecration.

I often go there simply to sit, to observe the scene, to think deep thoughts, to meditate over the meaning of life, to ask profound questions, to commune with Christ in the depths of my spirit.

These still waters are not a place of stagnation. Quite the opposite, they serve as a powerful magnet that attracts a startling array of wildlife. Their moisture provides a rich environment for all sorts of vegetation that lends lovely diversion to the dry arid region.

Here ducks dabble in the shallows. More often, they simply rest on the surface, looking almost like carved decoys reposing on a glass tabletop, their smooth shapes reflected to perfection in the surface. A heron will often stand as still as a miniature statue carved in stone, waiting at the water's edge for a careless bit of prey to come his way.

Overhead, cumulus clouds drift softly across the sky. Their white forms are caught in duplicate by the water. Like billowing white sails on the sea they drift slowly across the lake in steady procession. The blue skies and white clouds adorning the scene in exquisite patterns of pristine beauty add tremendous breadth to the scene.

Momentarily there is a splash at the water's edge. A muskrat moves out of the reeds that rim the shore. He swims across the water, fracturing its mirror surface into fragments of what may appear as broken glass. Then suddenly he stops. The ripples soon subside. And once again all is still as he lies there like a brown stone, soaking up the warmth of the morning sun.

A pair of swallows, graceful in flight, swift on wing, swoop over the quiet waters with splendid smoothness. Their acrobatics, so silent, so smooth, so swift, actually accentuate the quietude. Here amid such solitude they glean their harvest of insects without disturbing the stillness of the spot.

A fringe of graceful reeds encircles the little lake. Their slim foliage forms a delicate pattern of basketlike weaving in the water. Intertwined and criss-crossed by the breeze, it is as if they had been interwoven by the wind. Here and there a Red-Winged Blackbird makes his music amid their shafts. The mellow notes rippling across the little valley with purity and a touch of the wild on their edge, remind me that Red-Wings have come to this place of peace for a thousand years.

A Whitetail Doe steps out of the dim shadows of the Black Birches on the bank. Because I sit so still she has not spotted me. No stray eddy of air bears my scent to her twitching nostrils. Step by step, in silent but deliberate action, she moves into the strong sunlight. A fawn follows her. His spotted coat glistens gold and white in the bright light. Both doe and fawn dip their black muzzles in the cool waters. Only briefly do they pause to refresh their lips and throats. Then slowly they turn away and step back into the dim, dark shadows of the trees.

It is an instant of delight—a scene of supreme serenity. It is a moment of joy, an uplift of the spirit. All of it is unplanned; none of it is arranged by man. It is a pure but gentle gift from God. In our common lives such simple incidents come as treasures beyond calculation. They are cameos of beauty, healing, love and restoration that remain etched on the memory, never to be erased.

These incidents endure while all around time erases other events. The passing of the hours wipes away other transient concerns.

The joyous renewal that comes to the anguished soul in solitude assures me again and again of my Father's care that enfolds His earth children. If we are to know His compassion, if we are to sense His touch upon our torn spirits, if we are to feel the caress of His hand upon our wounded hearts, we must seek Him in solitude.

It is no accident that His Spirit speaks to us with such clear perception as the psalmist wrote: *"Be still and know that I am God. . . . I will be exalted in the earth"* (Psalm 46:10).

We modern people live so much amid turmoil, tension and the trauma of a fractured world. So, when death strikes or illness of terminal nature tears away the fragile fabric of one's thin veneer of invulnerability, most men and women know not where to turn for shelter. It is as if they stand exposed, naked, stripped and shattered by the suffering and sorrow that has swept over them in a whirlwind of horror.

Again and again I have been through the storms of suffering with other human beings who really wondered if there would or could be a way out. Was there a place of peace? Was there some spot of stillness for the soul?

My answer over and over is, "Yes!" But one must search, and seek, and find it in the presence of Jesus Christ, who is from everlasting to everlasting, who changes not across the centuries, who is eternal, Creator of heaven and earth, yet also Creator of my complex character.

We cannot find such assurance in the mayhem and madness of our great commercial complexes. Nor will we ever find it in the sophisticated skepticism of science and technology. Nor will it be found in our most august academic intellectualism. None of these philosophies can ever mend the soul torn with sorrow or the spirit seared with suffering. They are all cold, clinical and cruel!

But we can find renewal in the stillness of a lake; the drift of clouds against the sky edge; the flight of a bird across the water; the reflection of a deer coming to drink; the limpid, liquid notes of a blackbird in the reeds. These things have been ever of old. They are as ancient as the duration of days. They speak impressively of eternal values. They remind us that our Father is ever here, nor does He change.

In their constancy we see reflected something of His continuing care and compassion for us. We comprehend, even if only dimly, in the beauty of grass and trees and sky and sun, a little of the glory and wonder of our God who continually makes all things new. In our innermost beings we grasp again the enduring truth that if He can sustain all the earth in its pristine splendor from generation to generation, He can sustain our souls as well. It is He and He alone who can regenerate us in spirit both in this life now and in that to come.

In essence *to know Him* is *to know life eternal!*
This is that which surpasses our suffering.
It is this which overcomes even death.
So we are set free from all fear.
All is well. He is here.
Thank You, Father!

19
Return of the Birds

AS I WRITE these words the worst of winter is over. Though last night the temperature hovered down around zero, and the trees stood stiff and stark in the bitter cold, there is a change in the weather. Each day the sun is a little higher in the sky, a few more degrees above the sky edge. Its warmth increases steadily. Here and there on the south slopes there is a snow melt with brown earth and green grass showing between the white drifts.

Yesterday I took a long tramp in the brilliant, late winter sunshine. And though I have welcomed scores of springs in the north, it excited me again to notice the return of the birds. I had scarcely left the front door when a great black raven, shining like a polished boot, tumbled through the high cold air in glad abandon. His raucous cries rang across the ridges and came slanting down the airwaves to me. Already he was making his wild mating call.

Even more dramatic was a magnificent Golden Eagle soaring sedately above the great ragged firs on the sky line above our chalet. With powerful precision this monarch of the mountain winds etched perfect circles against the sky edge. Often I have stood spellbound watching a ragged band of crows try to mob one of these regal birds. With screams of outrage and cries of alarm they dive at the eagle which only turns its rapier beak or displays its fierce talons to send them off in terror.

Sailing serenely to some gnarled old crag on a rock ridge, the eagle will alight with dignity. Then composing itself in quiet strength it will sit calmly until the last of the crows exhausts its empty tirades and flies away in utter frustration. Then once again peace prevails.

As I hiked along the edge of a frozen streambed a small flock of my favorite chickadees called and fluttered through the undergrowth. Where the warming sun had bared the soil, they dropped to the ground and scratched busily among the decaying leaves. They are always harbingers of good cheer and better things to come, even when they work their way through the pine needles just outside our large patio windows. There the wind rocks them gently as they search for forage in the whispering foliage.

Always seeming so full of energy and joyous vitality, they did not appear the least concerned about what crisis tomorrow might bring. They had sufficient for this day. That was enough to cheer about.

Further on down the valley I heard the distant call of a Downy Woodpecker. This was another sure sign that soon all the woods and hills would ring with the songs of birds. I followed the sounds of his cry and saw his flight across some open ground to a grove of white-barked aspens shining in the sun.

He was searching for stalks of dry Mullen. The ragged brown plants appear so dead, so inert, so utterly useless. But locked tight in those shaggy stalks is a virtual banquet for the birds. And long ago the dainty little woodpeckers learned how to unlock the rich store of delicacies for their own survival in the spring.

I went on down the sun-drenched valley even further. It startled me to see that in some of the more sheltered spots all the snow was gone. Brown earth, sun-bleached grass from last year, gray rocks and sage were the muted tones that covered the landscape. But despite their apparent drabness all spoke eloquently of a long winter that was past and a new spring about to begin.

In the far distance there came that ecstatic sound of wild geese on the wing—not the high wild notes of a great wedge of the giant birds going to the arctic. This was the much more intimate "goose gabble" of a flock in search of local nesting grounds. These were the fore-fliers who came early from nearby open waters to find a marsh or open stream or even gentle spring which might lend itself as a home for a goose colony.

The strong birds straggled through the valley in a loose and untidy formation. Their excited calls were those of mating pairs surveying the land below for suitable homesteads. They had been this way before. It was familiar terrain. Still they searched it carefully for a suitable spot to set down and stay for the summer.

Yes, the birds were back. Their presence was a sure sign that winter was over. The dark days were gone; the long, dreary nights were behind. Each week it would become warmer. Every new day would be a little brighter. Each dawn held vivid promise of better things to come.

Contemplating all this it came home to me with formidable force that really it was all a precise replay of the recent, spiritual experiences we had passed through. There had been chilling days of sharp anxiety for those who faced death. We had known dark hours of sorrow for those who had bade loved ones farewell. There had been the grim vigil of those who endured the unknown future alone. All of these were akin to winter in the soul and night in the spirit.

Sometimes it seemed the long nights far, far outstretched the brief days. Despair and darkness far, far outweighed the brief interludes of hope and cheer. The forlorn fears were far worse than the bright promises of renewal.

Yet behind the scenes of sorrowing, pain and acute suffering our Father was still very much at work in the weariness of our winter. His faithfulness to His people would prevail over and beyond all the agony of their human despair. His concern and His care would change the impossible anguish into new and fresh opportunities to begin again.

That is how it was every spring.
That is how it was with Him.
The birds were back.
Hope came anew at the sky edge.

Here and there like a solitary rascal of a raven tumbling gleefully in the wind, a sudden spectacle of fun and good cheer would tumble through our thoughts. Borne on the wind of God's powerful Spirit some joyous word of encouragement or little experience of ecstatic delight would sweep into life to dispel a bit of the gloom.

There were hours, yes, sometimes even days or maybe weeks, when the crows of craven fear and apprehension seemed to crowd in upon us. The ragged cries of cowardice and black regret seemed to gang up on us. But we found a place of peace, a spot of strength as we settled down quietly to be still and know the presence of the Living Christ who abides with us always. Eventually the harassments of the opposition would fade away and we would know the rest of those who trust in God.

Some of the most unpromising circumstances became suddenly brighter when like the chickadees, they were invaded by unexpected bits of light. It astonished me to see how one unexpected knock at the door, a letter from a long-forgotten associate, a bit of fun with a friend, a hilarious cameo of humor could come winging into the day to drive away the despair.

There were a dozen ways in which our Father arranged for "birds of joy" to return, bringing with them hope and healing for the deep hurts of my wounded heart. In His mercy, love and compassion He had ways of bringing light and love back into the gloom.

Beyond this there were those quiet interludes when like the woodpecker, searching for the Mullen plants, I found a hidden banquet in the pages of God's own promises to me as His child. There was life and there was spirit imbedded in my Father's word for me. Where before it seemed death was so dominant, now suddenly vital life sprang up anew. Where previously despair prevailed, now, radically, incredible love came to my soul. Where in the winter of my darkness there was such a long night, now in wonder and joy the brightness of new light and hope came alive.

Nor were these just passing whimsies or transient sensations that would delude and discourage those of us who passed through the dark shadows of the valley of death. They were much more permanent and enduring than that. Like the straggling skeins of great winged geese searching for a spot to nest, so the coming of Christ's Gracious Spirit, the Comforter, had arrived to take up permanent residence in the labyrinth of my life.

With fresh awareness and acute intensity there swept over my spirit those ancient, unshakable, marvelous words of old:

> *"Be strong and of a good courage;*
> *be not afraid, neither be thou dismayed;*
> *for the Lord thy God is with thee whithersoever*
> *thou goest"* (Joshua 1:9).

There, in essence, was the secret to renewal. The presence of the Most High would enable me and my friends to surmount every sorrow. He it was who would bring spring to the soul again. Because of His great faithfulness joy would come once more to the spirit.

20
The Wonder of Spring

ONLY THE PERSON who has spent a severe winter in a northern latitude, at comparatively high altitudes, will ever fully comprehend the true wonder of spring. There really is no other physical experience on the planet which can quite match the magic of the melting of the snow. Nothing is so designed to stimulate the entire body and quicken all the senses as the return of warm weather, stronger sunlight and renewal of the earth.

As adaptable as man may be, the long winter nights, the deep freeze of unrelenting cold, the unmerciful winds bearing blizzards, tend to shrink one's soul and shrivel the spirit as if constricted in a prison. It is the coming of spring that sets one free. The gentle advent of strong, warm sunshine liberates one's locked-in life to wander at will once more.

This explains why ancient tribes of the north could not help but adore the return of spring. There is an aura of awe and worship in seeing green grass spring up anew from beneath the snowbanks. Strong men will sometimes fall down upon all fours to kiss the sun-warmed soil that has lain locked in frost for months. The tinkle of snow melting from glasslike icicles, the sweet singing of streams flowing free again, the ever-widening circle of bare ground around every tree trunk—all are powerful impulses that purge the soul of its dark reflections, giving glorious hope to the heart and new songs to the soaring spirit.

The final triumphant display of new life is the joyous return of the birds accompanied by the stirring resurrection of fresh foliage adorning the land. Turgid buds swell and burst into tender new leaves. Bare twigs and branches of willow, birch, poplar and a hundred lesser shrubs are dressed in glowing greenery. New grass and a thousand varied wildflowers push new shoots from the sun-warmed soil. Spring has come!

In our western mountains and desert valleys some four thousand diverse species of wildflowers carpet the countryside. In frontier days, before the advent of the pioneer's plow and the range rider's hordes of "hooved locusts," the earth glowed with the glory of fields and flowers. The display now is much less dramatic, much more subdued, altered by the invasion of cheat-grass, gray sage, knapweed and other noxious plants.

Still for those of us who search out the secluded valleys and climb the steepest slopes there are spots where the upland flower fields are a majestic spectacle. In some areas hundreds of acres are blanketed in blossoms of every possible hue. Whole ridges are alive with masses of blooms too beautiful to describe with mere words.

Where there was barrenness suddenly there is exquisite beauty. Where the mountains against the sky edge were a stark white, now they are dressed in vivid green, yellow, red and white flowers. Where there had been utter severity of scenery, now suddenly there has come softness and splendor as if painted with an artist's brush.

This total transformation of the high country from winter to spring dress remains one of the most magnificent spectacles upon the planet. The total transfiguration is a moving panorama that progresses with enormous power and perfect precision. It is governed by the celestial movement of the sun, moon, stars and planets, all in orbits ordained by the meticulous mind of our Father God.

There is nothing haphazard about spring. It is not a fickle affair that happens some years and not others. Its advent is sure; its impact is enormous. Its coming produces incredible changes. It ushers in a wondrous regeneration of life.

For those of us sensitive in soul to the changes around us, spring spells liberty, freedom and stimulation. Our spirits, attuned to the world around us, surge with new life. The urge to go out and explore, to hike, to climb a cliff, to roam at random, to wander free in the wind is a heady impulse that cannot be denied. Our hearts are set to singing. A bright light of excitement fills our eyes. Our muscles must move. Our strength must be spent in splendid exhilaration.

Though we scarcely seem to realize it, we too are being re-made, quickened, reborn in resurrection life. The winter is past, the darkness is gone, the cold has vanished under the warming sun. And we are free, free, free! No wonder we want to walk for miles, to climb a hill, to laugh in the sun, to sing in the breezes that blow so softly, to throw off our jackets and bare our faces to the touch of spring.

Everywhere there is new life. The zest of renewal reassures us: all will be well. The coming of April flowers, the refreshment of spring showers, the sheer loveliness of shining cumulus clouds towering high against the sky edge relaxes our pent-up bodies. We rejoice in the wonder of it all. Somehow, suddenly, we are at rest. An ancient saying suggests, "Our God is in His heaven, and all is at peace on earth."

But all of this takes time and thought and quiet moments to enjoy. Primitive people with long outdoor traditions fully understood the uplift and inspiration that came to them from gentle contemplation of the cosmos. It is an ancient aspect of life that has been pretty well lost in the madness of our modern society. Few indeed are those people of our generation who know anything at all about moments of meditation in which Christ can be given a chance to commune with them in the depths of their spirits.

The reader of this book may not have realized that its chapters have actually led step by step through the four seasons of the year. Unlike most such works, it began with the high noon of summer and now ends with the surge of spring. This was done deliberately to portray the parallels of our common human spiritual pilgrimage.

We begin our life with God in a strong and buoyant season, sometimes called our "first love." But it is usually followed by the subdued events of a fall season during which a much more mellow mood engulfs our souls. Then come those severe storms of sorrow, the tough trials of pain and parting, the winter winds of adversity. Our faith is tested. Our confidence in Christ is constricted. But as we endure, spring comes again. We are renewed. The truth and credibility of Christ's resurrection power engulfs us. We are assured of His everlasting hope and life. Love springs anew within our spirits. Faith flames bright again. All is well, for *He is here!*

The great cycle of the seasons goes on year upon year, enacted against the giant backdrop of the sky edge. We watch in humble awe and spellbound wonder as moon after moon the pageantry of the planet is played out upon the earth. The sublimely orchestrated script of the Divine Director is acted out in incredible detail by ten thousand participants. Each is directed by His will, guided by His genesis, moved by His inspiration.

If this can be true for lesser life forms, such as birds and bees and bears and Balsam Root or Bunch Grass, then surely it can be equally true for us human beings created in Christ's own image. The utter tragedy and terrible truth is it seldom does happen. For horror upon horror, most men's hearts (wills) have been deliberately set, and very purposely hardened, against the gracious good will of our loving Father.

This need not be so. There can be harmony between us and Him. It is not impossible for a person to come to *truly know Christ,* who to know is life everlasting. It is absolutely true that if men and women welcome Christ as wholeheartedly as they welcome the warmth of spring, new life, abundant life, the very life of the risen Lord, can pour into their beings.

It is this total availability of a soul to the impinging presence of the Living Lord that can set them free. Just as the sun of spring rising ever higher in the sky releases the earth from its winter bondage, so the new life of the Risen Sun, the Christ of God, sets our spirits free. Jesus, Himself, said without apology, "If the Son [Sun] therefore shall make you free, ye shall be free indeed" (John 8:36). Free to follow Him. Free to revel in His love. Free to find abundant energy, hope and life in Him.

All of us have our summer days of strength and bright assurance. All of us, too, have our autumn days when the shadows lengthen across our years. All of us will have our winters of deep despair and the dark pain of death. And all of us can know again the powerful resurgence of Christ's triumphant, overcoming life made real in our experience by His presence and resurrection power.

This book has been an impassioned plea for men and women to find their life, their strength, their love, their hope, their ultimate healing and wholeness in Christ. All other human philosophies will cheat us of the best. All other false religions, mysticism or spiritism of any sort are but a delusion that leads to darkness, despair and death.

But glory of glories, wonder of wonders, Christ brings His light amid our darkness. He brings His love into our despair. He brings His life to replace our death. *He is springtime to our souls!*